# AN INTRODUCTION TO SPORTS COACHING

*An Introduction to Sports Coaching* provides students with an accessible, informative guide to the theory underlying the practice of quality sports coaching.

This unique, readable text explains the practice of coaching from a variety of sports science perspectives, showing how such various knowledge strands underpin effective sports coaching.

Real-life coaching examples are used in every chapter to demonstrate theory in practice, and to show how athletes can benefit from a coach's broad understanding of sport.

The text provides full coverage of how Sport Psychology, Motor Learning, Physiology, Sports Medicine, Biomechanics, Notational Analysis, Sociology, History, Philosophy, Pedagogy and Sports Development can and should inform sports coaching.

*An Introduction to Sports Coaching* is edited by a team of senior sports coaching academics, all of whom are also experienced sports coaches. The text contains:

- Insights from practising international and club coaches
- Clear definitions of important themes and key concepts relating to the sports science knowledge that underpins coaching
- Seminar and self-test questions to help confirm your understanding.

*An Introduction to Sports Coaching* offers an ideal support text for today's student of sports coaching.

**Robyn L. Jones** is a Professor of Sports Coaching, **Mike Hughes** is Professor of Performance Analysis and **Kieran Kingston** is a Senior Lecturer in Sport Psychology. All are based at the Cardiff School of Sport, University of Wales Institute, Cardiff (UWIC), South Wales, UK.

# AN INTRODUCTION TO SPORTS COACHING

## From science and theory to practice

**EDITED BY ROBYN L. JONES, MIKE HUGHES AND KIERAN KINGSTON**

Routledge
Taylor & Francis Group

LONDON AND NEW YORK

First published 2008
by Routledge
2 Park Square, Milton Park, Abingdon, Oxon OX14 4RN

Simultaneously published in the USA and Canada
by Routledge
270 Madison Ave, New York, NY 10016

Reprinted 2008 (twice), 2009

*Routledge is an imprint of the Taylor & Francis Group, an informa business*

Typeset in Zapf Humanist and Eras by
Keystroke, 28 High Street, Tettenhall, Wolverhampton
Printed and bound in Great Britain by
the MPG Books Group

*British Library Cataloguing in Publication Data*
A catalogue record for this book is available from the British Library

*Library of Congress Cataloging in Publication Data*
An introduction to sports coaching : from science and theory to practice / [edited by]
Robyn L. Jones, Mike Hughes & Kieran Kingston.
p. cm.
ISBN 978-0-415-41131-8 (softcover) — ISBN 978-0-415-41130-1 (hardcover)
1. Coaching (Athletics) I. Jones, Robyn L. II. Hughes, M. (Mike) III. Kingston, Kieran.
GV711.I58 2007
796.07'7—dc22
2007014079

ISBN 978-0-415-41131-8 pbk
ISBN 978-0-415-41130-1 hbk
ISBN 978-0-203-93426-5 ebk

# CONTENTS

# LIST OF TABLES AND FIGURES

## TABLES

## FIGURES

# LIST OF CONTRIBUTORS

**Dr Nicola Bolton** is a Principal Lecturer at the Cardiff School of Sport, the University of Wales Institute, Cardiff (UWIC). Her research interests lie in sport development and management, public policy, strategy and evaluation. She is a board member of the Sports Council for Wales and the Institute of Sport, Parks and Leisure (ISPAL).

**Scott Fleming** is a Professor at the Cardiff School of Sport, University of Wales Institute, Cardiff (UWIC). His teaching and research interests are mainly in the sociology of sport and leisure, as well as in research methodology and research ethics. He is currently the Chair of the Leisure Studies Association (LSA).

**Dr Alun Hardman** is a Senior Lecturer at the Cardiff School of Sport, University of Wales Institute, Cardiff (UWIC). His research is conducted in the area of applied philosophy and ethics of sport, and is focused on understanding how sporting organisations from grass-roots to elite level can improve their ethical climate.

**Dr Michael G. Hughes** is a Senior Lecturer and Discipline Director in Sport and Exercise Physiology at the Cardiff School of Sport, University of Wales Institute, Cardiff (UWIC). His experience in the physiology of elite sports performance is partly based on previous employment as an exercise physiologist with both the British Olympic Medical Centre and Badminton England. He is accredited as a provider of sport science support work by the British Association of Sport and Exercise Sciences (BASES). His current research interests include the physiology of repeated-sprint sports, fitness assessment and training.

**Mike Hughes** is a Professor of Performance Analysis and Director of the Centre for Performance Analysis at the Cardiff School of Sport, University of Wales Institute, Cardiff (UWIC). He is also Director of UWIC Academy of Squash (Level IV coach) and a Fellow of the Royal Statistical Society. He is a Visiting Professor at the Universities of Zagreb, Ljubljana and Magdeburg. His principal research areas are: analysis of sports performance, the effect of fluid dynamics in sport, and developing methodologies in notational analysis. He has published in many leading journals, whilst founding and serving as initial General Editor of the *International Journal of Performance Analysis of Sport*. He is on the editing boards of the *Journal of Sports Science*, the *International Journal of Kinesiology* (Zagreb), the *International Journal of Computers in Sports Science* and the *International Journal of Sports Science and Engineering*.

**Dr Gareth Irwin** is a Principal Lecturer and Head of Biomechanics at the Cardiff School of Sport, University of Wales Institute, Cardiff (UWIC). He is a British Association of Sport and Exercise Sciences (BASES) accredited Sport Biomechanist. His research addresses theoretical issues associated with the development of skill, combining biomechanics, coaching science and the principles of training in a multiple paradigm approach. His applied research is facilitated by his background in international-level sport, previously as a competitor and currently as an international-level coach.

**Dr Carwyn Jones** is a Senior Lecturer in Sports Ethics at the Cardiff School of Sport, UWIC. He was the first person in the UK to gain a PhD in the subject. He teaches sports ethics, research ethics and professional ethics. His main research interests are role models, moral development, cheating, racism and other ethical issues in sport. He has published recently in the *Journal of the Philosophy of Sport*, the *Sociology of Sport Journal* and the *European Physical Education Review*.

**Robyn L. Jones** is a Professor at the Cardiff School of Sport, University of Wales Institute, Cardiff (UWIC), and a Visiting Professor at the Norwegian School of Sport Sciences, University of Oslo. His research area comprises a critical sociology of coaching in respect of examining the complexity of the interactive coaching context and how practitioners manage the inevitable dilemmas that arise. He has published in many leading journals including *Quest*, *Sport, Education and Society*, *The Sport Psychologist* and the *Sociology of Sport Journal*, whilst also serving on the editorial boards of *Physical Education and Sport Pedagogy* and the *International Journal of Sports Science and Coaching*.

**David G. Kerwin** is a Professor at the Cardiff School of Sport, University of Wales Institute, Cardiff (UWIC). His research focuses on the development and application of new technologies in the analysis of technique in sport. He is a Fellow of the Royal Society of Medicine (FRSM) and of the British Association of Sport and Exercise Sciences (FBASES), a College Member of the EPSRC and a member of the Science Commission of the Fédération Internationale de Gymnastique (FIG). David is also Principal Investigator for an Engineering and Physical Sciences Research Council (EPSRC) project investigating wireless sensor technologies in the training of elite athletes.

**Dr Kieran Kingston** is a Senior Lecturer and Discipline Director of Sport Psychology at the University of Wales Institute, Cardiff (UWIC). He received his PhD in 1999 from the University of Wales, Bangor. His research interests are focused primarily on the motivational aspects of sport, including goals, self-determination, burn-out and confidence, whilst also pursuing inquiry into the psychology of golf. Kieran has been a BASES accredited sport psychologist since 1997, and has acted as a consultant in a variety of individual and team sports.

**Dr Gavin Lawrence** is a Lecturer in Motor Control and Learning at the School of Sport, Health and Exercise Sciences, University of Wales, Bangor. His research interests include visuo-motor control with a focus on feedback processing, motor programming and the attainment of expertise.

**Dr Malcolm MacLean** teaches history in the Faculty of Sport, Health and Social Care, and is Deputy Dean of Modular Schemes in the Academic Development Unit at the University of Gloucestershire. His research focuses on sport in colonial and post-colonial settings with a particular focus on the relationship between sport as a cultural practice and social and political movements. He is Vice Chair of the British Society of Sports History, President of the International Society of Football Scholars and a member of the editorial boards for *Football Studies* and *Sport in History*.

**Dr Andy Miles** is a Principal Lecturer and Director of Enterprise at the Cardiff School of Sport at the University of Wales Institute, Cardiff (UWIC). His areas of interest and professional involvement include sports science support to elite athletes and the development and delivery of coach education materials. He is currently a member of the UKCC External Reviewers Group.

**Ian Mitchell** is a Senior Lecturer in Sport Psychology and Director of Football at the Cardiff School of Sport, University of Wales Institute, Cardiff (UWIC). As a former professional footballer, Ian's applied work has mainly been in performance enhancement and coaching behaviour within professional football. He is a UEFA qualified coach and regularly delivers on the UEFA 'A' and 'Pro' licence education courses for elite football coaches.

**Dr Kevin Morgan** is Senior Lecturer and Programme Director of the MSc Coaching Science at the Cardiff School of Sport, University of Wales Institute, Cardiff (UWIC). His research interests lie in pedagogy and motivational climate in physical education and sports coaching. He is a member of the association for Physical Education (afPE) and the British Educational Research Association (BERA) PE special interest group.

**Dr Ian Pritchard** is a Senior Lecturer and Programme Director of the BSc Sport and Physical Education at the Cardiff School of Sport, University of Wales Institute, Cardiff (UWIC). His principal research interests include sport and Neo-Marxist perspectives; sport, leisure and nationalism; and nineteenth-century sport and leisure history.

**Bev Smith** is a Senior Lecturer and Programme Director for the MA Sport Development and Coaching degree at the Cardiff School of Sport, University of Wales Institute, Cardiff (UWIC). She is a former national gymnastics coach and international judge, and is currently a board member of Sports Coach UK and the Institute of Sport, Parks and Leisure (ISPL).

**Dr Owen Thomas** is a Senior Lecturer in Sport Psychology at the Cardiff School of Sport, University of Wales Institute, Cardiff (UWIC). His main research interests include stress in sport and sport confidence. He is a British Association of Sport and Exercise Sciences accredited sports psychologist.

**Dr Richard Tong** is the Director of Learning and Teaching at the Cardiff School of Sport, University of Wales Institute, Cardiff (UWIC). He is a sports physiologist and also the Academic Co-ordinator for the MSc Sport and Exercise Medicine at UWIC. He has been accredited by the British Association of Sport and Exercise Sciences to provide physiological support to elite performers for over a decade.

# PREFACE

## BACKGROUND AND AIM

Although scholars agree that coaching is a complex, multi-faceted activity involving many different forms of knowledge, the literature that has informed it, particularly at the beginner or introductory level, has been roundly criticised (e.g. Jones *et al*. 2006). The disapproval has centred on the portrayal of coaching as a knowable sequential course of action to be delivered unproblematically and accepted by the athlete; a picture that grossly over-simplifies the process involved. Such a portrayal has also been fragmented or splintered in nature; presenting coaching as a series of isolated, discrete and largely unrelated components. The problem with such compartmentalisation is that those parts being analysed have been decontextualised, giving a very artificial account of events. As everyone who has coached or been coached can attest, coaching is just not that clear-cut. What has exacerbated the situation is that coaches and students of coaching have been left to make the links between the different theoretical strands and the thorny reality of practice for themselves, which they have consistently failed to do. Unsurprisingly, it has left the relevancy of such work open to question. The result is that much of coaches' knowledge remains rooted in implicit assumptions as opposed to explicit research and theory. No doubt authors of such introductory texts would rightly protest that there is a need to present coaching in a way that is both accessible and understandable for students and novice coaches. We couldn't agree more. Consequently, those wishing to write a foundational book in coaching are left with a dilemma; how to pen a clear, readable text suitable for undergraduate students and beginner coaches without dumbing down the activity so that it lacks any perceived application to the real world.

This book, written principally by academics from the Cardiff School of Sport at the University of Wales Institute, Cardiff (UWIC), is a response to that challenge. Subsequently, it has three principal goals: to introduce students to the multifaceted nature of coaching and the predominant knowledges that inform it; to highlight how they can and should be related to coaching practice; and, finally, to emphasise them as part of an integrated entirety that comprises the holistic nature of the activity. Although an introductory text, this is not a simple 'how to' book of coaching comprising a list of handy hints and quick fixes; indeed, this is where it differs from much of what has gone before. Rather, the significance of the book lies in better defining coaching's content knowledges and how they contribute to a collective body of understanding for beginner coaches and students of coaching. Clarifying in this way holds the potential to increase the perceived relevancy of explicit knowledge sources for readers, consequently reducing the gap between theory and practice.

## CONTENT

Although not claiming to cover all the possible knowledge sources available to coaches, the chapters included in this book examine coaching from a number of sport science related perspectives. We are aware that presenting the book in such a format can be seen as going against the argument just given in respect of fragmenting knowledge. However, taking account of the complexity of the subject and the introductory nature of the book, for the purposes of clarity and to counter fear and frustration among readers it was decided to bracket coaches' knowledge along the lines defined by sports science. This is not to say that we have sacrificed the multifaceted and knotty nature of coaching for an easy ride, as, although delivered as separate, each chapter discusses appropriate evidence and concepts directly related to coaching's messy and interpretive character. Additionally, in line with the complexity of the subject matter examined, an inescapable element of overlap exists between the notions discussed in many of the chapters. Far from being a bad thing, however, we see this emergent conceptual blending as allowing readers to clearly identify and grasp the most illuminating and consistent ideas that underpin coaching (Jones *et al.* 2007). For example, the chapters relating to psychology (Chapter 3) and philosophy (Chapter 6) both highlight the relative importance of developing intrinsic motivation in athletes, that is, an appreciation of the game for the game's sake, to maximise performance. The same could be said of deciding what comprises appropriate interaction with athletes, which is discussed (albeit in different ways) both in Chapter 1 ('Pedagogy for coaches') and Chapter 4 ('Sociology for coaches').

Furthermore, to encourage readers to make the required connections between the different chapters for themselves, we have deliberately clustered them so that each chapter is followed by another that relates to it. For example, 'Skill acquisition for coaches' (Chapter 2) is preceded by 'Pedagogy for coaches' (Chapter 1) and followed by 'Psychology for coaches' (Chapter 3). The chapters relating to 'Sociology for coaches' (Chapter 4), 'History for coaches' (Chapter 5), 'Philosophy for coaches' (Chapter 6) and 'Sport development for coaches' (Chapter 7) are similarly grouped, as are those related to 'Biomechanics for coaches' (Chapter 8), 'Notational analysis for coaches' (Chapter 9), 'Sports medicine for coaches' (Chapter 10) and 'Physiology for coaches' (Chapter 11). Grouping in this way, however, does not imply that cross-cluster connections cannot and should not be made, as the boundaries between the clusters are inevitably flexible and permeable. Indeed, the content of the chapter groups was very much our subjective decision around which there was plenty of enthusiastic debate. The point to be made, however, is that each chapter is inherently linked (in various degrees) to every other and should be read as such.

Each of these discipline-specific chapters is based on a similar format. This comprises a clear definition of the area in question followed by a discussion of a number of important constructs or sub-areas that inform it. For example, within the 'Sociology for coaches' chapter (Chapter 4), issues concerned with both micro (i.e. face-to-face interaction) and macro sociology (i.e. how wider social forces like race or gender affect behaviour) are discussed. Far from isolating the knowledge presented, however, we have tried to take account of its nature by contextualising it within coaching. Hence, as mentioned earlier, an attempt is made to illustrate how the knowledge presented in each chapter informs coaching both generally and uniquely. Each chapter, then, explicitly identifies insights within a particular strand of coaching knowledge and highlights how these insights can be used to understand the real world of coaching better. Each chapter also concludes with a series of discussion questions related to the information presented within it, which can also serve to check understanding. To close the book, the final chapter (Chapter 12: 'Tying it all together') outlines a means through which a more holistic and personal approach to coaching, incorporating all the differing knowledge strands previously discussed, can be considered. The aim here is to illustrate how the various information and knowledges presented in the earlier chapters need to be brought together, analysed and applied at an individual level to address unique, contextual coaching problems.

## WHO IS THE BOOK FOR?

An Introduction to Sports Coaching is a book true to its title in that it provides an introduction to the sport science knowledge behind coaching for undergraduate students. By design it is clear and manageable. For some students it will provide their only formal study of coaching, while for others it will serve as a foundation for further investigation. For all, however, it should enhance their general awareness of the various knowledges that underpin coaching and how each can be related to practice. A further valuable aspect of the book is that, whilst conveying to some extent the complex nature of coaching, it consolidates its principal knowledges into coherent sections, whilst, hopefully, conveying to students a little of what it means to be a coach. Our intention, then, is to introduce an element of reflection into the thoughts and practices of those beginning their study of coaching as an academic field of inquiry. This is specifically so regarding a heightened appreciation of what kinds of knowledges comprise coaching and how they can be better understood and developed to inform practice.

*Robyn L. Jones,*
*Kieran Kingston*
*and Mike Hughes*

# ACKNOWLEDGEMENTS

An anthology like this is obviously the work of many. In particular, we would like to thank the contributing authors, most of whom are colleagues at the Cardiff School of Sport at UWIC, for their hard work and diligence as the project unfolded, and to the coaches who provided us with considered words to begin each chapter. Thanks also go to Routledge and, especially, Sam Grant our commissioning editor, for her continued support in developing academic texts for students of coaching. Finally, we gratefully acknowledge the readiness of several authors and copyright holders in allowing their work to be reproduced here.

# PART 1

# CHAPTER ONE

# PEDAGOGY FOR COACHES

Kevin Morgan

*The best coaches are good teachers*

Sir Clive Woodward –
England Rugby Union 2003 World Cup winning coach
(Cain 2004: 19)

**Key sections:**

- Introduction
- Learning theories
- Teaching styles
- Multiple intelligences
- Motivational climate
- Conclusion

## INTRODUCTION

Traditionally, a divide has existed between perceptions of sports coaching and teaching, with coaching being viewed as training and the attainment of physical skills, whereas teaching has been seen to be about the total development of the individual (Jones 2006; Lee 1988). This divide is highlighted by such definitions of sport and physical education as: 'Sport covers a range of physical activities in which adults and young people may participate, PE, on the other hand, is a process of learning' (DES/WO 1991: 7); and 'PE is essentially an educational process, whereas the focus in sport is on the activity' (Capel 2000: 137). Pedagogy, defined as 'any conscious activity by one person designed to enhance learning in another' (Watkins and Mortimer 1999: 3) has, therefore, tended to lie outside the traditional concept of sports coaching (Jones 2006). Recent interview data from elite coaches, however, has demonstrated that they view their role not as physical trainers but as educators (Jones *et al.* 2004). For example, the former British Lions rugby union coach Ian McGeechan talked about establishing a learning environment to 'grow players' and coaching individuals 'to understand something'. Similarly, Graham Taylor, the former coach of the England Football team suggested that 'coaching really is a form of teaching' as it primarily involves communicating, learning and maintaining positive relationships with those being taught (Jones et al. 2004: 21). Other research has found that good coaches act like good teachers, as they care about those over whom they have responsibility and constantly engage in reflection on what they do and how they do it (Gilbert and Trudel 2001). This suggests that 'athlete learning as opposed to mechanistic performance is at the heart of coaching' (Jones 2006: 8) and that pedagogic theory should perhaps play a more central role in preparing coaches.

The purpose of this chapter is to identify some of the key pedagogical concepts that could be used to inform coaching practice and consequently enhance athlete learning. The first section deals with learning theories, beginning with the behaviourist perspective before progressing to social learning theory and constructivism, whilst presenting practical examples of how they may be applied to coaching. Teaching styles and multiple intelligence theory are then covered, with particular attention being paid to the work of Mosston (1966) and Gardner (1993). Finally, motivational climate theory (Ames 1992a, 1992b, 1992c) and associated research (Morgan and Carpenter 2002; Morgan et al. 2005a; Morgan et al. 2005b) are drawn upon, and related to coaching practice.

## LEARNING THEORIES

Learning has been defined as a change in an individual caused by experience (Mazur 1990). Two main schools of thought and their associated theories have predominated in educational and sport settings since the late nineteenth century, namely behavioural and constructivist. Behavioural learning theories focus on the ways in which the consequences of action – for example praise following improved performance – subsequently change individuals' behaviour (Slavin 2003). Social learning theory, which is a major outgrowth of the behavioural tradition (Bandura 1986), focuses on the ways in which individuals model their behaviour on that of others. Constructivist theories, on the other hand, contend that learners must discover and transform new information to learn effectively.

### Behavioural learning theory

Behavioural learning theories attempt to discover principles of behaviour that apply to all human beings (Slavin 2003). Behaviourists, such as Pavlov (1849–1936) in Russia, and Watson (1878–1958) and Thorndike (1874–1949) in the USA, were chiefly concerned with manipulating stimulus (S) and response (R) connections and observing the results. Thorndike's law of effect states that if an act is followed by a satisfying change in the environment, then it is more likely to be repeated in similar situations than an act that is followed by an unfavourable effect. For example, if an action is followed by praise from a coach it is more likely to be repeated than one that is followed by criticism.

Like Thorndike, Skinner (1904–1990) focused on the use of pleasant or unpleasant consequences to control behaviour, which became known as operant conditioning. Pleasant consequences, such as praise or rewards, were known as reinforcers and were considered to strengthen behaviour, whereas unpleasant consequences, such as public criticism, were known as punishers and were considered to weaken it (Slavin 2003). On this basis, behavioural learning theory suggests that if individuals enjoy the sports coaching and competition environments they are more likely to continue to participate and succeed within them, whereas if they find the consequences unpleasant they are more likely to drop out. Creating an enjoyable and rewarding climate, then, would appear to be an important element of good coaching, although what constitutes an enjoyable and rewarding climate will not be the same for everyone.

The most frequently used reinforcers in the sporting context include praise, attention, grades and recognition in the form of trophies, certificates and badges. However, although such reinforcers are generally considered to be important motivators they are individually perceived, so that we cannot assume that a particular consequence is a reinforcer for everyone. For example, some individuals enjoy being selected to demonstrate a particular sporting skill in front of their peers, whereas others may find it embarrassing and try to avoid being so chosen. If the coach, therefore, selects different participants to demonstrate without first asking or considering if they want to, the supposed reinforcer may, in fact, be acting as a punisher. This, in turn, may cause some participants to perform below their capabilities in order to avoid being chosen to demonstrate publicly.

Reinforcers that are escapes from unpleasant situations are known as negative reinforcers, e.g. not having to do extra training repetitions if the quality of the session is good. A further principle of reinforcement, known as the Premack Principle (Premack 1965) concerns promoting less desired behaviours by linking them to more desired activities. A commonly adopted use of this principle in the PE teaching and sports coaching context is to offer the participants the promise of a game if the previous skill practices are done well enough.

The main guidelines for the use of reinforcement to increase desired behaviours in the classroom setting and everyday life are also applicable to the coaching context (e.g. Baldwin and Baldwin 1998; Walker and Shea 1999). For example, one should firstly decide what behaviours are desired and reinforce these behaviours when they occur. Secondly, the desired behaviours, such as effort, improvement, a positive attitude and fair play, should be communicated clearly and an explanation given as to why they are important. Finally, the behaviours should be reinforced as soon as possible after they occur in order to make the connection between the behaviour and the consequence.

Intrinsic reinforcers are behaviours that individuals engage in for the inherent pleasure without any other reward, whereas extrinsic reinforcers are rewards given to motivate individuals to engage in behaviours in which they might not otherwise do so (Slavin 2003).

There is evidence to suggest that reinforcing children's behaviours that they would have done anyway can undermine intrinsic motivation that is essential for long-term participation in sport (e.g. Deci et al. 1999). Therefore, if coaching tasks are designed to be enjoyable and varied and to challenge athletes at their optimum level, extrinsic rewards may not be necessary to maintain interest and motivation, and could, in fact, harm intrinsic motivation. Slavin (2003) suggests that if extrinsic reinforcers are deemed necessary, self-reinforcement or praise should be used first before introducing certificates or prizes. However, practical reinforcers may be necessary to motivate individuals to do important things that they may otherwise not do.

Punishers are consequences that weaken behaviour (Slavin 2003). If an apparently unpleasant consequence does not reduce the behaviour it follows, it is not a punisher. For example, shouting at someone for perceived bad behaviour might give them the attention they desire and enhance their status amongst their peers, thus increasing the likelihood of that behaviour being repeated rather than reducing it. A frequently and successfully used punishment in PE and junior coaching settings is 'time out', where an individual is required to sit out of the activity for a set time. White and Bailey (1990) found that the use of a 'sit and watch' consequence for PE classes virtually eliminated misbehaviour for primary school pupils.

The withdrawal of reinforcers can also be an effective means of weakening behaviours. Take, for example, the situation where one child is continually shouting out the answers in group sessions, thus not giving any of the others an opportunity to contribute. Simply ignoring that child and insisting on 'hands up' for answering will weaken and eventually eliminate the shouting-out behaviour. However, before elimination there may be an increase in the behaviour, known as an extinction burst (Slavin 2003). If the coach recognises this increased behaviour and allows the individual to answer, then the worst possible message will be sent and the individual will think that shouting out works, if he or she keeps doing it.

In behavioural learning theory, new skills are taught or shaped through a series of small reinforcing steps towards the desired final action (Walker and Shea 1999). For example, when teaching a tennis forehand shot to complete beginners, the coach would not simply demonstrate the full shot and then wait until it is performed perfectly to reinforce the learner. Rather, the coach would first reinforce the correct grip of the racket, then the stance, then the contact point, and so on until the complete stroke is performed. Thus the individual's technique is being improved by reinforcing the individual steps towards the final goal. After a point, reinforcement for the early steps may not be necessary to maintain the behaviour because the final outcome of the shot is successful and desirable. Therefore, once the technique has been established, reinforcement for correct responses should become less frequent and also less predictable. The reason for this is that variable schedules of reinforcement, where reward is given following an unpredictable amount of time and behaviour complexity, are much more resistant to extinction than are fixed schedules (Slavin 2003). For example, if the coach praises the tennis player following every good shot and then stops the commendation, the player may become demotivated. However, if the coach gradually allows the player to increase the number of good shots played before praising, and praises the player at random intervals (variable ratio-schedule), then the player is more likely to continue playing with little or no reinforcement from the coach.

Thus behavioural learning theory can explain and justify many behaviours adopted within the sports coaching context. However, applying the theory is seldom a simple process. For example, what acts as a reinforcer for one person may be a punisher for another. Some players prefer intrinsic reinforcers, whereas others may respond more positively to extrinsic rewards. Individual levels of self-esteem and competence may influence perceptions of, and reactions to, different reinforcers and punishers. Previous experiences with significant others such as parents, teachers/coaches, peers and siblings may also play a part in an individual's response to praise and criticism. Furthermore, some players judge their success in comparison to others (i.e. a normative perception), whereas others are more self-referenced in their personal definition of success (Nicholls 1989) (see Chapter 3: 'Psychology for coaches' for a fuller discussion of this). All these considerations and others may influence the coach's application of behavioural learning theory. Subsequently, it is only through a thorough knowledge of individuals and situational variables, along with reflection on previous experiences, that the best coaches learn to adopt the most effective behaviours and strategies to suit different coaching situations.


**Social learning theory**

Social learning theory accepts most of the principles of behavioural theories but concentrates more on observational learning or modeling (Bandura 1986). Although it is relevant to athlete learning, it has to date been more commonly cited as an explanation of how coaches develop their own coaching methods and style. In this latter respect, it is akin to serving an apprenticeship (Cassidy et al. 2004). In relation to the teaching and learning relationship, Bandura (1986) describes modelling as a four-stage process: attention, retention, motor production and motivation. In the attention stage, the best coaches position themselves appropriately for the group, communicate effectively whilst focusing on a few key coaching points, and demonstrate several times whilst letting the learners know exactly what to look for (Weinberg and Gould 2003). The second stage of retention involves memorising the observed act, which might include mental practice or question-and-answer by the coach to help the learners remember the key points. Physical practice is then required for an effective motor reproduction stage, so that individuals learn to co-ordinate their muscle actions with their thoughts. In order for this phase to be effective, skill progressions and optimal practice time is required. The final stage is motivation, without which the other phases will not be effective. This involves the learners imitating a model because they believe it will increase their chances of gaining success.

Self-regulation is another important concept in social learning theory (Schunk 1999). According to Bandura (1977a), people consider their own behaviour, judge it against their own standards and reinforce or punish themselves accordingly. In order to achieve this we need an expectation of our own performance. Coaches can foster self-regulation by getting athletes to set self-referenced goals before and during competition and training sessions (Ames 1992b). Such goals could be to improve performance of a particular technique or skill, or to reduce the number of errors made. Thus, self-regulation involves thought processes and begins to bridge the gap between the behavioural perspective and the constructivist approach to learning.

## Constructivist learning theories

There is now a consensus of opinion that we do not learn by receiving passively and then recalling what we are taught. Instead, learning involves actively constructing our own meaning linked to what we already know. Constructivist learning theory draws heavily on the work of Piaget (1896–1980) and Vygotsky (1896–1934), both of whom argued that a process of disequilibrium in the light of new information is required in order for effective learning to take place (Slavin 2003). Four key principles from Vygotsky's ideas have helped shape constructivist learning theories. Firstly, he proposed that children learn through social interaction with adults and more capable peers, which links closely with social learning theory. Thus, mixed-ability groups and co-operative learning situations, where individuals are exposed to the thinking of a range of others, are promoted by constructivists. An example of this in the coaching situation would be to set a group task that involves mixed-ability teams working co-operatively to identify the strengths and weaknesses of the opposition, and devising strategies and tactics to outwit them.

A second key concept is the idea that children learn best when they are engaged in tasks that they cannot do alone but can with the assistance of adults or peers; a learning space known as their zone of proximal development (Vygotsky 1978). Individuals should be challenged at different levels as the zone of proximal development will differ between them. Differentiation by task or outcome is, therefore, a key aspect of coaching when a constructivist approach is adopted. Such differentiation could take the form of designing tasks at various levels of difficulty or allowing flexible time for completion of tasks.

The third concept is known as cognitive apprenticeship. This derives from the first two as it refers to the process by which a learner gradually acquires expertise through interaction with an expert, either an adult or a more advanced peer. Within coaching, this could involve a process of mentoring, whereby newly qualified or trainee coaches learn from more experienced practitioners. Similarly, less experienced players can benefit enormously from the guidance of their more experienced teammates.

Finally, Vygotsky's concept of scaffolding or mediated learning sees the teacher or coach as facilitating learning by initially providing a great deal of assistance in the early stages and then gradually reducing it as the learners become more able. In practical terms, this might involve the coach giving more structure to the sessions in the early part of the season and then allowing the players to take more responsibility and leadership roles as the season progresses. A further example of the application of the scaffolding concept in coaching is the use of practical tasks and associated questioning by the coach to enable the athletes to discover solutions for themselves. This is consistent with a guided discovery teaching style, which will be discussed in the following section. Questioning should be thought-provoking, focusing on why, how and judgement questions rather than just simple recall, thus requiring athletes to construct their own conceptions and, in doing so, enhance their learning.

## TEACHING STYLES

There is some confusion over the use of the terms teaching styles and teaching methods in the physical education and sports coaching literature. Siedentop (1991) defines teaching style as the interaction between teacher and pupils, whereas he describes teaching method as an instructional format. Contrary to this, Mosston (1966) contends that teaching styles are independent of personal idiosyncrasies, hence viewing them as methods. For the purpose of this chapter, and in order to avoid confusion, Mosston's definition of teaching style will be adopted, which is synonymous with teaching method.

Mosston's Spectrum of teaching styles is a continuum categorised according to the decisions made by the teacher or learner in the planning (pre-impact), teaching (impact) and evaluation (post-impact) phases of a lesson (Mosston 1966). At one end of the Spectrum is the Command style in which the teacher makes all the decisions across all three phases. At the other end is the Learner Initiated style in which the learner makes almost all the decisions and the teacher acts as a consultant. Between these two, Mosston and Ashworth (2002) systematically identified a series of other styles, each with its own decision-making anatomy (see Table 1.1).

The Spectrum can be further categorised into two distinct clusters, one associated with reproduction and the other with production. In the Reproductive cluster (methods A–E) the central learning outcome is for pupils to reproduce or recall motor skills and known information. Alternatively, in the Productive cluster (methods F–J), the central learning outcome is for pupils to discover new information or unique solutions to problems. The Reproductive and Productive clusters are, therefore, consistent with behavioural and constructivist learning theories respectively, as reviewed earlier in this chapter.

In a study that focused on teacher education, Pichert et al. (1976) found that teachers trained in how to use Mosston's teaching Spectrum gave more individual feedback, displayed less domination of lessons and allowed more time on task. Similarly, Ashworth (1983) found that teachers who had been given Spectrum training engaged learners in more time on task, used more feedback, engaged in more private and individual inter-actions with pupils, gave fewer negative statements, circulated more among children and altered their teaching method more frequently. These behaviours are closely associated with a positive motivational climate (Ames 1992b), as discussed later in this chapter.

9

*Table 1.1* Teaching styles adapted from Mosston and Ashworth (2002)

| Style | Essential characteristics | Focus |
|---|---|---|
| A. Command | Teacher makes all decisions | Motor development |
| B. Practice | Pupils practise teacher prescribed tasks | Motor development and autonomy |
| C. Reciprocal | Pupils work in pairs, one as the teacher and one as the learner | Social, motor and cognitive |
| D. Self-check | Pupils evaluate their own performance against set criteria | Motor, cognitive, independence |
| E. Inclusion | Teacher provides alternative levels of difficulty for pupils | Differentiation, motor, cognitive |
| F. Guided Discovery | Teacher plans a target and leads the pupils to discover it | Cognitive and motor development |
| G. Convergent Discovery | Teacher presents a problem and pupils find the correct solution | Cognitive, motor, social and affective development |
| H. Divergent Discovery | Teacher presents a problem and pupils find their own solution | Cognitive, motor, social and affective development |
| I. Individual Programme | Teacher decides content and pupils plan and design the programme | Cognitive, personal (autonomy) and motor development |
| J. Learner Initiated | Pupils take full responsibility for the learning process | Personal (autonomy), cognitive and motor development |

According to Metzler (2000) the selection of a particular teaching style is dependent on a number of factors including the intended learning outcomes, the teaching context and environment, and the learner's developmental stage. For example, two coaches may have different learning outcomes for a football session. Coach A may want to focus on developing the players' decision-making in games, whereas Coach B may want to concentrate on improving the players' techniques. Based purely on these learning outcomes, a more Productive style, such as Guided Discovery (see Table 1.1) may be more appropriate for Coach A, as his or her aim is to develop players' ability to understand the game and make appropriate decisions in different situations. In order to achieve this, he or she could set up different game situations and guide players through a series of practical tasks whilst asking searching questions, thus allowing the players to work out the most appropriate responses for themselves. Coach B, on the other hand, may be better selecting a style from the Reproductive cluster, such as the Practice style, in order to maximise the opportunity for players to improve their techniques through repetition and practice drills.

Although the learning outcomes are the most important reason for selecting the appropriate style, as Metzler (2000) suggests, the coach should also consider the learner's developmental stage and the teaching environment. If, for example, the learners in Coach B's session are more experienced players, a Reciprocal style may work better for the technique practices, as they are likely to have the necessary technical knowledge to pass on to others. However, in poor weather conditions, or where Coach B is dealing with large numbers of inexperienced players, the more direct Command or Practice styles may be better employed to keep the session active and to demonstrate appropriate techniques. Metzler (2000) also suggests that when safety is a key consideration, as in situations such as javelin throwing and swimming, the direct instruction or Command style of delivery may be the best one to adopt. However, if developing understanding is more important, the Reciprocal or Discovery styles are better choices.

An important factor in deciding how to coach is that a session may include several different delivery styles depending on the intended learning outcomes of each phase of that session. In fact, the best practitioners can change their style to suit the situation and have the flexibility to use several different styles in one session (Mawer 1995). Therefore, returning to the football examples in the previous paragraphs, a Reproductive style such as Practice may be the most appropriate method for the delivery within a physical conditioning phase. Alternatively, a tactical phase may be best delivered using a more Productive, Discovery method to develop the players' ability to make decisions during the game without relying on the coach.

In discussing the teaching and learning relationship, Tinning et al. (1993) suggest that teaching styles should not simply be viewed as strategies to be implemented by the teacher but more like a set of beliefs about the way certain types of learning can be achieved. In which case, they are 'as much statements about valued forms of knowledge as they are about procedures for action' (Tinning et al. 1993: 123). This is a firm reminder that coaching or teaching is a social practice that involves the values and philosophy of the individual coach and athletes, the objectives of the activity and the context.

Consistent with a learner-centred philosophy of coaching, Kay (2003) argues that effective learning in sport and PE should involve participants in planned activities that develop four central domains: the physical, social, cognitive and affective, which he terms 'whole learning'. Such an approach echoes Jones' (2006) aforementioned concept of coaches as educators as opposed to physical trainers. The development of the physical domain is the most obvious one and should involve the development and application of core techniques and skills and the application of these to competition-specific situations (Kay 2003). In order to develop the social domain, participants should be involved in interacting with others in co-operative situations, as already discussed under constructivist learning theories and teaching styles such as Reciprocal and Discovery. Cognitive development refers to knowledge and understanding of physical concepts, strategies and tactics, and can be developed by the implementation of Productive styles of teaching such as Guided and Divergent Discovery, or Individual Programme (see Table 1.1). Finally, development of the affective domain should involve helping all pupils to develop self-esteem through successful individual experiences of social, cognitive and physical aptitude (Kay 2003). Teaching styles to facilitate such a development could include Inclusion and Self-Check (see Table 1.1). Arguably, the more traditional direct teaching styles have focused on developing the physical domain to the exclusion of the social, cognitive and affective domains. Consequently, in order to promote whole learning, coaches and teachers need increasingly to adopt teaching styles that focus on the individual being taught and not on the activity.

## MULTIPLE INTELLIGENCES

The differing intelligences of participants are an important consideration in selecting the most appropriate teaching styles (Gardner 1993). Gardner identified several intelligences (see Table 1.2), and suggested that to maximise the learning environment practitioners should use a range of styles to engage them all. Individuals can be high or low in each intelligence with some intelligences being more prominent than others.

In order to exemplify the use of Gardner's multiple intelligences theory in teaching tennis, Mitchell and Kernodle (2004) developed a variety of strategies to maximise learning for the different intelligences. For example, they suggested that linguistic learners could keep a tennis journal to describe the new strokes and strategies they have learned, or discuss the key points of a tennis stroke with the coach. More visual learners might prefer to create a mental image from video or demonstration, whereas more kinaesthetic learners might prefer to shadow-practise the coach.

*Table 1.2* Multiple intelligences adapted from Gardner (1993)

| Intelligence | Learner characteristics |
| --- | --- |
| Verbal/linguistic | Capable of using words effectively. Learns most effectively by reading writing, listening and discussing |
| Visual/spatial | Perceives spatial relationships and thinks in pictures or mental images. Learns most effectively through visual input such as demonstrations, video or viewing diagrams |
| Kinesthetic | Can manipulate objects and uses a variety of gross and fine motor skills. Learns most effectively through practical participation and interacting with the space around |
| Musical/rhythmic | Is able to communicate or gain meaning through music. Learns most effectively by listening to and creating music or rhythms |
| Mathematical | Thinks in, with and about numbers. Learns most effectively through activities that promote logical thinking or using numbers |
| Interpersonal | Interacts successfully with others. Learns most effectively in co-operative group situations |
| Intrapersonal | Is introspective and focuses on internal stimuli. Learns most effectively when given time to process information individually, formulate own ideas and reflect on these |

From a practical coaching perspective, however, it is a difficult challenge to devise practices to suit all the different intelligences and their various possible combinations. Furthermore, although questionnaires do exist to test for the different intelligences (Gardner 1993), assessing all players and then interpreting their profiles to work out the most effective teaching styles to adopt for each would prove to be a very time-consuming and perhaps unrealistic process. That said, there is certainly potential in a coaching strategy that takes better account of such considerations. Hence the more innovative and creative coaches may find this area worthy of further consideration and exploration.

## MOTIVATIONAL CLIMATE

Throughout this chapter links between the various pedagogical concepts presented and the motivational climate created by the coach have been made. The reason for this is that the pedagogical concepts discussed are only useful if they can be applied to the everyday role of a coach, and creating a positive coaching climate where every athlete is encouraged and given equal opportunity to achieve his or her full potential is the key to successfully fulfilling that role. This final section, therefore, deals specifically with how such a climate can be created.

Motivational climate is defined as a situationally induced psychological environment influencing the goals that individuals adopt in achievement situations, such as within a coaching session (Ames 1992a). According to Ames, two types of motivational climate predominate in such situations: a comparative (performance) climate that focuses on normative ability comparisons, and a self-referenced (mastery) climate that focuses on self-referenced effort and improvement. Research on motivational climate in sport and physical education (Carpenter and Morgan 1999; Ebbeck and Becker 1994; Kavussanu and Roberts 1996; Ntoumanis and Biddle 1998; Ommundsen et al. 1998; Papaioannou 1997; Spray 2002; Walling et al. 1993) has revealed that perceptions of a mastery climate are associated with positive motivational responses, such as: perceived competence, enjoyment, effort, learning, intrinsic motivation, a preference for challenging tasks, beliefs that success is due to effort and the development of lifetime skills. In contrast, perceptions of a performance climate are linked with potentially negative responses, such as: high levels of worry, a focus on comparative ability and a preoccupation with enhancing one's social status.

Based on Epstein's (1989) work, Ames (1992b, 1992c) suggested that the task, authority, recognition, grouping, evaluation, and time structures (TARGET) of the learning environment can be manipulated by the teacher to promote a mastery motivational climate (see Table 1.3). In accordance with Ames's suggestion, in order to develop a mastery climate the tasks within coaching sessions should be designed to emphasise self-referenced improvement goals, variety, novelty and differentiation. Consistent with a constructivist perspective and the concepts of empowerment (Kidman 2001) and shared leadership (Jones and Standage 2006), the authority structure involved here should include participants in the learning process by providing them with choices and opportunities to make decisions. The grouping structure should focus on co-operative group learning and the use of mixed-ability and varied grouping arrangements. Recognition and evaluation should be focused on individual effort and improvement, and be given privately whenever possible, thus providing all participants with equal opportunity for success. Finally, activity and learning time in sessions should be maximised and individuals should be allowed flexible time to complete tasks. Such a mastery-focused teaching intervention has been found to enhance pupils' motivational responses in physical education and sport settings (Morgan and Carpenter 2002; Solmon 1996; Treasure 1993). In contrast, a performance climate emphasises uni-dimensional (i.e. the same task for all) competitive tasks, teacher authority, normatively based public recognition and evaluation, ability groups and inflexible time to practice (see Table 1.3).

Recently, Morgan et al. (2005a) have used the Behavioral Evaluation Strategies and Taxonomies (BEST) (Sharpe and Koperwas 1999) software to develop a computer-based observational measure of the TARGET behaviours (Ames 1992b). This measure allows researchers to film coaching sessions and to systematically code and analyse the coaching behaviours that impact upon athletes' perceptions of the motivational climate. In a study that combined motivational climate and teaching styles in physical education, Morgan et al. (2005b) used the behavioural measure to investigate the effects of different teaching styles on motivational climate and athletes' subsequent responses. Results revealed that Reciprocal and Guided Discovery teaching styles resulted in more mastery-focused TARGET behaviours leading to enhanced athlete motivation. In a subsequent study,

*Table 1.3* TARGET behaviours that influence motivational climate (Epstein 1989; Ames 1992b)

| TARGET behaviour | Mastery | Performance |
| --- | --- | --- |
| Task | Self-referenced goals, multi-dimensional, varied and differentiated | Comparative goals, uni-dimensional and undifferentiated |
| Authority | Students given leadership roles and involved in decision-making | Teacher makes all the decisions |
| Recognition | Private recognition of improvement and effort | Public recognition of ability and comparative performances |
| Grouping | Mixed ability and co-operative groups | Ability groups Large groups |
| Evaluation | Self-referenced. Private diaries and consultations with teacher based on improvement and effort scores | Normative and public |
| Time | Flexible time for task completion | Inflexible time for task completion |

Morgan and Kingston (in press) developed a mastery intervention programme for physical education practitioners and assessed its effect on TARGET behaviours and pupils' motivation. This intervention was found to improve teachers' reflective abilities in developing their own contextual strategies in relation to utilising mastery-focused TARGET behaviours whilst enhancing the motivation of the more disaffected pupils in the class.

## CONCLUSION

The purpose of this chapter has been to establish that, conceptually, coaching is about teaching and learning, and to identify some of the key pedagogical concepts, theories and research that could be applied to coaching. It does not claim to cover all the pedagogical concepts that could be applied to coaching, or that the examples chosen are necessarily the most important ones. It does, however, aim to contribute to the re-conceptualisation of coaching as teaching and to further inform coach education and practice. It is acknowledged that many successful and experienced coaches may not consciously be familiar with the teaching and learning theories presented in the different sections. However, it is suggested that an awareness and knowledge of the key concepts discussed will result in a deeper level of coach reflection and assist coaches in developing a greater understanding of how individuals learn and of the impact their coaching behaviours can have on the learning and motivation of their charges.

Although it is suggested that individuals learn most effectively in a constructivist way, it is important to acknowledge that good coaching practice also draws on many aspects of behaviourist and social learning theory, particularly in the feedback and evaluation processes. Similarly, the best coaches draw from a whole range of learning theories and from both Reproductive and Productive teaching styles to achieve their learning outcomes in successfully dealing with different coaching scenarios. The key message of this chapter, therefore, is that coaches should continually evaluate their sessions within a broad pedagogical theoretical framework which will allow them to become more reflective, better practitioners.

1. Sir Clive Woodward is quoted as stating that the 'best coaches are good teachers'. Do you agree? Why?
2. Compare and contrast behavioural learning theory with constructivist learning theories. Which do you most agree with? Why?
3. Imagine you are taking your first coaching session with a new team. From a teaching perspective, how do you approach it? What style do you adopt? Why?
4. What are the proposed advantages of adopting a TARGET motivational climate?

# CHAPTER TWO

# SKILL ACQUISITION FOR COACHES

Gavin Lawrence and Kieran Kingston

*Appropriate organisation of practice, and the ways in which you provide feedback are pivotal to improving skills.*

Dave Pearson –
Head Coach, England Squash

**Key sections:**

- Introduction
- Structuring the practice environment
- The nature and administration of feedback
- Attentional focus
- Conclusion

## INTRODUCTION

As active human beings we hardly ever stop moving. Most of these everyday movements are initially acquired with the help of parents or teachers, while others we gain through trial and error. In sporting situations, many of these basic movements act as foundational skills for more complex actions that may take years to master. The effectiveness of the coach in facilitating the learning of such skilled movements can be enhanced through a more detailed understanding of how athletes learn and how best to structure the environment to support this learning. How people learn to execute skills effectively poses an interesting set of questions, questions that researchers continue to wrestle with in an attempt to illuminate the sometimes misty world of effective coaching. The aim of this chapter is to discuss some of these questions and to illustrate the value to coaches of knowledge about the acquisition of skills. Further, it seeks to provide a framework for understanding and applying that knowledge that will, it is hoped, have a positive impact on the coaching and learning experience.

Schmidt and Wrisberg (2000) recently developed an academic road-map for providing instructional assistance. The upper layer of their map or model guides readers to a number of open-ended questions relevant to addressing skill acquisition and subsequent performance issues. These include: Who is the learner? What is the task the person must perform? and, What are the conditions under which the performer wants to be able to perform? Although this information is critical, most coaches seldom ask such questions as they appear to implicitly understand athletes, the sport and their requirements. Consequently, our objective in this chapter is not to examine individual differences between participants and across tasks, but to concern ourselves with the second layer of Schmidt and Wrisberg's model – the learning experience. Specifically, we will examine three aspects of this experience to illustrate how coaches can (a) structure the practice environment, (b) provide effective feedback, and (c) identify an appropriate attentional focus (i.e. what one should concentrate on) for performers whilst executing motor skills. For each of these areas we present the main principles and contemporary research findings and discuss the application of this knowledge. Finally, we conclude with a brief summary that brings together the main points raised.

## STRUCTURING THE PRACTICE ENVIRONMENT

Often, the time constraints placed upon coaches require them to teach more than one skill in a single training session. Thus, most sessions demand that athletes practise a number of activities. In football (i.e. soccer), for example, a training session may well include the practices of dribbling, crossing and shooting. Therefore, it is important that coaches understand how to schedule different activities within a training session so that learning is maximised. Two types of practice scheduling that have been widely referenced within the skill acquisition or motor learning literature are blocked and random practice (see Magill 2004).

### Blocked versus random practice

Blocked practice can de defined as a practice schedule in which the performer repeatedly rehearses one task before moving on to another. It is typically observed in repetitive drills and is often adopted by coaches as it is seen as allowing the learner to refine and, if necessary, correct a skill before beginning another. For example, a squash coach wanting to teach the forehand, the backhand and the serve in one session would choose to devote a fixed block of time to practise each on the premise that the uninterrupted time on one task will cement the movement skill into the learner's memory. Alternatively, in a random practice schedule the session is structured so that the learner practises a variety of skills in no particular sequence. Here the coach organises the practice session so that there is large variation in skill rehearsal, i.e. the athlete alternates amongst the skills to be learned in an assorted or intermingled fashion and, in extreme cases, never practises the same skill consecutively.

An important misconception between these two practice schedules is that because blocked practice often leads to more proficient performance during training, it also leads to greater learning (i.e. the retention and/or transfer of skills over time). However, research investigating practice scheduling challenges this, and actually reports greater learning when practice occurs in a random, rather than a blocked, sequence (e.g. Battig 1966, 1979; Lee and Magill 1983; Perez et al. 2005). This counter-intuitive pattern of results – that is, where conditions of practice associated with poor performance also lead to better learning – has been termed the contextual interference effect. This phenomenon has been explained using a variety of theories, but the two most commonly cited are the action plan reconstruction hypothesis (Lee and Magill 1985) and the elaboration hypothesis (Shea and Zimny 1983).

According to the action plan reconstruction hypothesis, continually reconstructing a plan for new movement, as occurs in random practice, undermines performance. However, since the learner has devoted more mental effort to developing a memory representation for each skill (i.e. remembering how to do), learning is enhanced. In essence, the extra cognitive effort required for random practice enables the performer to create a library of action plans in memory and to retrieve the appropriate one to meet specific task demands at a later date (e.g. during a game situation). Conversely, in blocked practice, a given action plan can be constructed on the first attempt of a movement skill and simply applied to subsequent attempts over an entire block of trials. This uninterrupted repetition of the same action plan leads to good performance during practice, but the minimal experience learners have in reconstructing action plans means that applying that learning in a variety of contexts is poorer.

The principal idea behind the elaboration hypothesis is that random practice forces the learner to engage in a variety of cognitive processing activities, the result of which means information about each to-be-learned skill is more distinctive. That is, when the learner switches from practising one skill to another during random practice, they compare and contrast the separate tasks, which results in the establishment of more meaningful or distinctive memories, thus making retrieval easier at a later time. In contrast, the continued repetition of a single skill in blocked practice does not provide the learner with the opportunity to engage in such cognitive activity. Therefore, learners develop less distinctive memory representations of each practised skill.

### Factors influencing the contextual interference effect

Although there is a large body of research supporting the contextual interference effect, it is not a completely robust phenomenon and does not apply in all situations. Thus, the degree to which the contextual interference effect influences skill learning may depend on a number of individual and task-related factors (Magill and Hall 1990). The two most probable individual factors here appear to be age and skill level. Experiments utilising children as participants are rather limited, but those that have been conducted have failed to find greater skill retention under conditions of random practice (Del Rey *et al.* 1983; Pigott and Shapiro 1984). Similarly, in a recent review of the literature it was concluded that practice schedules of lower contextual interference (i.e. blocked practice) led to greater skill learning in children (Brady 2004). With regard to the skill level of the learner, it has been observed that individuals with very low skill levels perform better on a retention test when subject to blocked practice (Herbert *et al.* 1996), whereas it is more beneficial for higher-skilled performers to experience random practice (Hall *et al.* 1994). Although these findings are at odds with the contextual interference effect, they can be explained by the performers' stage of learning and the practice schedule adopted (Guadagnoli *et al.* 1999). For example, in the early stages of learning, athletes often struggle to understand the movement to be learned (Gentile 1972, 2000). In an attempt to do so, they simplify the required task's demands by trying to reduce the number of potential moving body parts involved in the skill (Fitts 1964; Bernstein 1967). Thus, constructing the learning environment to include high levels of contextual interference at this stage of learning may be overwhelming and may actually interfere with the development of a stable action plan for movement (Wulf and Schmidt 1994). Therefore, before progressing to random practice, children and beginners alike may need time to explore and develop the basic required co-ordinated pattern of movement (Gentile 1972, 2000).

In relation to task factors, Magill and Hall (1990) hypothesised that the beneficial learning effects associated with practice schedules that include high levels of contextual interference are more consistent when the skills practised are controlled by different generalised motor programmes (GMPs) (Schmidt 1975, 1991). A GMP is essentially a memory mechanism that a learner uses to control particular actions, such as throwing, kicking, catching, and jumping, that have common (i.e. the rhythm of the movement, in terms of timing, force, and the order of the components) yet unique features (i.e. the overall timing and force of the movement). Therefore, according to Magill and Hall (1990), when the learner practises a number of movement skills that require different patterns of co-ordination adopting a high, as opposed to a low, level of contextual interference within the practice schedule, better learning will result. However, if the practised skills are generally similar or from the same GMP (i.e. swinging the same golf club to hit the ball different distances), then a practice schedule with a high level of contextual interference will not benefit learning over one with a low level of contextual interference.

## Constant versus variable practice

If random practice benefits the learning of skills from different GMPs, how would a coach structure a practice environment to enhance the learning of a variety of movements from the same class of actions or GMP? One option is to ensure that only one variation of the skill is practised in any one session (i.e. throwing a ball to a single, unchanged target that is always positioned the same distance away). This type of practice schedule is not dissimilar to blocked practice and is often referred to as constant practice. However, if the learning goal is to produce a number of versions of the same skill, then it is important to have learners practise different versions of the action in each practice session; something referred to in the literature as variable practice. Indeed, research has consistently demonstrated the learning benefits of variable over constant practice, both in laboratory tasks (Shea and Kohl 1990, 1991) and in experiments involving sports skills (Shoenfelt *et al.* 2002).

To summarise this section, whatever the skill to be learned, coaches should be aware that it is important to introduce practice variability into sessions, and also to organise the practice environment according to the principles of contextual interference. Although practising under conditions of high contextual interference (i.e. random practice) does not always lead to immediate good performance, research suggests that it often leads to better long-term skill learning. However, the level of contextual interference that is likely to lead to optimal learning depends on a number of task and individual factors, namely: whether the to-be-learned tasks are from the same or different GMPs, and the age and skill level of the learner. Finally, while there is no agreement as to how the structure of the practice environment influences skill learning, both the action plan reconstruction and the elaboration hypotheses concur that making practice more cognitively demanding (i.e. making individuals work problems out for themselves) forces athletes to process skill-related information in a more active and independent manner that, ultimately, facilitates learning.

## THE NATURE AND ADMINISTRATION OF FEEDBACK

Augmented feedback is information provided to the learner from an external source. It is the general term used to describe information given about the performance of a skill that enhances the intrinsic feedback that is naturally available from performers' senses (i.e. their auditory, proprioceptive and visual systems). Augmented feedback can be provided verbally or non-verbally, during (concurrent feedback), immediately following (terminal feedback), or some period after the completed skill (delayed feedback), and can include information about the movement outcome (knowledge of results [KR]) and/or the movement pattern (knowledge of performance [KP]).

From the coach's perspective, the most important question when considering whether to use augmented feedback is: can it help in the acquisition of the to-be-learned skill? Unfortunately, the answer to this question is not simple as (similar to the earlier discussion on how to best structure the practice environment) it is dependent on both individual and task factors. Firstly, there may be situations where augmented feedback is not required, as the task-intrinsic feedback alone provides sufficient information for skill learning to occur. In these situations, athletes can make appropriate future adjustments to their movements based on their own sensory feedback from either their individual performances or by observing others of the same (Herbert and Landin 1994), or higher, skill level (Magill and Schoenfelder-Zohdi 1996). However, if athletes cannot utilise intrinsic feedback to enhance their performance, then augmented feedback is essential for skill acquisition. This situation can occur due to a number of reasons, such as injury, task constraints and skill level. For example, when an individual who, through injury, has damaged essential mechanisms for the detection and/or utilisation of task-intrinsic feedback, or where the constraints of the task mean that critical intrinsic feedback is not readily available, augmented feedback must be presented if learning is to occur. In addition, there may be situations where task-intrinsic feedback is readily available, yet it is not immediately useful to the learner due to his or her limited experience in perceiving its meaning. These situations often occur during the early stages of learning. Here, then, augmented feedback can help the novice learner better understand the meaning of the task-intrinsic feedback. However, this process can sometimes be problematic as, if the task-intrinsic feedback is minimal or perceived as overly difficult to understand, augmented feedback may actually reduce learning. This occurs if the learner substitutes the intrinsic feedback with the offered augmented feedback, subsequently becoming reliant on the latter for accurate performance. Consequently, when augmented feedback is not available, such as in a game situation, a decrease in performance is likely to occur. This is referred to in the motor learning literature as the guidance hypothesis (Salmoni et al. 1984) and will be further discussed later in this chapter.

## Types of augmented feedback

Verbal feedback provided by coaches is perhaps the most commonly used form of augmented feedback in the practice environment. However, there are a number of other ways of providing augmented feedback. An increasingly utilised form is through video. However, for videotape feedback to be effective at least two important factors need to be considered: the learner's skill level and the period of time for which this type of feedback is utilised (Rothstein and Arnold 1976). Here, research suggests that skilled performers benefit from unaided video replays of their performance, whereas novices tend to be overwhelmed by the information available in the video and require the addition of specific verbal cues to point out critical information (Newell and Walter 1981; Rothstein and Arnold 1976).

Research has also suggested that learners need sufficient time to familiarise themselves with video replays as a form of augmented feedback so they can understand what information is important to extract and act upon. Whilst it may be possible to reduce this time period by providing attention-focusing cues as described above, it has been recommended that video replays should be utilised for at least five weeks in order to become an effective teaching/learning tool (Rothstein and Arnold 1976).

Another useful form of augmented feedback is biofeedback. Here information is presented to the athlete about internal physiological actions such as heart rate, muscle activity and/or joint movement. This form of augmented feedback is generally used in the clinical setting for the purpose of rehabilitation (Brucker and Bulaeva 1996; Intiso et al. 1994; Shumway-Cook et al. 1988). However, it has also been used in the sporting environment to enhance the learning and performance of both skilled swimmers, by providing audible signals about their stroke rate (Chollet et al. 1988), and elite rifle shooters, by providing audio signals enabling them to shoot between potentially disruptive heartbeats (Daniels and Landers 1981).

## The frequency and timing of augmented feedback

While the skill level of the performer and the characteristics of the task need to be taken into account when deciding if and what type of augmented feedback is required for skill learning, it is also important to consider the amount and frequency of such feedback as well as its timing (i.e. when it should be given). Early views regarding the presentation of augmented feedback suggested that 'the greater the amount the better the learning', and that it should, therefore, be presented after every practice. However, this view is no longer tenable following the emergence of the guidance hypothesis (Salmoni *et al.* 1984). According to the guidance hypothesis, if the learner receives augmented feedback after every trial they may develop a dependency on it, thus undermining the benefits of important intrinsic sensory feedback required for error detection and correction (Bjork 1988; Schmidt 1991). Consequently, when augmented feedback is not available, performance suffers, as the learner has come to rely upon it to produce the required skill effectively. A number of studies have been carried out examining augmented feedback using a variety of techniques (e.g. Winstein and Schmidt 1990, Janelle *et al.* 1995), the results of which appear to support the guidance hypothesis. Specifically, the research indicates that low-frequency feedback schedules are advantageous to skill learning because they promote problem-solving and encourage learners to explore the dynamics of a skill while utilising task-intrinsic feedback.

A common misconception with regard to the timing of augmented feedback is that it should be provided as soon as possible after completion of the practice trial, because any delay results in the learner forgetting the skill. Research, however, does not support this. Rather, it has demonstrated that there must be a minimum time period given to the learner before augmented feedback is presented (Swinnen *et al.* 1990). This is in accordance with the principles of the guidance hypothesis, which suggests that if the KR delay is too short the learner is unable to fully engage in important intrinsic error detection and correction mechanisms, thus compromising the learning.

A second important timing issue relates to the interval between the presentation of augmented feedback and the beginning of the next practice trial (the post-KR delay). Whilst there is no evidence indicating an optimal period for this interval or an upper limit, the general conclusion is that it can be too short (Gallagher and Thomas 1980; Rogers 1974). This is because the learner requires sufficient time to process both the augmented feedback and the task-intrinsic feedback from the previous trial to produce an action plan for the subsequent response. Thus, for optimal learning, the post-KR delay should be long enough to permit these important learning processes to occur.

To conclude, primary considerations when using augmented feedback are to assess both the characteristics of the learner (e.g. the skill level) and the nature of the to-be-learned skill (i.e. the amount of available task-intrinsic feedback during execution of the skill). These will determine what role additional feedback could play in learning (e.g. is it necessary for learning to occur?). If augmented feedback is deemed necessary for skill learning, a number of different types of presentation techniques are available to the coach. These include verbal, video replays and biofeedback, the merits of which again depend on individual and task factors. For example, video replays are particularly useful to skilled performers (Rothstein and Arnold 1976), although in order to be effective for beginners, videos should be supplemented with cues designed to focus the learners' attention on critical aspects of the skill (Kernodle and Carlton 1992; Newell and Walter 1981). Finally, in line with the guidance hypothesis (Salmoni *et al*. 1984), the frequency and timing of presenting augmented feedback should be considered in order to facilitate optimal learning.

## ATTENTIONAL FOCUS

The first two sections of this chapter have looked at ways in which the learning environment can be manipulated to facilitate learning. The third will focus specifically on the instructions given to learners regarding their focus of attention, the objective of which is to help them produce the appropriate action to realise the desired movement goal. The question of what learners should concentrate on when executing motor skills has received a good deal of recent attention. Traditionally, learners have been given instructions to direct attention towards aspects of the required movement and the co-ordination of their body to achieve it. It has long been assumed that making learners aware of what they are doing is a requisite for successful performance (Baumeister 1984). Indeed, underpinned by research in the field of sport psychology (e.g. Kingston and Hardy 1997), performers are frequently persuaded to adopt a process or task focus, which encourages them to pay explicit attention to technical aspects of the skill. This, it is argued, will enable them to successfully complete the skill. Such instructions, however, are being increasingly questioned in the context of learning and coaching (Baumeister 1984; Hardy *et al*. 1996; Jackson *et al*. 2006; Masters 1992; Mullen and Hardy 2000). Indeed, there is mounting evidence suggesting that instructing performers to be consciously aware of their body movements during skill execution is not a very effective learning strategy, and can actually undermine performance. Wulf and her colleagues (see Wulf and Prinz 2001 for a review), for example, 'demonstrated that directing learners to focus on their body movements, i.e. inducing an "internal" focus of attention, resulted in no learning benefits or even in learning decrements, relative to not giving learners instructions at all' (McNevin *et al*. 2003: 22). Others, however, continue to espouse the merits of giving athletes the what and how of a particular skill to be performed (Masters 2000). The obvious question arising, therefore, is what should athletes be directed to focus upon in order to facilitate learning and the execution of complex sport skills?

### Support for an external focus of attention

One reasonable objective for a coach is to help athletes execute skills in an automated fashion because this is the most efficient manner to perform (and characterises many expert performers). However, because attempting to perform a skill as though it were automatic is very difficult for beginners, Singer (1985, 1988) proposed a five-step approach (Readying, Imaging, Focusing, Executing, Evaluating) to help learners maintain a desired process or task focus, yet distract them from their own movements. The important point here is that, while having the athlete mentally imagine the act before executing it promotes awareness (self-focused attention), the cues used to focus attention need to be external (e.g. the dimples of a golf ball, the anticipated trajectory of a basketball), thus taking attention away from the required movement pattern (Wulf *et al.* 2000). Similarly, related research into the efficacy (i.e. the performance benefits) of using internal cues indicates that, contrary to traditional beliefs (and in comparison to not focusing on how to perform the required skill), 'instructing learners to focus on the details of their movements during performance can be detrimental to performance and learning' (Wulf *et al.* 2000: 230). In expanding and refining this line of research, Wulf and colleagues found that directing learners' attention to the effects of movements (i.e. the result of kicking a ball) was more effective than focusing on the movements themselves. Indeed, in Wulf's tennis-forehand experiment, she found specific learning benefits for those instructed to focus on the anticipated trajectory of the ball (the movement effects) as opposed to the action of hitting the ball itself. A possible explanation for these benefits is provided by Prinz's (1997) action effect hypothesis, which suggests that actions are planned and controlled most effectively by their intended effects.

In order for coaches to buy into using external foci of attention, it is important to justify why the proposed benefits of doing so may occur. According to Wulf *et al.* (2000), focusing on the effects or the consequences of movement allows unconscious control processes to take over. This results in more effective performance and learning than would occur if individuals consciously tried to control their movements or concentrate on something else. Similarly, McNevin *et al.* (2003) argued that consciously intervening in movement production is likely to disrupt the co-ordination of a number of relatively automatic (reflexive and self-organising) processes that normally control the movement, further supporting the efficacy of unconscious control processes in learning and controlling movements.

The negative self-focused attention effect is not exclusive to beginners. Masters (1992) suggests that under certain conditions (e.g. elevated levels of stress) the automatic control processes utilised by expert performers are overridden by the desire to ensure task success. He coined the phrase 'conscious processing' to describe this behaviour. In such cases, individuals adopt a mode of control primarily associated with the early stages of learning (Fitts and Posner 1967), resulting in less effective performance.

While the learning and performance benefits of using an external focus of attention appear robust, McNevin *et al.* (2003) proposed that the advantages of doing so were more profound and appeared earlier in the learning process as the distance of the external focus from the body increased. This was because, at a distance, such foci are more easily distinguishable from the body movements that produce them and, hence, facilitate the utilisation of more natural control processes. These suppositions, however, seem to contradict the results of a second experiment by Wulf *et al.* (2000) using a golf chip-shot task. They found that performers focusing on the swing of the club (a proximal [close to the body] focus) experienced performance and learning benefits compared to those who focused upon the anticipated trajectory of the ball and the target (a distal [away from the body] focus). In trying to explain this apparent anomaly, the authors suggested that focusing upon the club movement (less distal) produced better learning as it provided the learners with more salient information regarding the movement technique (Wulf et al. 2000; Wulf and Prinz 2001). This indicates that complete novices who have yet to grasp the fundamentals of complex tasks may, therefore, benefit from some form of self-monitoring of the action, such as focusing on the details of their movements during performance (Perkins-Ceccato et al. 2003).

## Practical implications

So what does all this mean for coaches? We will now summarise the implications of the preceding discussion and provide some guidance for coaches in relation to attentional focus while considering the broad skill level of those being coached and the complexity of the task itself. The weight of evidence currently suggests that there are benefits to learning motor skills in the absence of internal or self-focused attention on the desired body movements. This internal focus leads to a build-up of explicit rules about task performance that has the potential to hinder learning (Hardy et al. 1996; Poolton et al. 2006). Furthermore, Liao and Masters (2002) provided evidence that learning under self-focused attention appears to lead to more vulnerable (i.e. weaker) performance under stress. Therefore, it is necessary to identify coaching techniques that minimise the tendency of athletes to engage in self-focused attention.

An implicit or unconscious learning strategy, by definition, encourages the development of implicit (non-verbalisable) knowledge that is unavailable to consciousness. Learning under such conditions negates the potential for poor performance due to self-focused attention because there are no explicit rules for self-focused attention to access. One strategy to promote implicit learning is to coach by analogy. The objective of analogous coaching is to encourage athletes to perform the skill being learned using a general analogical rule that acts as a movement metaphor and that, by default, incorporates the technical rules necessary for successful execution of the skill (Masters 2000). For example, the top-spin forehand in tennis can be taught by using the right-angled triangle as an analogy. The learner is asked to imagine following the outline of the triangle using their racket from the preparation of the racket head at the highest (acute) point of the triangle to dropping the racket to the ninety-degree angle, before drawing back along the base of the triangle in order to strike the ball as the racket head returns squarely to the hypotenuse. Embedded within the analogy are many of the rules often associated with teaching this stroke to beginners. Similarly, learner golfers might be asked to replicate the grip used on a hand-axe (in carrying out a chopping action) when being taught the position of the lower hand (right hand for right-handed golfers) of the golf grip. The key with analogies is for the coach to be creative while the metaphor itself should be clearly understood by the athlete.

While analogies give learners the general idea of the movement without the use of explicit rules, they may not enable the learner to garner sufficient information to evaluate effectively and then alter an unsuccessful performance (Bennett 2000). Consequently, for more complex skills it may be important that learners have a knowledge of the fundamentals of the skill to be performed in order that they can monitor and evaluate their performance effectively should problems arise. For example, Bennett illustrated (in golf) the value of some fundamental knowledge associated with the stance and club-head approach that would enable a slicing golfer to make adjustments to remedy that problem. Such fundamentals can be taught by coaches through facilitating an intrinsic or kinaesthetic (i.e. bodily movement) appreciation in athletes of the desired technique without recourse to explicit rules.

For more capable/skilled performers, coaches can be left in a tricky situation. With too much explicit knowledge, players are likely to be susceptible to negative stress effects caused by conscious processing (Masters 1992). However, without it it is unlikely that players will achieve high levels of performance. A solution is to ensure that players have strategies in place to negate the tendency (under stressful conditions) to use explicit rules inappropriately when attempting to ensure task success (as these undermine rather than support successful task execution). One coping strategy that has received widespread support in this respect is that of pre-performance routines (Jackson et al. 2006). These are most relevant in sports that have closed-skill elements (i.e. where the environment is stable, as in golf). Here, absorbing one's self in a given set of behaviours designed to support task performance may provide a means of resisting the effects of self-focused attention.

While there is widespread support for focusing on a set of processes that are chunked together to form a pre-performance routine (see, for example, Boutcher 1990), an alternative strategy is to focus on an isolated aspect of the skill that, if executed effectively, will permit successful performance. This describes what has been coined in the sport psychology literature as a process goal (Kingston and Hardy 1997). However, despite supportive evidence that focusing on isolated aspects of technique might facilitate performance (e.g. Filby et al. 1999; Kingston and Hardy 1997; Zimmerman and Kitsantas 1996), such a process focus has been questioned. Primarily it has been challenged on the premise that promoting step-by-step monitoring and control of complex procedural knowledge, which typically operates automatically, results in performance impairment (e.g. Hardy et al. 1996; Jackson et al. 2006; Masters 1992). Furthermore, and more specifically, Jackson et al. (2006) provided strong evidence that movement-related process goals were detrimental to performance regardless of individual tendencies for self-focused attention and situational pressure. However, in line with Kingston and Hardy (1997), Jackson went on to suggest that subtly different process goals may have different attentional functions. For example, process goals that take attention away from the physical movements being performed (e.g. functioning as holistic cues for the desired action) do not encourage explicit monitoring (Jackson et al. 2006). To illustrate, holistic-process goals (as distinct from isolated- [or part] process goals), which are less rule-based representations of the to-be-performed skill (for example, holistic process goals describing the 'whole' movement could take the form of 'smooth', 'extended' or 'controlled') may encourage performers to execute skills using more automatic control structures (Jackson et al. 2006). Finally, more global strategies to reduce the tendency for performers to engage in self-focused attention during potentially stress-inducing situations might be to promote trust (Moore and Stevenson 1994) and self-confidence. The issue of developing self-confidence is examined in greater depth in Chapter 3: 'Psychology for coaches'.

In closing this section on attentional focus, it is important to acknowledge that this area of research continues to develop. What we have attempted to do is highlight a body of research that brings into question traditional notions of coaching where athletes are instructed to focus on their movements while executing skills. It is equally clear that subtle differences in athletes' focus of attention can have significant effects on both learning and performance. Furthermore, these effects vary (and in some cases will produce the opposite to the desired effect) according to the skill level of those to whom the instructions are given.

## CONCLUSION

The aim of this chapter has been to identify the current state of play regarding three of the central issues pertinent to the acquisition of skills as specifically related to what Schmidt and Wrisberg (2000) coined the learning experience. For each, a contemporary review of relevant literature was presented, accompanied by an illustration of how this knowledge can be applied by coaches. Broadly speaking, we have tried to illustrate how learning has the potential to be facilitated by a number of factors. These include: practice schedules that promote cognitive (mental) activity; the appropriate use of certain types of feedback, with particular consideration given to frequency and timing; and the utility of an appropriate focus of attention that encourages learners to allow natural control processes to run free. Although we believe such suggestions provide lines of good practice in relation to skill learning, it is important to remember that coaches still need to consider carefully the characteristics of both the individual performer and the task to be performed in structuring optimal learning environments.

**REVIEW QUESTIONS**

1. Why is random practice important for developing skills? What are the reasons for its positive effects?
2. The use of augmented feedback should be tailored to the individual athlete and the specific task in question. Discuss with reference to the types, as well as the frequency and timing, of such feedback.
3. Why is it important for coaches to promote a focus of attention that allows natural control processes to run free?

# CHAPTER THREE

# PSYCHOLOGY FOR COACHES

Kieran Kingston, Owen Thomas and
Ian Mitchell

*Competitive sports are played mainly on a five-and-a-half-inch court, the space
between your ears.*

Bobby Jones –
(the only person to complete golf's Grand Slam
of all four major championships in one year)

## Key sections:

- Introduction
- What is sport psychology?
- Motivation
- Self-confidence in sport
- Stress and anxiety in sport
- Conclusion

## INTRODUCTION

The formal application of psychological principles to sport has increased tremendously over the past 20 years. This has been evidenced by the number of athletes and coaches now looking to sport psychology to gain an edge over their competitors (Williams and Straub 2001). Despite this recognition, coaches' application of sport psychology has been, and often remains, ad hoc and unstructured in nature. The aim of this chapter is to further illuminate the value of sport psychology to coaches and, rather than simply providing a 'how-to' of techniques, to illustrate how appropriate theoretical principles can be systematically applied to maximise athletic performances. We start by defining the discipline of sport psychology before focusing on the areas of motivation, self-confidence, and stress and anxiety. Each of these is examined in terms of selected, pertinent theories, their implications for coaching and their potential application by coaches, taking into account certain mediating factors. Finally, we conclude with a summary that highlights the collective value of the applied implications of the constructs discussed for sports coaches.

## WHAT IS SPORT PSYCHOLOGY?

One would think that defining what has become a recognised field of academic pursuit would be a simple enough exercise. This is not, however, the case. Indeed, Dishman (1983) has suggested that sport psychology sometimes suffers from an identity crisis. The reason for this is the many and varied perspectives that exist within the field. Nevertheless, a summary definition (based on a number given by Feltz and Kontos 2002) describes sport psychology as the study of people's behaviour and thoughts in sporting contexts. Furthermore, the general goal of applied sport psychology is to provide athletes and coaches with the necessary mental skills to manage the demands of training and competition, thus helping each realise his/her potential.

Under the broad umbrella of sport psychology, we have identified three principal areas for attention, namely: motivation; self-confidence; and stress and anxiety. A reasonable question might be, Why these and not others? In response, we believe that, as applied practitioners (i.e. sport psychology consultants), a high proportion of the issues we come across either falls within or is underpinned by these aspects. That is, much of the work we do focuses on developing and sustaining athletes' confidence and motivation, whilst providing them with tools to regulate anxiety and arousal. Consequently, in identifying the areas most pertinent to cover, we have been led by the needs of athletes and coaches. Furthermore, whilst one might reasonably expect a section on team issues, we determined that when working in such environments most of the psychological issues that arise do so at an individual level. Readers interested in the psychology of teams, therefore, are guided to other, more specific texts (for example, Carron et al. 2005).

## MOTIVATION

Understanding the dynamic and complex psychological processes of motivation is critical to understanding human behaviour, especially in sport (Roberts 2001). Motivation refers to the personality factors, social variables and cognitions that act in situations where one is evaluated, competes against others or attempts to attain a standard of excellence (Roberts 2001). In an applied context, it can be thought of as 'the personal drive that leads individuals to initiate, direct, and sustain human behaviour' (Kingston et al. 2006: 2). Similarly, according to Ryan and Deci (2000), motivation lies at the core of biological, cognitive and social regulation and is, therefore, a pre-eminent concern for those whose roles involve mobilising others to act (e.g. coaches).

Within sport and exercise psychology, motivation can be viewed from a number of vantage points. Two of the most popular from an applied perspective are self-determination theory (SDT) (Deci and Ryan 1985) and achievement goal theory (AGT) (Nicholls 1989). Both adopt a social-cognitive perspective (i.e. they emphasise that the way individuals perceive social factors determines both their application to an activity and the quality of their engagement in that activity), and each have extensive applications to sport and exercise psychology. Subsequently, they have facilitated our understanding of the dynamics of motivation and its related cognitive, affective (i.e. emotional) and behavioural outcomes.

## Self-determination theory

Self-determination theory (SDT) is based on the premise that individuals have innate tendencies toward psychological growth and development, to master ongoing challenges and, through their experiences, to develop a coherent sense of self (i.e. who they are as individuals) (Deci and Ryan 2000). Specifically, Deci and Ryan (1985) have argued that three universal psychological needs are fundamental to motivation and psychological well-being. These are the desires for competence, autonomy and relatedness. The need for competence encompasses people's strivings to interact effectively with their environment (Harter 1978), to seek control over outcomes and to experience mastery (Kingston et al. 2006). The need for autonomy refers to the desire to be self-initiating in determining one's actions (Vallerand and Losier 1999), while the need for relatedness concerns the wish to feel connected and to have a sense of mutual respect and reliance in relation to others (Baumeister and Leary 1995). The extent to which these needs are fulfilled by the social context (e.g. the sporting environment) influences the degree to which an individual's motivation is self-determined (Deci and Ryan 2000). More self-determined forms of motivation (via the satisfaction of innate needs) produce positive consequences (e.g. performances) (Vallerand 1997). Within sport settings, research has supported the importance of satisfying innate needs upon motivation (Kowal and Fortier 2000; Standage et al. 2003; Hollembeak and Amorose 2005). Consequently, promoting high levels of self-determination is desirable for coaches interested in facilitating both the motivation and performances of athletes. Although Deci and Ryan (1985) distinguished between a number of motivational styles, we will focus exclusively on methods to promote the most self-determined form of motivation – intrinsic motivation.

Intrinsic motivation describes an inclination towards assimilation, mastery, spontaneous interest and exploration (Ryan and Deci 2000). It involves people engaging in activities voluntarily in the absence of material rewards or external pressures or constraints (Deci and Ryan 1985, 2000). Athletes who practise because they find it interesting, satisfying and for the pleasure associated with striving to overcome challenges are considered to be highly intrinsically motivated (Vallerand 1997). Not surprisingly, therefore, the promotion of high levels of intrinsic motivation should be a primary objective for anyone interested in the development and maintenance of sporting skills (i.e. coaches).

Cognitive evaluation theory (CET), a sub-theory of SDT, was proposed by Deci and Ryan (1985) to illustrate and explain variability in intrinsic motivation (Ryan and Deci 2000). According to CET, social-contextual factors (e.g. rewards, feedback and the nature of communication) can facilitate or forestall intrinsic motivation by supporting or thwarting the innate psychological needs of autonomy and competence. For example, threats, deadlines, directives, pressured evaluation and imposed goals have been shown to undermine intrinsic motivation, whereas choice, acknowledgement of feelings and opportunities for self-direction have been associated with increases in intrinsic motivation (for a fuller review, see Ryan and Deci 2000). An important facet of CET is the proposal that feelings of enhanced competence will not promote intrinsic motivation unless accompanied by a sense of autonomy for the behaviours that caused that competence. Finally, while autonomy and competence have been found to be the most powerful influences on intrinsic motivation, Deci and Ryan (2000) also support the value (albeit somewhat distal by comparison) of relatedness in its maintenance.

According to CET, then, to promote intrinsic motivation coaches should attempt to create an environment (1) where athletes' feelings of competence are promoted by successful achievement of agreed athlete-controllable goals; (2) where rewards give information about competence and effort rather than being perceived as controlling behaviours (undermining autonomy); (3) where feedback is individualised and focuses on effort; and (4) where athletes are given choice, and are at least partially responsible for strategic decisions regarding training and competition. Implementing such policies, however, is not as easy as it sounds. This is because elite sport is, by-and-large, a full-time profession with those involved being subject to many external pressures, which include financial rewards, public and corporate image, public expectations and increasingly difficult competition. Many of these factors are not conducive to developing and satisfying autonomy, competence and relatedness (Deci and Ryan 2000). Nevertheless, it is incumbent upon coaches at the elite level to work hard in searching for ways to provide an environment that continues to support the innate needs of athletes if optimal performance is to be obtained.

## Achievement goal theory

Achievement goal theory (AGT) (Nicholls 1989) has evolved into one of the most popular theoretical approaches for studying achievement motivation in sport and physical activity (Roberts 2001). According to achievement goal theorists (e.g. Nicholls 1989; Dweck and Leggett 1988), the primary intent of individuals in achievement contexts (i.e. situations where performance is likely to be evaluated) is the demonstration of ability. The way individuals judge and interpret their ability, and subsequently define success, determines variations in achievement-related thoughts, behaviours and affective responses (Duda 2001). In developing the theory, Nicholls (1989) suggested that two principal states of involvement exist in achievement contexts; namely, task and ego. Task involvement operates when competence is judged according to some self-referenced criteria (e.g. effort, learning, level of enjoyment, or the degree of self-improvement). Conversely, a state of ego involvement operates when success is based upon some normative reference (e.g. performing well relative to others). Individual differences in the tendency to adopt these states of involvement are usually expressed as task and ego goal orientations (Spray *et al.* 2006). Early goal orientation research indicated that a predominant task orientation relates to selection of moderately challenging tasks, high levels of effort and persistence, intrinsic interest in the activity and sustaining or improving performance (Hodge and Petlichkoff 2000).

According to Nicholls (1989), an individual's perceived competence is central to deter-mining his or her motivation for engaging in a task. The research findings here, however, are a little ambiguous. For example, on the one hand, it is assumed that the adaptive (i.e. positive) motivational outcomes associated with high task orientation function regardless of the accompanying levels of perceived competence (Duda 2001). Contrastingly, however, Nicholls (1989) suggests that perceived competence can change the nature of the effect of ego orientation on motivation (i.e. it acts as a moderator variable). Therefore, when high ego orientated athletes hold high perceptions of competence they are likely to exhibit the adaptive motivational outcomes associated with high task orientation (Hardy 1997; Hodge and Petlichkoff 2000). However, when high ego orientation is combined with low perceived competence, negative outcomes have been demonstrated (Cury *et al.* 1997; Vlachopoulos and Biddle 1997). For example, such athletes might demonstrate a lack of effort, devalue the task when success seems unlikely, and are more likely to drop out of an activity. These individuals are motivationally vulnerable because they define success and competence primarily in relation to others.

Based on the fact that task and ego orientations have different motivational implications (e.g. Duda *et al.* 1992), examining combinations of both could be more appropriate than considering them in isolation (Hardy 1997). Recent research has been dominated by studies adopting this premise (i.e. examining goal profiles) (e.g. Duda *et al.* 1992; Roberts *et al.* 1996; Hodge and Petlichkoff 2000). Such work has found that individuals who exhibit high ego and low task orientations coupled with low perceived competence were most likely to display maladaptive (i.e. negative or counter-productive) behaviours and cognitions (Fox *et al.* 1994). Support has also gathered for the potential cognitive-behavioural benefits of a combination of, or a complementary balance between, moderate to high levels of both task and ego orientation (e.g. Roberts *et al.* 1996; Hodge and Petlichkoff 2000). This complementary balance represents athletes that are motivated both by the desire to demonstrate superior abilities relative to others and to develop and master their own personal skills. The benefit of this is that it guards against the potential maladaptive consequences of a high task orientation (i.e. perfectionism) and a high level of ego orientation as described in the previous paragraph (Gould *et al.* 1996).

The applied implications of achievement goal theory for coaches lie in the need to promote a high level of task involvement for athletes. This, however, is easier said than done in a sports culture that places an overwhelming emphasis on normative comparisons (i.e.

competition). Nevertheless, performers should be guided towards developing a more adaptive, positive representation of what is regarded as a successful performance in achievement settings; the emphasis being on personal skill development and role execution rather than judging performance relative to others. Similarly, the coaching environment, that is the climate created by coaches, should be task-involved, with the emphasis being on effort, improvement, co-operation, and personal targets and objectives.

## SELF-CONFIDENCE IN SPORT

Confidence in sport has been defined in several different ways (Hardy et al. 1996). This section, however, focuses on two approaches that have direct relevance to coaches and sport performance, namely self-efficacy (Bandura 1977b) and sport-confidence (Vealey 1986, 2001).

Bandura's (1977b) self-efficacy theory is concerned with an athlete's perceived ability to perform specific sport skills at a given time (Hardy et al. 1996). Although relatively few studies have directly assessed the relationship between self-efficacy and sports performance, the general consensus indicates support for the proposal that self-efficacy is a key determinant of success (Hardy et al. 1996). Essentially, Bandura's theory indicates that self-efficacy will predict performance if the athlete perceives appropriate skill levels and incentives for personal success are present. According to Bandura (1977b), efficacy expectations (i.e. one's belief that a certain level of performance can be attained) are based on four sources of information: (1) *Performance accomplishments* have the most influence over self-efficacy due to the fact they are based upon an athlete's previous successes and performance of sports skills; (2) *Vicarious experiences* relate to a performer gaining self-efficacy through watching others perform sporting skills; (3) *Verbal persuasion* refers to information conveyed to the performer by the self (i.e. through self-talk) or significant others (i.e. the coach) that helps manipulate behaviour; and (4) *Physiological and emotional arousal control*, the least powerful predictor of self-efficacy, relates to levels of control the performer believes he/she holds over his/her physiological and emotional states (e.g. anxiety). The major implication for coaches here is that they should expose athletes to sources of information that relate directly to these four efficacy domains with a focus towards the top of the hierarchy. For example, coaching strategies that foster accomplishment will have more impact on efficacy than those designed to target emotional arousal control.

Several factors influence the effectiveness of these four sources of information on the level of self-efficacy a performer holds. For instance, the difficulty of the task, the amount of guidance received and effort expended all influence the amount of self-efficacy gained through performance accomplishments. Coaches should, therefore, acknowledge that success by a performer on a difficult task, with relatively little guidance early in the learning experience, facilitates development of self-efficacy more than success at an easy task that is highly dependent on guidance following a series of early failures (Feltz 1988).

Additionally, the relative authenticity of the model, that is the individual being observed, effects the efficacy gains realised through vicarious experience. Consequently, efficacy gains are suggested to be greatest when viewing a model of similar age, gender and athletic ability perform skilled demonstrations (Lirgg and Feltz 1991). Finally, the perceived credibility and expertise of the persuader is suggested to influence potential gains in self-efficacy. These mediators, then, are critical for the coach to consider when modifying the climate athletes are exposed to during training and competition.

Although self-efficacy theory has obvious application for competitive sport, it also has shortcomings. Primarily, critics have argued that self-efficacy may just be a by-product of the anxiety response. Hence, it is the anxiety response rather than efficacy expectation that is the major determinant of behaviour (i.e. performance) (Borkovec 1976). The limitations identified within self-efficacy theory prompted Vealey (1986) to propose a sport-specific model of confidence. In this original model she indicated that state sport confidence (i.e. situation-specific confidence) would be the primary predictor of performance. However, empirical support for this hypothesis has remained scarce. Subsequently, in an attempt to overcome some of the perceived deficiencies evident in the original model of sport-confidence, Vealey et al. (1998) proposed a new one which reconceptualised or collapsed the notion of sport-confidence into a single construct. This was in contrast to the original state-trait distinction previously outlined (Vealey et al. 1998). Additionally, the new model indicated that self-regulation, achievement and social climate were predictors of performance via their impact on effect, cognition and behaviour. Further, she acknowledged the indirect influence of individual difference variables (e.g. gender, personality) as well as social and organisational factors on the development and maintenance of sport-confidence.

As part of their work, Vealey et al. also proposed nine sport-specific predictors that athletes could draw upon to develop their confidence. These included: (1) *Mastery*: information derived from personal mastery or improvement of sport skills; (2) *Demonstration of ability*: demonstrating more ability than opponents in competitive settings; (3) *Physical and mental preparation*: where the athlete feels physically and mentally prepared with an optimal performance focus; (4) *Physical self-presentation*: based on an athlete's perception of their physical self or body image; (5) *Social support*: received in the form of positive feedback and encouragement from coaches, teammates and/or friends; (6) *Vicarious experience*: based on the contentions that observing or seeing other athletes perform successfully serves to foster confidence; (7) *Coach leadership*: where the athlete gains confidence from believing in the coach's decision-making and leadership qualities; (8) *Environmental comfort*: a source of confidence derived from feeling comfortable with the competitive environment (e.g. competing with home advantage); and (9) *Situational favourableness*: where the performer gains confidence from the perception that the breaks or the benefits of the situation are in his or her favour (e.g. umpire decisions).

Having identified these nine sources, Vealey (2001) categorised them to fit within three broad domains: (1) *Achievement* (i.e. mastery and demonstration of ability); (2) *Self-regulation* (i.e. physical/mental preparation and physical self-presentation); and (3) *Social climate* (i.e. social support, vicarious experience, coach leadership, environmental comfort and situational favourableness). Essentially, Vealey indicated that these three domains could act as a framework to guide coaches' attempts to target and develop athletes' confidence. Such a standpoint echoes that of self-efficacy theory and the notion that the four sources of information used for efficacy expectations (i.e. performance accomplishment, vicarious experience, verbal persuasion and emotional control) provide a theoretical base from which to underpin the construction of applied interventions. Consequently, the following section details such possible interventions and coach behaviour issues according to the constructs of achievement, self-regulation and social climate.

Both Bandura's theory of self-efficacy and Vealey's theory of sport-confidence give us considerable insight into how confidence can be gained in an achievement context. Unsurprisingly, the coach has a significant role to play here in creating a sense of achievement in both the training and competitive environments. Lines of accepted practice in this context include acknowledging the athlete's perception of prior competitive success, introducing game scenarios within training sessions (e.g. performance-related scenarios), encouraging athletes to use reflective logbooks detailing past competitive success, considering the use of highlighted DVD footage that demonstrates skill execution, in addition to engaging in effective goal-setting programmes that alter the perceived difficulty of performances (Vealey 2001). In relation to the latter, it is important for the coach to set goals that are controllable for the performer in both competition and training, and to evaluate these in terms of personal performance rather than social comparison (Kingston and Hardy 1997).

Self-regulation (i.e. the management of one's behaviours, thoughts and feelings) provides a further domain through which the coach and psychologist can strive to foster performers' confidence (Vealey 2001). This links to mental skill training through the self-regulatory strategies of goal-mapping, imagery and self-talk. Coaches could promote the use of goal-mapping through the creation of a goal plan that incorporates systematic and ongoing assessment of progress towards achieving these goals (Burton *et al.* 2001). Effective monitoring of programmes allows athletes to gain confidence through self-regulation, whilst imagery, or visualisation, of successful performance provides them with confidence gains through vicarious information. Imagery can either be used within a self-regulatory capacity (i.e. imaging control of the self, emotions, and behaviour within the competitive environment) or within an achievement context through imaging successful performance and accomplishment of specific sports skills (Vealey 2001). The effective management of self-talk by athletes can also foster confidence through verbal persuasion. Here coaches and sport psychologists could assist athletes through self-talk programmes that provide control over negative thought processes and promote the use of positive self-affirmation (Zinsser *et al.* 2001). It should also be noted that successful implementation of these skills may impact confidence through the achievement domain.

A coach can also enhance athlete confidence through the leadership style they adopt and the consequent social climate created. In particular, coaches need to be flexible in order to influence an athlete's perception of control. For example, the adoption of a collaborative style, if used appropriately, could facilitate confidence to achieve shared goals and allow the coach to provide contingent reinforcement and informative feedback. Ensuring effective social support to the athlete also serves as an important source of confidence in terms of his or her perception of the resources available to cope with the various demands of competitive sport. These issues can be targeted through team-building activities and the education of significant others (e.g. spouse, parents, peers). A coach can facilitate this process through an awareness of the social context and the individual situations of athletes.

## STRESS AND ANXIETY IN SPORT

The area of competitive anxiety has received unrivalled attention within sport psychology literature (Woodman and Hardy 2001a). Before identifying some of the specific interventions, it is important to consider the research that provides the theoretical base for them. For reasons of clarity, we begin this section with a definition of two key terms of particular relevance, namely: *Competitive stressors*: the environmental demands (i.e. stimuli) associated with competitive performance; and *Competitive anxiety*: a specific negative emotional response to competitive stressors (Mellalieu *et al.* 2006).

Perhaps the first major development within competitive anxiety was the distinction made between trait and state anxiety. Consequently, anxiety symptoms were considered both as responses to situation-specific stressors or stimuli (i.e. state-like), as well as a dispositional response that exists across all settings (i.e. trait-like). A further advance was the development of multi-dimensional anxiety theory (MAT: Martens *et al.* 1990), which saw state anxiety responses separated into cognitive and somatic components. Cognitive anxiety was defined as the cognitive elements of the anxiety response, characterised by thoughts of worry, concern and negative self-evaluation (Martens *et al.* 1990). Somatic anxiety was, in contrast, described as the physiological or affective (i.e. emotional) effects of the anxiety response (e.g. butterflies, sweaty palms), and was manifest through experiencing feelings such as nervousness and tension (Martens *et al.* 1990).

In terms of working with athletes, and understanding anxiety responses, one of the more important areas of research (adopting this multi-dimensional framework) is concerned with the antecedents (i.e. the precursors and/or causes) of anxiety and the changes in anxiety's intensity and frequency over time. Here, studies have identified different antecedents for cognitive and somatic anxiety. Years of experience, perceived readiness and attitudes towards previous performance are reported as the major factors influencing cognitive anxiety, while levels of trait anxiety are believed to be the major antecedent of somatic anxiety (Woodman and Hardy 2001a). Support for a distinction between cognitive and somatic anxiety has led to interventions that match the construct to the required treatment (Morris *et al.* 1981; Maynard and Cotton 1993). For example, techniques such as progressive-muscular relaxation programmes (Ost 1988) have been used to target somatic anxiety symptoms, while thought stopping and positive thought control (Suinn 1987) have been employed to target cognitive anxiety. The primary function of these techniques is to reduce the level (i.e. the intensity) of anxiety symptoms experienced by athletes.

A further conceptual development within anxiety literature was provided by Hardy and colleagues (Hardy 1990; Hardy and Parfitt 1991) through their catastrophe model of anxiety, physiological arousal and performance (see Woodman and Hardy 2001a for a complete review). In comparison to MAT, this model included actual physiological arousal rather than somatic anxiety (i.e. the perception of this state), and attempted to explain the relationship between the three variables through a series of interactive rather than additive effects. Some of the key implications from the model indicated that cognitive anxiety does not always have a negative influence over competitive performance and that, under conditions of high cognitive anxiety, it is performers' ability to deal with increases in physiological arousal (e.g. through relaxation techniques) that determines whether their performance levels remain high (Hardy 1990).

The notion that anxiety is not always detrimental to performance links to recent developments where, in addition to the intensity (i.e. level or amount) of anxiety experienced, interpretations of anxiety symptoms have been considered (Jones 1991). These interpretations have been labelled directional perceptions and relate to the extent to which performers interpret the intensity of their anxiety symptoms to be positive (facilitative) or negative (debilitative) (Jones 1995). Research in this area has indicated that elite athletes, in addition to using more psychological skills (Fletcher and Hanton 2001), are highly competitive (Jones and Swain 1992) and more confident (Hanton and Jones 1997) than non-elite athletes, and also better able to interpret the symptoms associated with anxiety as being more facilitative towards performance. This has led to a shift in practitioners' approaches. Specifically, applied sport psychologists are starting to move towards adopting techniques that foster facilitative interpretations of anxiety symptoms (i.e. reinterpreting anxiety symptoms as positive rather than negative) over techniques that are designed to solely reduce the intensity of the anxiety a performer experiences (Hanton and Jones 1999a and b). From a coaching perspective, the implication is that it is not the amount of anxiety but rather the way in which the athlete interprets that anxiety that is critical for performance. This point becomes more important when considering the demands of certain sports. For example, some sports (e.g. contact sports) may require higher levels of anxiety (or activation as it is labelled when describing the cognitive and physiological activity that is geared towards a planned response [Pribram and McGuinness 1975]) to achieve the desired performance. Consequently, it may be illogical in this context to reduce the anxiety symptoms via traditional stress management techniques. Rather, coaches should recognise the need for a restructuring approach through, for example, encouraging athletes to view their symptoms as reflective of an optimal level of preparedness as opposed to ones that may debilitate performance (Mellalieu et al. 2006).

Another important consideration for the coach is that the stress response is not static. Hence, anxiety symptoms have the potential to change during the time leading up to competition (Mellalieu et al. 2006). Here, both the intensity and the frequency of anxiety symptoms tend to increase as competition moves closer. Within this context it has become apparent that, in comparison to intensity, frequency is more sensitive to fluctuations during the seven days directly preceding competition (Swain and Jones 1993; Hanton et al. 2004). Consequently, those athletes with more facilitative interpretations of anxiety experience lower frequencies of anxiety symptoms and higher frequencies of confidence symptoms during the time preceding competition. For the coach, these findings suggest that athletes can alter the way they view their mental states during the time leading up to performance (Hanton et al. 2004, Thomas et al. 2004).

Coaches and athletes, then, could, or perhaps should, seek to integrate psychological skills (e.g. imagery, goal-setting, and cognitive restructuring) into their preparation within seven days pre-competition, focusing specifically towards the final 48 and 24 hours before the competitive event. This could offset increases in the intensity and frequency of experienced cognitive and somatic anxiety and (with an appropriate restructuring strategy) lead to a more facilitative interpretation of cognitive and somatic symptoms during the time leading up to performance (Hanton et al. 2004).

In addition to experiencing stressors that are characterised as competitive in nature (i.e. demands associated with competitive performance), contemporary research within sport psychology has indicated that athletes are also readily exposed to, and thus need to consider, organisational stressors (Fletcher et al. 2006). Organisational stressors are defined as 'environmental demands (i.e. stimuli) associated directly and primarily with the organisation within which an individual is operating' (Fletcher et al. 2006: 329). Within this context, four major stress-related domains have been identified, namely: environmental, personal, leadership and team issues (Woodman and Hardy 2001b). Fletcher and Hanton (2003) provided support for these constructs in addition to identifying several other related issues. These included accommodation, travel, and competition environment and safety. Taken collectively, these findings suggest that it is important not only to consider performers' anxiety responses in relation to competitive demands, but also to take into account organisational and environmental pressures when preparing athletes for competition.

It has been proposed that interventions addressing organisational stress should be targeted at three specific levels (Fletcher et al. 2006). At a primary level, coaches should focus on the overall demand placed on athletes as a consequence of their performance environments (i.e. training and competition). For example, by clarifying roles within the organisational hierarchy, a more proactive approach is adopted that can lessen certain organisational stressors. At a secondary level, specific stress management issues for the athlete can be addressed that may include team members generating 'what if?' scenarios, where coping with problematic situations is discussed together with contingency plans to deal with them (Fletcher and Hanton 2003). Finally, at a tertiary level, interventions should focus on the treatment of problems once they have transpired. In these cases, practitioners (i.e. coaches and/or sport psychologists) should promote educational coping programmes, clinical counselling and athlete assisted programmes (Fletcher et al. 2006).

## CONCLUSION

The objective of this chapter has been to illustrate the value of psychological knowledge to coaches by providing a theoretical context for its application. While writing in a text such as this precludes us from covering every eventuality, in focusing on the three areas of motivation, confidence, and stress and anxiety, we have tried to target the types of issues that coaches are most likely to come across in their dealings with athletes. So what can we conclude as we draw this chapter to an end? Firstly, in reviewing what we consider to be some of the most salient and robust theories in relation to the performing athlete that currently exist in sport psychology, we conclude that coaches should provide athletes with a sense of control in an environment that promotes personal perceptions of competence, and the opportunity to set goals and judge performance against self-referenced objectives. Secondly, in terms of confidence within sport, coaches need to recognise the value of creating environments that permit athletes to gain confidence not only through achievement but also through personal management skills (self-regulation) and positive social interaction (e.g. with coaches, peers, parents). Thirdly, with regard to the area of stress and anxiety, coaches should attempt to account for and manage anxiety at an environmental and organisational level, whilst recognising it as a multi-dimensional, changeable and potentially beneficial (to those performers with the tools to harness it appropriately) facet of competitive sport. Finally, a pervasive message to coaches seeking to help create an environment supportive of optimal athlete performance is that, whatever the issues that arise, consideration must be given to athletes' (often) changing perceptions of task demands and their individual differences in psychological make-up.

### REVIEW QUESTIONS

1. Why is it important that coaches promote a high degree of self-determination within their athletes? What methods can they use to achieve this?
2. Vealey (2001) identified a number of sources of athlete confidence. Describe the three broad domains into which these fall and illustrate strategies that coaches might use to facilitate such confidence.
3. Why is it limiting to consider only the intensity of anxiety responses?

# PART 2

# CHAPTER FOUR

# SOCIOLOGY FOR COACHES

Scott Fleming and Robyn L. Jones

*We work in an environment which involves us continually managing interactions with people. In this respect, social knowledge is absolutely essential.*

Chris Davey –
Wales Rugby Union U21 coach (1997–2006);
Grand Slam winners (1998–9; 2002–3 and 2004–5)

**Key sections:**

- Introduction
- What is sociology?
- How can sociology help coaches?
- Macro-sociology and how it can help coaches
- Micro-sociology and how it can help coaches
- Conclusion

## INTRODUCTION

Some years ago, a tentative case was made by one of the authors and colleagues (Jones 2000; Potrac and Jones 1999) related to sociology's relevance to coaches. Indeed, sociology was claimed to be the invisible ingredient in coaches' knowledge, which built on an earlier article by Jarvie (1990a) arguing for the application of sociology to the real world of the sport practitioner. The case made was based on the premise that, as sport (and those who partake in it) happens within society as opposed to some social vacuum, it must be influenced by wider social factors. Consequently, it would be a very unwise coach who did not pay heed to the powerful shaping forces of class, ethnicity and gender (among others) on individual identities as he or she seeks to enhance the performances of athletes. Since then, the argument for sociology as being useful for coaches has been developed to include a more refined theoretical position (e.g. Jones *et al.* 2002), and by empirical studies directly supporting it (Cushion and Jones 2006; Jones *et al.* 2004). This includes an investigation into the power-ridden coach–athlete relationship, the interaction that both shapes and is shaped by it, and the subsequent context or climate created (Purdy 2006).

Despite the value of sociological considerations to coaches being increasingly high-lighted, it is obvious that many still question their worth. Indeed, this scepticism is clearly seen both in existing professional coach education programmes and academic coaching courses. Here, recourse to and discussion of such notions as coaches' agency within structural constraints – that is, what coaches choose to do and how they are influenced to choose what they do – are conspicuous by their absence. The question, then, appears to remain: of what value is sociology to coaches? The aim of this chapter is to address this issue by further clarifying the relevance of sociology and the related notion of sociological competence to coaches, whilst also suggesting ways in which coaches can better develop such competence. Following a brief definition of sociology, and in particular the ongoing debate surrounding the influence of agency (i.e. a person's free will) and social structures (i.e. education, family etc.) on behaviour, a general case for how sociological knowledge can help coaches is presented. This is followed by a discussion of both macro- and micro-sociological perspectives with, again, their particular relevance for coaches being outlined. Finally, a conclusion summarises the principal points made.

## WHAT IS SOCIOLOGY?

According to Lemert (1997), most of the time we have no reason to think about such an abstract concept as society. Indeed, most of us have a good enough common sense of what goes on in the social world, otherwise we could never survive within it. Such sense refers to our logic of social things, of our personal sociologies; that is, our knowledge of how to manage our lives in terms of our interactions with others. Sociology, then, refers to our understanding of how we live with others, thus comprising a society. Similarly, social life works because most people live their sociologies or exercise their sociological competence (Lemert 1997). Lemert (1997) defines such competence as the highly practical, seemingly always present, capacity that we have to sustain relations. For him, everyday acts such as greeting strangers, getting deadlines extended and even asking for a Big Mac without fries all entail exercising one's sociological competence, in that such situations require certain social rules be adhered to in order to get what we desire.

Most people, however, take such knowledge for granted. Hence, they are unwilling or unable to describe and understand the often complex social relations and interactions that affect them. This is the difficulty often faced by sociologists; to make real for people the link between personal (individual) and public (social) issues. The ability to do this was famously referred to as one's 'sociological imagination' (C. Wright Mills 1959), and is a concept we will return to later. The value of sociology and sociological knowledge, then, is to increase social competence, that is to better understand why we behave in the ways we do. This involves developing an understanding of the social structures through which power is exercised, and how to better deal with them (Jones 2000). Indeed, an explanation of power and the ways it is manifested or expressed is central to the sociological enterprise that, in turn, seeks to explore the tensions between an individual's agency or free will and the forces that act upon and affect that will. Consequently, within sociology there exists an ongoing debate between two principal schools of thought; on the one side are those who consider that a person's behaviour is shaped principally through the influence of social forces, such as education, race, gender and the family – such theorists are said to lean towards a structural explanation of behaviour; and on the other side there exist scholars who are more prepared to give weight to individuals' agency, or free will, in determining their actions. Most sociologists, of course, acknowledge that individuals are who they are partly because of what they do with what they have, *and* partly because of what the wider social world gives them or takes away (Lemert 1997). The debate then is one of leanings and relative positions, as opposed to absolute ones.

## HOW CAN SOCIOLOGY HELP COACHES?

Now that a definition of sociology and what can be described as sociological competence has been outlined, let us examine how such knowledge can be of use to coaches. The argument given here is not based on some armchair theorising, but on what coaches themselves say about the nature of their job. For example, recent work has tentatively concluded that many elite coaches consider their work as being very social in nature (Jones *et al.* 2004; Potrac *et al.* 2002). Here greater importance was given to managing the coach–athlete relationship in establishing and maintaining the respect of athletes than any other aspect of coaches' work. This is not to say that other forms of knowledge related to, for example, sport specifics or psychological insight are not needed, but that without appropriate social interaction to ensure athletes do what is asked of them, such additional knowledge fields are of little use. This interaction involves the way that athletes are treated both individually and as part of a collective group. It also includes a recognition that power in many ways is given to coaches by athletes who, therefore, can withdraw their consent if they so desire. A social tightrope, then, often needs to be walked by coaches between establishing direction for athletes and involving the latter in the decision-making process (or giving them the illusion that they are!), whilst at all times projecting an image that they are in control of every situation (Potrac *et al.* 2002). Of course, this is where coaches' sociological competence comes in, that is the knowledge of how to manage situations that comprise many athletes, each of whom may have his or her own agenda for being there (Jones and Wallace 2005). Such questions as: How should I treat this athlete? What are the consequences for him/her and my relationship with the rest of the group if I do that (or not)? and, How can I convince everyone of my strategy? all relate to managing social interaction with others in an unavoidably power-influenced context. Hence, the value of sociology and of developing coaches' sociological competence becomes increasingly clear. After all, far from being an easy-to-follow, step-by-step sequence, coaching involves the messy business of getting others to do what you want them to when maybe they don't want to. It involves manipulating and managing relationships and social environments to achieve desired ends. Yet, in spite of this evidence for the value of sociology to coaches, sociological knowledge has yet to find its way into established coach education programmes. Consequently, the following section makes the case that it should in greater detail, through an examination of both macro- and micro-sociological perspectives.

## MACRO-SOCIOLOGY AND HOW IT CAN HELP COACHES

Macro-sociology is concerned with the systematic study of human societies. At the risk of over-simplification, it is about understanding societies as wholes and focuses on the big picture. Inevitably this includes human behaviour and interaction, the contexts in which they occur, as well as social institutions. Typically, then, macro-sociologists focus their attention on particular aspects or institutions of society, for example education, media, religion, work, and so on. Importantly for our purposes, they are also concerned with sport.

Macro-sociologists, therefore, are interested in the structures that shape the social experiences and life-chances of people. Broadly, there are those who are concerned with consensus and adopt a structural-functional approach, and others who are concerned with conflict, seeing the social order as characterised by inequality. Within these divisions there are further sub-groups of social theory (for further discussion of these and their application to sport, see Giulianotti [2004] and Jarvie and Maguire [1994]). At first sight, these theories can appear to be a bewildering array of ways of viewing the world, and there are times when sociologists' jargon can make the material almost impenetrable. A helpful way forward, however, is to explore macro-sociology through some examples.

Over forty years ago, Peter Berger (1963)[1] wrote about what he called the sociological perspective. More recently, John Macionis (2007) has identified three main features of this perspective: (i) seeing the general in the particular; (ii) seeing the strange in the familiar; and (iii) seeing personal choice in social context. In examining each one in greater detail, it is widely acknowledged that sociologists often attempt to see the general in the particular. That is to say, sociologists often seek to establish patterns in human behaviour based on an understanding of particular people. In a study of South-Asian youth, one of us (Fleming 1995) spent time in a secondary school and as an assistant coach in London, in order to get a better understanding of such a group's experiences of sport. It was not claimed that this understanding would apply to all South-Asian youth, not even to all South-Asian youth in London. Rather, the context and circumstances of the school were described and, based

1. As with Wright Mills's (1959) *sociological imagination*, Berger's (1963) *sociological perspective* might seem a rather dated theoretical construct, especially when contrasted with the rapid and recent theoretical advances made in other coaching sciences disciplines (e.g. psychology). However, the works by Wright Mills and Berger are examples of classic theoretical contributions to sociology that have not lost their currency with the passing of time.

on this evidence, inferences and implications were drawn about similar schools in similar kinds of places.

Indeed, the exploration of race and ethnicity in British sport illustrates plainly this more general approach. From Cashmore's (1982) work based on elite sports*men*, through Jarvie's (1991) edited collection to a recent volume by Carrington and McDonald (2001), the effects of ethnicity and racism on sportspersons are clearly highlighted. Some relate to the social processes of stacking (where members of particular minority ethnic groups are disproportionately represented in certain positions in team sports) and channelling (where stereotypes about young African-Caribbeans result in them being encouraged to dedicate themselves to sport). Other examples include more explicit manifestations of racism in football (Merkel and Tokarski 1996; Burley and Fleming 1997; King 2004), cricket (Carrington 1999), and rugby league cultures (Long *et al.* 1997). These all illustrate, to some extent at least, the ways in which macro-sociological analyses are derived from empirical research, and how an understanding of particular instances or evidence is generalised more widely.

Secondly, macro-sociologists often look for the strange in the familiar. Rather than accepting those experiences that are routine in our lives and the lives of others, such sociologists often question those things that are sometimes taken for granted. In other words, they often start from the understanding that things are not always what they seem. Celia Brackenridge's (2001) investigative sociological enquiry into some of the abusive practices that exist in sport illustrates this. For example, the feminist sociologist Kari Fasting (2001: xv) notes in the Foreword to Brackenridge's book, 'For many young people sport is an enjoyable activity'. Indeed, for most participants it is, where many admirable virtues and qualities are cultivated. Similarly, it is often described as fun, presenting what we recognise as the familiar face of sport. However, Fasting continues:

> but not for everyone. Some . . . will have their lives destroyed during those years when they are active in sport. These are the girls and boys, young women and men who are exploited sexually by peers and/or authority figures.

This is the less familiar face of sport; the strange face, and some coaches are implicated. A small number have even been prosecuted and convicted of criminal offences.

As familiar as sport itself is the broadcast media coverage of sport. At first glance this might seem to be merely a matter of presenting the sports action and offering opinion about it. But as Garry Whannel (1992) has demonstrated, it is much more complicated than that; it involves particular representations of institutions and ideologies. For example, the way that women's sport and sportswomen are treated by the print and broadcast media often betrays a marginalised and trivialised status for female athletes, not to mention their objectification and sexualisation (Hargreaves 1994). Such examples illustrate the way that macro-sociologists look beyond the obvious, seek alternative (often critical) perspectives and deploy their own sociological imagination by examining afresh those everyday features of sport that are often taken for granted.

Thirdly, macro-sociologists also see personal choice in social context. That is to say, they are interested in how society and societal factors shape the personal choices that individuals make. The history of sport in Britain is one of class relations (see Hargreaves 1986; Holt 1992; Polley 1998), and Ken Roberts's (2004: 50) analysis of General Household Survey data shows the ways in which social class continues to shape participation levels. As he explains, the higher socio-economic strata participate more, and the reasons for the skew are straightforward: 'the better-off are the most likely to possess the transport, equipment, interest, skills and social networks that allow them to take advantage [of the opportunities available]'. Moreover, as well as the participation levels, social class also affects the participation choices that can be made. At an intuitive level, as Armour (2000) has noted, it is possible to attach class labels to many sports. Inevitably, there have been different attempts to make sense of the social status of particular sports and these have yielded different interpretations. Yet it is clear that, in general, those who participate in three-day eventing, polo and real tennis are from a different socio-economic background from those who participate in boxing, darts and football (Adonis and Pollard 1997).

Let us now briefly consider how this sociological knowledge might inform coaches and coaching practice. In the aforementioned *The Sociological Imagination*, C. Wright Mills (1959) noted the importance of history and biography and the relation between the two. As Knuttila (1996) elaborates, each of us has an individual life story, with each of us being situated in, and shaped by, the socio-historical context. In short, humankind displays astonishing social diversity, and it is important (even essential) for coaches to recognise this diversity in their interactions with athletes. We recognise that it appears common practice today to acknowledge that children are not merely mini-adults, and are not treated as such by good coaches. But are other aspects of social diversity identified and accommodated with the same awareness and understanding? Finally, in this context, Wright Mills (1959: 14) also noted the connection between personal troubles and public issues: 'an essential tool of the sociological imagination and a feature of all classic work in social science'. Thus, when *one* aspiring young athlete living in a rural area is unable to access high-quality coaching because of geographical remoteness, that is a regrettable personal trouble. If however, *many* (perhaps even *all*) aspiring young athletes living in rural areas encounter the same difficulty, that is then a public issue of social structure and needs to be tackled on a societal level (see Jarvie 1990b).

## MICRO-SOCIOLOGY AND HOW IT CAN HELP COACHES

As distinct from macro-sociology, micro-sociology is often concerned with face-to-face interaction (Powers 2004). Consequently, rather than emphasising the influence of social structures on the experiences, behaviours and life-chances of people, such a perspective focuses on individuals' behaviour usually in response to the behaviour of others (Marsh *et al*. 1996). It is often associated with theories such as social and symbolic interactionism, which examine how people understand one another, 'interpret what is going on around them and choose to behave in particular ways' (Marsh *et al*. 1996: 71).

Recent work utilising this approach has recently been carried out into the coaching context (e.g. Cushion and Jones 2006; Potrac et al. 2002). This has been done from both the perspective of coaches (Jones et al. 2003; Purdy 2006) and athletes (Jones et al. 2005; Purdy 2006). A common theme that has emerged throughout this work is the social complexity of coaching, that there is no one-size-fits-all magic formula of how to coach. Instead, both coaches and athletes have to work hard at establishing respectful relationships where each party is aware of what the other requires and is willing to fulfil that need. Naturally, each relationship requires different levels of investment and return, often highlighting the exchange nature of the interaction. Consequently, findings here have highlighted the importance of acting, talking and responding in certain ways when in positions of power (as coaches often are); actions that have the potential to inspire or demotivate followers.

This knowledge can help coaches in a number of ways. The findings from a recent study are drawn upon to illustrate them. Here, an investigation by Jones et al. (2005) focused on the experiences of a former elite swimmer, Anne (a pseudonym), whose career was interrupted and finally terminated by an eating disorder. The aim was to explore how the interaction Anne had with her coach not only led her to develop a strong yet brittle swimming identity, but also how that identity was broken, leading to the onset of *bulimia nervosa* for her. The story begins in earnest when a new coach arrived at Anne's swimming club. In her own words:

> My new coach promised exciting things and had a lot of new ideas and philo-sophies. He showed a lot of enthusiasm about my potential, so I took a lot of effort to please him. I was constantly encouraged by him as he seemed to have big plans for me. I wanted to do so well for him.
>
> (Jones et al. 2005: 383)

Through their initial interaction a strong bond was soon established between Anne and her coach as she bought into his ideas, knowledge and methods without question. Her self-identity and self-esteem became increasingly centred, not on the social person she was, but on how well she swam. Consequently, her times, and perhaps more importantly, what the coach thought and said regarding them, really mattered.

Then came what Anne terms 'the meeting', which was intended to bring swimmer, coach and parents together to discuss progress, future goals and ways of achieving them.

> He [the coach] told me that I was doing well, that I was showing progress with my swimming . . . but then he said 'it would probably be more beneficial if you were lighter and slimmer and could lose a bit of weight'. It just shot me down completely. And I remember feeling so embarrassed, in front of my parents and all. I came away feeling really down. I wanted to do so well for him [the coach] and I thought that I was. And that was the only thing that he could say. My body

was [now] the problem. I was judged by my body shape not just how well I could do in the pool. It [my body] became the focus and I became very conscious of it.

(Jones *et al*. 2005: 384)

The comment sparked a downward spiral for Anne, as she became increasingly obsessed by her body image. Consequently, what she ate and the amount of exercise she took became fixations for her. Eventually she was diagnosed with *bulimia nervosa*, a condition she continues to struggle with.

Although it would be a gross oversimplification to attribute Anne's subsequent eating disorder to a single comment by her coach, we should not ignore the coach's comment as unimportant. This is because, in many ways, it was (and remains) reflective of a general coaching culture driven by measurable times, appearance and weight. Undoubtedly, Anne was vulnerable to such criticism, a vulnerability created in large part by the heavy reliance upon her identity as a swimmer and upon her coach as an important person in creating that identity. What the coach said and did, then, had come to matter so much to Anne that it left her exposed and defenceless to the subsequent negativity expressed by him about her weight and appearance. Having sacrificed other aspects of her identity and the person she was, she had nothing to resist it with. This position is supported by previous research on disordered eating in female athletes, which concluded that pressure from coaches was an influential factor in the onset of such illnesses (Griffin and Harris 1996; Patel *et al*. 2003).

What can be learned from Anne's story? Principally, that coaches have a great deal of power over their athletes. Fed by the dominant language of measurable and observable performance, many coaches, albeit unconsciously, tend to treat athletes like machines to be trained and monitored. In turn, athletes, viewing coaches as knowledgeable experts, often carry out their coaches' wishes and demands without question. This is not to say that a hierarchical relationship between coach and athlete is always a problem, but that coaches should take great care when interacting with athletes, thus better respecting the elevated position they hold. Since human relationships lie at the heart of sociology, a sociological analysis can help in accurately describing and explaining such and similar situations, thus making both coaches and athletes question and become aware of why they act in the ways they do. The development of a coach's sociological competence, then, in considering the consequences of his or her words and actions would appear to be vital for the establishment of a healthy, progressive relationship with athletes.

## CONCLUSION

Sociology provides coaches with a perspective that enables them to ask the kinds of questions that will ultimately make them more thoughtful and perceptive as practitioners, more sensitive and empathetic as communicators and more effective as coaches. By drawing on the distinction between personal troubles and public issues, as Wright Mills

(1959) does, matters of social structure can be problematised (i.e. questioned) meaningfully. Furthermore, by adopting Berger's (1963) *sociological perspective* and seeking to see the general in the particular, the strange in the familiar and personal choice in social context, coaches can actively engage in understanding more deeply the social worlds of coaching and the athletes they coach.

Coaches and athletes both produce, and are products of, their own history and biography (Wright Mills 1959). In this respect, they are creations of their experiences. There are factors that characterise the socio-historical context in which coaching occurs – age, class, disability, ethnicity, gender and sexuality among them. The importance of each varies. For example, whilst one person may have her or his experiences affected most by disability, for another sexuality might be the key variable. Of course, the variables do not operate in isolation; rather, they intersect in ways that account for much more subtle and nuanced social difference. Yet, by embracing the importance of personal sociologies, histories and biographies (including their own), coaches will understand athletes better and be able to interact with them more effectively. This is because such engagement enables them to think about each athlete, even in team sports, as an individual with different wants and needs. This is not to say that each athlete should be treated so individualistically that no coherent pattern of behaviour emerges from coaches, as this leaves the door open to accusations of inconsistency or, worse, favouritism. Rather it makes coaches more aware of the consequences of what they do and say, thus helping them to reflect a little about the best course of action before impulsively jumping and then having to deal with a worse situation. Finally, embracing sociological concepts also allows coaches to develop a deeper appreciation of the power they hold in relation to athletes and how it can best be utilised to the benefit of all.

## REVIEW QUESTIONS

1. If sociology refers to our sense of social things (Lemert 1997), of how to manage our interactions with others, how is the discipline of value to coaching and coaches?
2. Consider a conversation or interaction you have had recently with your coach or fellow athletes. How was it structured? Who took the lead? Why do you think this was? How did you act and react within the interaction? Why?
3. How can an awareness of macro- and/or micro-sociology help coaches in their practice?

# CHAPTER FIVE

# HISTORY FOR COACHES

## Malcolm MacLean and Ian Pritchard

*Knowing the historical and cultural baggage a sport carries with it is vital if you are to succeed as a coach. You have to know where your athletes are 'coming from' in addition to the boundaries you're working within and what's expected of you.*

Lyn Davies –
former Olympic gold medallist and current President of UK Athletics

### Key sections:

- Introduction
- The sports coach in history
- History and national identity
- Sports coaching and national identity
- Conclusion

## INTRODUCTION

The cultural status of various sports in any society is the product of historical processes. Consequently, individuals involved in those sports, in any capacity, are influenced in many ways by the latter's cultural standing. Similarly, key aspects of coaching practice are influenced by historically constructed sporting cultural identities. This chapter draws together the fluctuating status of the sports coach and the emergence of sport-related national identities to consider the positive and negative effects that sporting cultural centrality may have on coaches, particularly those involved in so-called national sports. In doing so, the role of the sports coach in history is examined initially. This is followed by a discussion of history and national identity and, in particular, the role of the sports coach within it. The next section further explores this issue by outlining the importance of the socio-cultural context in understanding the current place of the sports coach in society. Finally, a conclusion draws together the principal points highlighted. The value of the chapter lies in making explicit the social expectations on coaches, particularly those who work at the national level. Such knowledge is important as it can make coaches aware of the boundaries within which they work and the pressures they face, so that they can manage them better.

## THE SPORTS COACH IN HISTORY

For most of the medieval period, practices that we would recognise as sporting or leisure related were often functional in that they were based in military or economic activities. This began to change after the seventeenth-century restoration of the English monarchy that influenced the aristocracy to revel in their recently rediscovered leisure diversions. The newly fashionable and overt consumption of leisure by the upper echelons of British society contributed to the first wave of sports codification (i.e. formalisation) and to the emergence of the modern sports coach. The first wave of this codification included the sports of horseracing, cricket, boxing and golf, all activities that were technically complex enough to require formalised skill-learning procedures. Aristocratic patronage and the prospective financial gains resulting from gambling meant that individuals organising these sporting activities were willing to pay for expert performance and/or tuition, while those involved as instructors and performers were of a lower social status than their wealthy patrons. These conditions resulted in a public perception of the coach as little more than a semi-skilled artisan.

Throughout the nineteenth century, the growth of the British middle class, with its moral code of respectability, led to a shift in leisure patterning and to a further cultural belittling of the sports coach. An important element in the dominance of the aristocracy and its upper-class allies was a masculinist and élitist public school system characterised by rigid in-class discipline with minimal supervision elsewhere. In these environments, sporting activity was dominated by disorganised games. Two nineteenth-century socio-economic developments brought about major changes in the English public school system, with related changes in the emerging world of organised sport. Firstly, the rapid industrialisation that began in Britain in the mid-eighteenth century had created a growing and increasingly affluent, socially ambitious middle class. Parts of this new class saw access for their sons to the public school system as a way to enhance and secure their social status. This ruthless, ambitious and energetic capitalist class included a large element that prioritised and expected discipline and value for money. In the second development, these expectations coincided with those of a new group of public school headmasters who shared an outlook that better management of all aspects of school life would improve the moral, spiritual and academic development of their charges. The enthusiastic reformatory zeal of these headmasters, plus the demands and concerns of the fee-paying middle class, led to the regeneration of the English public school system where it became infused with value-laden moral and ethical imperatives, many of which were embodied in games.

As various groups of public school old boys sought to continue competition, there emerged another wave of sports codification during the second half of the nineteenth century

(Chandler 1991). The moral imperative these middle-class groups wove into this codification of sport undermined formalised instruction. Here, the value system within public school sports demanded both a strict adherence to an amateur ethos and, despite the seriousness with which these activities were taken, a relaxed, devil-may-care attitude and a desire not to be seen to try too hard. This amateurist ideal meant that practice, training or consistent advice from non-participants both contradicted the British notion of sport and was dishonourable and unpatriotic. This fusion of moral earnestness, feigned physical laziness, and class-based superiority – characteristics of the Cult of Athleticism – stigmatised sports coaches and undermined organised coaching structures in Britain for the best part of a century.

Many working-class athletes were still willing, or needed, to earn 'a spare bob or two' from any activities outside work. In their sport, this clashed with the middle-class amateurist ideal. Once association football became professional in 1888, and after the rugby schism of 1895, when the clubs of the Northern Union broke with the Rugby Football Union, the middle-class mandarins of sport withdrew to their bastion of amateurism and maintained their own sports with a stringent policy concerning appropriate gentlemanly standards. Despite the social class divide in British sport, the middle-class cultural hangover concerning sport's values and morals lingered through the twentieth century, even in those activities that attracted the greatest level of working-class involvement and interest, such as association football.

Apart from the payment received for participation, association football remained amateurist and resisted organised skill learning and tactical applications until well after the Second World War. The middle-class distaste for professionalism meant that most association football clubs were financed by the *nouveau riche* (i.e. new rich) made wealthy through trade in Britain's expanding industrial towns and cities. Their capitalist outlook ensured that they were willing to support limited professionalism (such as player payments), but as upwardly mobile, aspirational and patriotic members of the community their cultural dissent was limited. In most cases, association football clubs maintained a management and coaching structure based upon and rooted in amateurist ideals: they employed an administrator-secretary, but formalised skill learning was *ad hoc*, unorganised and remained the responsibility of the senior players.

This restricted opportunities to coach even for those with the inclination to do so. Herbert Chapman in football, and others like him, began to change this situation in the 1930s, but recognised manager-coaches in any sport did not appear until after the War. Even then, Walter Winterbottom, who became English football's first national coach in 1946, was both team manager and FA director of coaching for 16 years without ever selecting any of the players in his teams. In the amateurist world of middle-class sports, resistance to any form of team management, coaching or tactical development, outside of that provided by the team captain and senior players, remained embedded until much later; e.g. the Welsh Rugby Union only appointed David Nash as its first national coach in 1967 (Morgan and Fleming 2003). Consequently, even in the home of contemporary codified sport (i.e. the UK), the period that saw its rapid emergence and establishment as a major cultural institution was marked by the marginalisation and often vilification of tactical development and formalised skill learning (i.e. coaching) because of a cultural obsession with social class allied to the stereotypical fantasy of the British national character.

These contradictions within modern, formalised coaching were not the same worldwide. Whereas in Britain, training and coaching during the later nineteenth and early twentieth century was associated with working-class sports, in North America a more complex relationship emerged. In both the United States and Canada there was a class-based, amateurist rejection of coaching similar to that seen in Britain. There were, however, two significant differences: the financial benefits of college sport, and the commercial basis of sports leagues. These two factors increased the need for a team to have some comparative advantage over its rivals. In the case of college sport, this advantage became an important element in boosting the institution's profile, attracting students, increasing income and enhancing alumni (i.e. former students') contributions.

Despite the class differences between college and professional league sports, the imperative for comparative advantage was similar: financial security. In North America leagues tended to be organised centrally with closed membership and with league members dependent on each other for financial security. For the most part, there was no promotion and relegation system, and the league was governed by commercial considerations where a club owner or franchise holder had to ensure their own security and that of the league. In Britain, sports leagues tended to be more amateurist in outlook and practice. The (English) Football League continued until the middle of the twentieth century to be governed by the ethos of a class-linked national character, with commercial considerations less important (Taylor 2005). The more complex circumstances of North American leagues meant that as soon as one team sought comparative advantage through, for instance, a professional staff to enhance skill development and tactics, others quickly followed suit. This form of commercial demand in North America meant that the development and history of coaching followed a very different path and trajectory from that in Britain, at least for significant components of popular and commercial sport.

After a century of effort to drive out the perceived corrupting influence of coaching from sport, the final third of the twentieth century saw British sport institutionalise formal provision for coaching. A system providing for formally qualified coaches is now nearly universal. Four changes in and beyond sport contributed to this shift. First, sports organisations in Britain recognised not only that sport had become more complex but also that increases in skill levels meant that specialist knowledge was needed beyond that which could be provided by captains and senior players. Second, changes in the commercial structure of professional sports since the 1960s meant that individual sports organisations were carrying greater financial risks, so greater skill development was required to minimise that risk. Third, the structure of British education and vocational training changed markedly during this period, with extensive development of more specialist awards, more staged qualifications and a growing demand for recognised credentials. Whereas this was not necessarily directly related to formalised systems of coach training and qualifications, it was a sign of a broader cultural shift. Finally, since the early 1990s there has been a growing concern about issues such as child protection and the abuse (physical, mental and sexual) of athletes by coaches at all levels. Formal systems of coach education and credentialisation became widely seen as one mechanism by which sports organisations could exercise their duty of care to sports participants.

The contemporary coach, then, in a world of centrally regulated, credentialed, stratified and rationalised sport can be seen as working in an environment shaped by the limits and logic of contemporary capitalism and a view of sport as entertainment. In many ways, these roots continue to influence how coaches and others perceive their job. They are, however, not the only limits, as there is an additional set of restrictive cultural and social factors that can be seen broadly as identity-related. One of the most far-reaching of these ways of having an identity is based on assumed national traits and characteristics, and it is to a discussion of these that we now turn.

## HISTORY AND NATIONAL IDENTITY

The way in which social worlds were organised, especially in western Europe, altered markedly during the nineteenth century. Two factors were crucial in this change, namely: the spread of capitalist economic and social relations, and the development of nation-states that, in turn, had profound effects on national identity. As the historian Eric Hobsbawm has noted, '"the nation" [is] a very recent newcomer in human history, and the product of particular, and . . . localised or regional historical conjunctures' (1992: 5). The reasons for the formation of nation-states (Hobsbawm's 'particular . . . historical conjunctures') are varied. In England it was, in part, related to the development of improved communication technologies – new road and railway systems, and improved postal and newspaper networks; meanwhile France as a single national entity was driven primarily by cultural and political forces during the latter half of the nineteenth century.

The identities related to these new nation-states were not the same as older local identities (Smith 1991), although it is important to remember that identities, be they based in localities, socio-economic relations, gender, ethnicity or any other factor, are social. For example, the cultural characteristics of masculinity and femininity can only be explained with reference to each other. Similarly, there is only a middle class because there are upper and lower classes; there are only slaves because someone else owns them. The most important difference between most other forms of social identity and national identities is that 'nation' is a much more abstract or intangible concept than locality or most other forms of social identification. There is no chance of an individual knowing or even having met many of the people with whom they share a national identity. Indeed, it is becoming increasingly common for analysts of national identity to accept Benedict Anderson's (2005) case that nations are best understood as 'imagined communities', the members of which assume that there are shared characteristics that give them a common basis for community membership.

These shared characteristics of community membership tend to be either language-based or related to a specific icon. That is, nationalism and national identity are either lingua-centric or iconocentric. In Anderson's approach, a national community may be imagined, but its members are not free to imagine that community in any way they want. Lingua-centric nations are easy to recognise: language revival was central to the revitalisation of Welsh nationalism in the second half of the twentieth century, while the spread of a uniform French language to replace a diverse set of dialects was central to the nineteenth-century creation of a single French nation.

Iconocentric nations on the other hand are not always so obvious. One of the markers of the United States of America is adherence to its constitution as a series of political principles. In Australia, the 'first fleet', the four convict ships that arrived in 1788, has, since the 1980s, emerged as a powerful icon of Australian national identity. These icons are distinctive because they are taken to signify the formation or founding of the nation: they are often an 'emblematic singularity', that is they mark a singular moment of origin (Morris 1998: 100). Other iconographic markers are more complex: for instance, rugby union is often seen as an icon of New Zealand. Rugby union's clear identification as a British game means that it suggests both a distinctive sense of New Zealand, often claimed through styles of play, and an inclusion in Britishness, through rugby's role in imperial expansion and relation. South African rugby's basis in Afrikaans-speaking communities means that it performs a different iconic function there.

These linguacentric and iconocentric claims to national identity are closely related to the problem of defining national identity. National identity is one of those things that many people know they have, but have no idea about what it might be in real terms. Definition is even more complex because the English language does not clearly distinguish between a state and a nation. The United *States* of America function as if they are a nation, with a head of state, a flag and a national anthem (that all 50 states share, although most also have their own anthem, flag and head of state), whereas the United *Nations* has only a flag, and is made up of states, but does not include all the world's nations. For example, Wales, Catalonia and Chechnya, despite having most of the characteristics of nations and having clearly identifiable national identities, are nations that do not have states. What is more, these three nations (Wales, Catalonia and Chechnya) are parts of bigger states (United Kingdom, Spain and the Russian Federation), one of which (Russian Federation) is fighting a war to prevent its member nation (Chechnya) becoming a state, while the other two recognise degrees of political autonomy. This means that there is not a simple relationship between states and nations, so to begin to talk about and explore national identity we need to have a different way of understanding the two: enter history.

Nationality and national identity can combine with sport to become a powerful social force and a way of defining ourselves and the groups to which we belong (Cronin 1999). The key way that sport does this is to provide shared social memories that give substance to national identity. These memories can be drawn from spectacular public events or from ordinary and everyday occurrences. Such events become commemorative rituals that provide a sense of who the nation is and, more importantly, what the nation does and stands for: they 'flag the homeland' (Billig 1995). What is more, sport fills up the empty vessel of nationhood in a subtle way, ensuring that commemorative rituals, through sites of social memories, seem natural and normal (Connerton 1989). Association football in England is a case in point; although the Football Association (FA) had agreed the rules of football in 1863, by 1871 it had barely a dozen members, while the rules it had agreed upon were still not the only ones by which football was played. For example, the members of the Sheffield Football Association played by slightly different rules, and it was still the case that there were often negotiations over which rules to follow before a game started. Yet by the end of the 1880s football had acquired an identifiable set of 'institutional and ritual characteristics' (Hobsbawm 1983b: 288). The FA Cup competition had been launched, professionalism had been accepted and the Football League had been formed. Alongside these institutional developments had come a set of rituals: regular attendance at the match on Saturday afternoon; groups of supporters had started to form; an annual outing for many to London to watch the FA Cup Final; club rivalries were intensifying. Football, then, became distinctive in England because, unlike other sports such as rugby union, it had rapidly acquired a national organisation (i.e. after 1895 rugby was even less national because of the regional and class division associated with the Northern Union's separation from the Rugby Football Union). As Hobsbawm has noted: that power that sport had as a means to fill up the vessel of national identity was the

> ease with which even the least political or public individuals can identify with the nation as symbolised by young persons excelling at what practically every man wants, or at one time in life has wanted, to be good at. The imagined community of millions seems more real as a team of eleven named people. The individual, even the one who only cheers, becomes a symbol of his nation himself.
>
> (Hobsbawm 1992: 143)

The effect was that not only was football seen by the English as an English game, it was also (and continues to be) seen as such by many others as well. In Denmark, for instance, it is not uncommon to hear football discussed as the English game, even though it has acquired Danish characteristics.

These commemorative rituals and similar events that 'flag the homeland' are often seen as traditional. Many of these traditions, however, have been invented, in that they can be seen to have emerged at a particular time under specific circumstances. Once again, Hobsbawm provides an approach that allows us a better understanding of this issue. In his analysis, these invented traditions are

> taken to mean a set of practices, normally governed by overtly or tacitly accepted rules which seek to inculcate certain values and norms of behaviour by repetition, which automatically implies continuity with the past. In fact, where possible, they normally attempt to establish continuity with a suitable historic past.
>
> (1983a: 1)

Sport is full of invented traditions. Leaving aside the Olympics, with its cornucopia or wealth of fabricated truths, one of the most powerful of these is the notion that in 1823, at Rugby School, William Webb Ellis picked up the ball and ran, thereby inventing rugby football. The claim first appeared in a Rugby School magazine in the 1890s, citing as its source the recollections of a former schoolboy. No earlier source has been located and no evidence has been provided that it ever happened. The timing is significant: during the 1890s there was a struggle for control of rugby football between the middle- and upper-class clubs of the south, and the working-class clubs in the north, leading to the split in the Rugby Football Union in 1895, and the creation of the Northern Union that eventually became the Rugby League. Being able to link the formation of the game to an event at a public school allowed the middle- and upper-class clubs to claim to be the authentic representatives of the game's traditions (Collins 1998). The reality is very different. Most public schools played their own version of football, only some allowed handling. During November and December 1863 there was a series of meetings organised by what became the Football Association that agreed the rules of football. Subsequently, a number of clubs left the FA to eventually agree, in 1871, rules of a form of football that became known as Rugby Football and which allowed handling (Harvey 2005). This history is well-known, yet in the mid-1990s, when launching a World Cup for men's rugby, the International Rugby Board called the trophy the Webb Ellis Trophy and, in doing so, continued to grant legitimacy to the myth of the game's origins.

Other countries have their own national sporting myths. A linguacentric example may be seen in the nineteenth- and early-twentieth century role of the Sokol gymnastic movement in nationalist politics in the Austro-Hungarian Empire (Nolte 2002). In Bohemia and Moravia there were often (Czech-speaking) Sokol and (German-speaking) Turnverein gymnastic groups in the same localities. In some places these groups linked to other parts of civil society as well. For example, in the Bohemian town of Budějovice/Budweis, an attempt in 1865 by the German-speaking group to form a volunteer fire brigade was overruled by the mayor who insisted that the brigade be made up of both Turnverein and Sokol members (King 2002). The Sokol form of gymnastics was presented as distinctively Czech (or Slavic) as opposed to the German Turnverein style, so that gymnastics became a weapon in nationalism and imperial politics and part of a set of body practices that were seen as nationally distinctive. It is difficult to see how these claims to Sokol's inherent Czech-ness or Turnverein's inherent German-ness can be substantiated, other than in the context of the emerging spirit of nationalism in the Austro-Hungarian Empire during the latter half of the nineteenth century.

Widespread adoption of national identities is relatively recent, and can be understood as being linked to nineteenth-century developments in industrialisation, urbanisation, technological advancement and rationalisation. Central to the justification and legitimation of these newly identified nations were historical traditions (authentic and invented). Many of these traditions were provided and supported by newly emergent organised sport, which established and continued to reinforce instant (invented) traditions inferring ideals of cultural, ethnic and/or racial superiority, and in doing so promoted imperialism. Equally importantly, these sports sponsored national unity and created and maintained so-called commonsense ideas about national sports and cultural characteristics.

## SPORTS COACHING AND NATIONAL IDENTITY

National identity is a double-edged sword in the context of coaching. There are both positive and negative consequences regarding the impact of national identity on coaching, although as with most things it is seldom the case that a consequence is entirely negative or positive. An appeal to national identity can enhance access to the best athletes. Paradoxically, this can often be difficult to ensure in the most popular and commercialised sports, which are also the clearest markers or carriers of an ideal of national identity. In the UK, for instance, players and clubs in both football and rugby union are caught between several sets of demands. Playing seasons in recent years have been around ten months' duration. As the number of national and international club-based competitions has increased, so have international matches. Additionally, clubs have more financial investment in players. The honour of representative sport in some cases, therefore, has come to clash with the commercial demands of professional sport. As a result, there have been a number of intense disputes between national bodies and clubs during the later 1990s and early 2000s over the availability of, and threat of injury to, internationally representative players.

Although these sorts of commercial considerations can, and often do, weaken the positive impact of national identity on coaches, there are more general beneficial impacts. For instance, when issues related to national identity are clear, and when the sport in question is seen as a marker of national identity, athletes and coaches may find themselves in positions that are culturally central, resulting in a high profile for both the sport and individuals (e.g. the English football team at the 2006 World Cup). However, this can also result in greater pressure for success that may not be at all positive or beneficial. It is something coaches should be aware of and, accordingly, plan for.

It is often the case that less immediately obvious or direct support is developed in association with national identity markers and alongside certain sports as nationally distinctive. For example, the development in the last quarter of the twentieth century of mass formalised coach education systems is linked to the demands of high-performance sport to be internationally competitive. It is increasingly common for coaches to take the blame for team failures, and the complexity of contemporary commercialised elite sport often means that there is more than one team coach. These systems of coach education, linked to a broader sense of the need for specific credentials in a range of occupations, have intensified rapidly. Consequently, in many sports there are now strict limits on who may do what, in that an aspiring coach will require certification by the relevant governing body to coach at a specific level. Although there is a debate to be had about whether these mass, formal coach-education systems are necessarily a good thing, there is little doubt that their development is, in part, the result of concerns about elite sports performance and comparative national standings.

A less obvious effect of the link between national identities and sport is related to popularity and participation rates. Sports that carry with them the weight of national identity tend also to be popular and to have relatively high participation rates. In this respect, well supported and popular sports tend to provide more opportunity for full-time employment (for coaches and others), although this is more so for sports traditionally seen more as men's than women's. For example netball, by far the most widely played women's sport in the UK, has proportionally far fewer opportunities for full-time, or even paid, coaching work than traditional men's sports and fewer opportunities in real numbers than men's sports with fewer participants, such as rugby union. Gender, then, disrupts a sense that sport and national identity are linked in an obvious or standard manner (Williams 2003). Even allowing this gendered differential, when combined with a system of formal coach education and qualifications, the sport, popularity and national identity dynamic makes clearer the mechanisms for upward mobility for coaches and contributes to the growing potential for full-time, secure employment.

As coaches and athletes have discovered over the years, however, a close association between their sport and national identity is not always a good thing; in many cases this association can have definite negative consequences for coaches. As many coaches have discovered to their cost, in sports heavily invested with a sense of national identity there is a great and often over-emphasis on success at all levels. Closely related to this heightened emphasis is an exaggerated media focus not only on coaching decisions and skills but also on all aspects of a coach's life. Consider, for example, the attention paid to Nancy Dell'Olio during Sven-Goran Eriksson's time as the coach of the English men's national football team. This media focus can become intrusive to the extent that coaches lose credibility, while they can be affected in many ways by the intensive and distracting focus on their abilities as measured by the team's performance.

In the main, however, sports (and by implication, coaches) tend to benefit from a close association with a national identity in terms of enhanced support, a greater allocation of resources from the state and other sources, and more secure career structures. These benefits have disadvantages for other sports not so central to national identity. In a context where financial and other resources are limited, these other sports will be marginalised not only by the media but also by central and local government as well as other financial agencies. Sometimes this is a direct product of the normally close fit between gender and national identity, as seen in the previous rugby union–netball example. More often than not, most of us remain unaware of this marginalisation. For example, it is common for migrants to recognise the extent to which the English sports media is dominated by football (soccer). This domination by football often extends to coverage of the semi-professional, fifth-division Conference League at the expense of national and international success in other mainstream, although less popular, sports such as gymnastics, hockey, netball and women's football (both soccer and rugby union). In these cases, and many others, the close association between other sports and English national identity means that financial resources are directed elsewhere, undermining professional, commercial and career structures and, in effect, maintaining the under-development of those sports themselves.

A further, less obvious problem, although one that is becoming more real, is the over-formalisation of learning processes leading to an exclusion and/or alienation of both potential and lower-level coaches. Many national governing bodies now have a system of coaching awards that apply at all levels of a sport, meaning that a parent who has skills in a specific sport and who may want to coach their child's team (and in doing so become a sport volunteer and the backbone of mass sport globally) may find themselves obliged or under pressure to study for a coaching qualification. There is, therefore, a risk that high-profile sports success and popularity leading to a formal career structure may end up placing obligations beyond those that such parents consider necessary for coaches or potential coaches at mass and entry level. It would be reasonable to assume that this alienates people willing, happy or wanting to be part of a mass sport experience. Here, then, investment in national identity-related factors can actually drive people away from the sport.

The final issue to be discussed here is that the cultural centrality of a sport can, and often does, lead to general constant over-expectations of success and rapid recrimination upon failure. In recent years a number of national team coaches have fallen on their swords in the wake of perceived failure, which is often a failure to meet expectations. John Hart resigned as the All Blacks' coach on the day the team lost to France in the play-off for third place in the 1999 men's rugby world cup. This was the lowest placing the team had ever achieved in the competition, and they had been expected to make the final. Late in 2006 Andy Robinson resigned as the English men's rugby coach after a series of losses by the 2003 World Cup winners that matched their worst run ever. This could also be seen as a failure to meet expectations, although it could equally be argued that English rugby had merely returned to a level of performance seen through most of the last quarter of the twentieth century.

## CONCLUSION

Coaches work in a world where they need to balance demands as diverse as the nutritional needs of their athletes and the expectations of supporters. A significant, but not the only, factor shaping supporter expectations is the role that the sport in question plays in the particular national identity and its relationship to the myths and traditions (authentic and invented) of nationhood. This is in addition to the class, gender and ethnic associations of the sport in the context of the nation, as well as the underlying linguacentric or iconocentric bases of assumed nationhood. A sport central to a sense of national identity will present as many issues to be managed and problems to be controlled as a sport marginal to that sense of national identity. These national identity-related factors do not only have an impact on the context of sporting action, but also on the day-to-day business of team selection, systems of coach education, funding, social and political support, and facilities and sporting infrastructure. In none of these cases is the relationship with national identity (central or marginal) entirely positive or entirely negative; in all cases it is extremely influential, and ignored by coaches at their peril.

1. The traditional amateur ethos of, and the cult of athleticism in, British sport has mitigated against the development of sports coaching as a profession in the UK. Discuss.

2. How does national identity affect individual sports? Think of the sport you most often partake in; how does its standing in society affect the available opportunities to work within it? How much media coverage does it get? Why do you think this is? Compare this experience with a sport that is equally as popular but has either a much higher or much lower standing in society.

3. What is meant by the authors' statement that 'National identity is a double-edged sword in the context of coaching'?

4. How valuable is historical knowledge to coaches and coaching? Justify your answer.

# CHAPTER SIX

# PHILOSOPHY FOR COACHES

## Alun Hardman and Carwyn Jones

*A coach's practice is founded on his or her philosophy; it will affect their choices of what is right and wrong. This is extremely important in top level sport, because there are many temptations to make short cuts.*

Atle Kvålsvoll –
Coach of Thor Hushovd, winner of the
Green Shirt (sprint) in the Tour de France, 2005

### Key sections:

- Introduction: what is philosophy and how can it help us understand coaching?
- The tools of philosophy and how they can be used in coaching
- Applying philosophy to coaching
- Conclusion

## INTRODUCTION: WHAT IS PHILOSOPHY AND HOW CAN IT HELP US UNDERSTAND COACHING?

The term philosophy is often used both in everyday life and coaching to refer to a world view or approach, or even a kind of personal ideology. Here, 'my philosophy of life' or 'my coaching philosophy' are fairly familiar pronouncements. In the context of this chapter and this book, however, a far more precise and formal use of the term will be discussed. Philosophy is often about seeking clarity and drawing distinctions, and we will immediately distinguish between philosophy as a noun and as a verb before analysing the value of both to coaching (Best 1978). The chapter is divided into three parts. The first section provides a detailed understanding of philosophy as a discipline and its relevance to coaching generally. The second identifies and explains three philosophical concepts that we consider to be particularly relevant to coaching. A final section demonstrates the application of philosophical ideas in a practical coaching scenario.

Philosophy, literally the love of wisdom, has a long and distinguished history. It is one of the oldest academic disciplines and is considered the forefather of others, including science and mathematics. Philosophy poses and answers questions about values (axiology), morality (ethics) and meaning (ontology). So, for example, a philosopher of sport might ask: What is the value of youth sport? How should children conduct themselves when playing sport? and How might sport contribute to a meaningful and happy life?

The term philosophy as a verb describes a process or method. One can philosophise as well as study philosophy in the same way that one can be a coach as well as study the practice of coaching. The philosophical process can be encapsulated in reference to two crucial and important questions: 'What do you mean? and, How do you know?' (Best 1978: 8). Both these questions encourage reflection about all sorts of claims and statements. The first question is essentially related to clarification, and in asking the question one seeks more detail. The second is a justificatory question, where the questioner looks for evidence to support the statement made. The difference between these two types of questions from a philosophical point of view is apparent in the following example. The statement 'Sport is good for your health' is commonly heard. However, using philosophy, the statement can be further interrogated. For example, one might ask what is meant by sport and whether there is universal agreement on what counts as sport? Are chess and darts included? One might also legitimately ask what is meant by health – mental? physical? emotional? all three? By thinking philosophically, then, one can clarify meaning in relation to all sorts of important issues.

Asking the justificatory question (How do you know?) is about seeking evidence. Hearsay, rumour, gossip and opinion are not generally thought to be sufficient. What is required is relevant and appropriate evidence that is valid (true) and reliable (dependable). The evidence for the previous statement – sport is good for your health – is likely to be empirical in the shape of facts and figures, trends, health indices and so forth, but this will not always be the case. Indeed, where empirical facts provide evidence, there may be different interpretations or weight given to such facts. For example, what should we make of the fact that a significant number of injuries and even deaths occur in sport each year and are a drain on the National Health Service? Here the discussion gets messy and careful philosophical analysis can be very helpful. What precisely do we mean by the term 'health' and what form of sport is compatible with such an account? (McNamee and Parry 1990). A coach should, therefore, be encouraged to use philosophical tools to develop a more coherent and sophisticated understanding of their own coaching and of coaching in general. What is coaching? What are the key values of coaching? Does coaching differ from teaching? If so, in which ways? Is coaching about the process or the product? Does coaching enrich children's lives? Ought coaches to specialise early or later? These and many other questions are crucial for coaches and coaching organisations to address, because they help establish a clear agenda for both individual and collective aims, and the appropriateness of the manner in which such aims are to be achieved. There are no off-the-shelf responses to such questions, but there are better and worse answers. Philosophy and philosophical reflection can help coaches to establish a clear rationale for what they are doing and provide the tools to deal with these and other questions in a clear and justified way (Drewe 2000).

# THE TOOLS OF PHILOSOPHY AND HOW THEY CAN BE USED IN COACHING

Our introduction has attempted to emphasise that philosophy's contribution to the practice of coaching is an embedded and holistic one that sees reasoned, principled and reflective thinking as an ongoing skill that provides a cornerstone to coaching practice. However, there are a number of specific philosophical concepts that, when understood better, can help to promote greater self-awareness for practitioners. The concepts articulated below, therefore, represent distinct philosophical content knowledge relevant to the practice of coaching. The concepts are selective rather than comprehensive, but none the less represent, in our view, the most helpful to develop philosophically informed coaching.

## Axiology (values)

All coaches must and will ask themselves at some stage what is good about sport? What is it about sport that makes them, the players and all others who contribute to the production of sports performances do what they do? After all, for most, coaching is a matter of choice as there are other, more lucrative, equally enjoyable ways of earning a living or spending free time. In answering this question, coaches may point to one or more things of value that can only be acquired by being a sports coach. In so doing they will be engaged in discussing the branch of philosophy concerned with values that is called axiology.

Once again, in order to further our understanding of the concept of value and its relationship to sport and the coaching process, distinctions need to be drawn. It could be argued that there are two sources of value in both sport and coaching. First, there are subjective values that relate to what is of importance to individuals or groups of individuals such as a coach or players. Second there are objective values that relate to the importance and significance of things as objects in themselves, such as a hockey game, or the role of a coach. The distinction means, for example, that a coach may have personal or subjective reasons for wanting to coach that may or may not coincide with the objective values appropriate for the role of a coach. Conflicts of interest in coaching are often the result of a clash between objective and subjective values. Coaches choosing representative sides, for example, must ensure they use objective selection criteria to avoid any favouritism to their own players. The objective selection criteria used should be based on a clear, justifiable and persuasive (to other coaches) account of what a good player looks like, and clear evidence (through the selection process) that those selected best fit such a description.

The distinction between subjective and objective values helps us to judge the appropriateness of different coaching motivations and coaching practices. A coach of a junior football side may value his or her role because it demands the application of certain qualities like empathy, concentration, pedagogic skill, inspiration and motivation. This coach sees the coaching process as having intrinsic value (i.e. having a value in and of itself). Similarly, such a coach would regard football for its specific qualities such as the skill, tactical acumen, co-operation, speed and commitment required to play the game well. The coach gains satisfaction from getting players to do the best they can and to develop their football abilities in order to gain the enjoyment attached to playing well.

On the other hand, a rival football coach may value sport and the coaching process for very different reasons. For him or her, playing football might be seen in terms of a means to achieve other valued ends such as demonstrating superiority by developing masculine values or achieving recognition through winning trophies. Similarly, the coach may be motivated by the social status or the financial rewards and career opportunities that coaching provides. Coaching for him or her has become a vehicle for achieving rewards external to the purpose of both football and coaching. This coach can be said to perceive football and coaching in terms of its extrinsic value. To borrow from psychology, it could be said that the first coach is intrinsically motivated to coach and fosters intrinsic motivation in his/her players, whereas the second coach is extrinsically motivated to coach and encourages his/her players to focus on extrinsic or tangible rewards. Consequently, their source of motivation and the reasons why they coach are different. The first is motivated by the activity itself, its goods and values, whereas the second is motivated by goods that are external to, or contingently related to, the activity of football and coaching. Thus, playing and coaching sports can be said to be valuable in two ways. First, they have instrumental value in that they may be used as instruments to secure a number of goals like money, fame, esteem and so forth; secondly, they have inherent value – that is they can be said to be valuable for their own sake or in their own right (McNamee 1997).

For the most part, individuals' motives to coach will be made up of intrinsic and extrinsic reasons. Consequently, they will appreciate both the values inherent to sport and the manner in which it has instrumental value when used as a means to pursue other ends. While the mix is a legitimate one, it is important to understand how an emphasis on a particular set of values and motivations impacts upon what is deemed important to coaches (Kretchmar 1994). In turn, this reflects on how coaches make decisions in terms of what is emphasised and how they get their message across.

## Ethics (morality)

The philosophical sub-discipline of ethics is closely related to axiology in that it deals with values. Ethics, however, focuses specifically on certain types of values, namely moral values. Moral values are, in essence, to do with how we treat ourselves and others and what counts as good and bad, right and wrong in these contexts. Clearly, moral values play a central role in coaching given the interpersonal interaction involved. Ethicists attempt to articulate a value framework for a given practice (e.g. coaching) and identify a list of prescriptions (actions that are encouraged), proscriptions (actions that are discouraged) and qualities of character that promote and sustain that practice and those who participate in it. The ethics of coaching, therefore, is to do with what goals coaches aim for and how they behave towards themselves and others in pursuing these goals.

Often the coach's moral obligations are outlined in a code of ethical conduct. A code of conduct is generally a list of dos and don'ts that spell out the rights and duties of both the coach and the athletes. This focus on rights and duties is associated with a particular tradition in ethics called *deontology* (DeSensi and Rosenberg 2003). Deontology defines the moral arena in terms of a number of rights or entitlements that persons have. When an individual claims they have a right, it means that other individuals have corresponding duties that they must perform to ensure that such rights are established. For example, a young player's right not to be bullied by the coach is closely related to the coach's duty not to act in a threatening and intimidating manner. Codes of conduct are essentially a list of rights and duties that aim to promote certain moral principles or values like freedom, autonomy, fairness and justice. Such codes are useful, but knowing their content is not sufficient in itself. Knowing what is right is no guarantee of right action. Hence, additional qualities of character such as compassion, wisdom, courage, fairness and honesty may be required for such (i.e. right) action. For the deontologist, right and wrong are understood in terms of the inherent qualities of actions; for example, lying and causing physical harm are deemed inherently wrong whereas honesty and fairness are inherently right.

Another branch of ethics, namely *utilitarianism* (often used interchangeably with the term *consequentialism*) approaches the nature of moral goodness from a different perspective (DeSensi and Rosenberg 2003). For a utilitarian, actions are right insofar as the action contributes to an increase in overall good, pleasure or satisfaction, or a decrease in pain, suffering or badness. Actions are wrong insofar as they result in an overall decrease in good, pleasure or satisfaction or an increase in pain, suffering or badness. According to the utilitarian approach the ends may justify the means. For example, a gymnastic coach may justify robust physical treatment of junior gymnasts in terms of the eventual overall pleasure and satisfaction that will be derived from their future success. Similarly, a coach may encourage aggressive and intimidating play as a strategy for winning an important game. Deontologists would be concerned about the appropriateness of using such approaches regardless of the possible outcomes because the infliction of pain is inherently wrong. Coaches, therefore, often face difficult decisions about the means they use to achieve their goals.

Another approach to ethics, namely *virtue ethics*, focuses more specifically on the qualities of individuals rather than right actions (McNamee 1995). Virtue ethics aims for the development of good habits, character traits and dispositions such as courage, fairness and integrity (MacIntyre 1984). A coach who is compassionate, fair, just, honest, committed and dedicated will try to produce a responsive moral climate when coaching, and will seek to cultivate similar dispositions in their athletes. A virtuous coach should be sensitive to moral impropriety. For example, a virtuous coach not only knows that bullying is wrong but is aware enough to spot bullying, be sensitive to the victim's suffering, courageous enough to tackle the bully and able to resolve the issue in a fair and appropriate way.

### Ontology (the meaning of coaching)

Ontology is the branch of philosophy that deals with the nature of existence in terms of what actually exists. It asks fundamental questions about the meaning of life and, as such, ontological questions can be the most complex and frustrating of all. For the purposes of this discussion, however, we will focus on the ways in which coaching is a meaningful practice that can provide persons with a rich and rewarding pursuit or vocation. Here the notion of how coaching and being a coach might come to exemplify the so-called good life or *telos* is an important consideration. Our overall outlook, then, seeks to understand and recognise how coaching can contribute to the pursuit of a meaningful life (MacIntyre 1984).

We find meaning in our lives through performing social roles or when engaged in certain social practices that we either have or acquire through choice. The idea of a social practice is that of a coherent, complex and meaningful human activity through which individual and collective goals and values are realised. Social practices are usually formally supported by institutional mechanisms such as associations, organisations or companies whose responsibility it is to ensure that the well-being of such practices are safeguarded. Through related social interactions, communal bonds are formed, which provide the fabric that underpins society. Social practices include such things as education, law, commerce and, for our purposes, sport, including the more specific sporting practice of coaching. Such practices are supported by the respective institutions of schools and universities, the criminal justice system, banking and stock markets, and in the case of sport, by organisations such as the Football Association, the International Olympic Committee and, in coaching, by bodies such as Sports Coach UK.

In order for a social practice to thrive as a meaningful aspect of our lives we undertake various social roles. Our most immediate and recognisable roles involve being a partner, son, daughter, brother, sister or grandparent. These roles all derive their meaning and significance within the institutional framework of the family. Elsewhere, we have other roles as a friend, a colleague, or in the context of sporting practices, as a player, a coach, a mentor, an administrator, an official or a supporter. The type and number of roles and practices we undertake are likely to be products of a number of factors that may or may not be under our control. The roles and practices we choose will depend on the extent to which we have the opportunity and wherewithal to undertake them. For many, socio-economic circumstances, for example, may limit our opportunities. Fortunately, for those who are interested in coaching, sport is, relatively speaking, socially inclusive, providing a mix of practices in which the vast majority of people can engage and find enjoyment. As a result, there are ample opportunities to become involved in coaching sport, particularly at its foundational levels.

Once we understand that coaching can, and perhaps should, be understood as a social practice, we begin to recognise that it can become a way of life for any who do it, impacting much of what they do and how they think of themselves. Rather than recognise coaching as a set of techniques and skills, therefore, coaching's ontological significance lies in the manner in which it has the potential to shape a coach's life and who they are. While it is true that each individual coach, due to his or her personality, experience and particular circumstances, will be different in many ways, there will none the less be a core set of features to coaching that provide personal significance and a central source of meaning, self-understanding, social expression and self-esteem to that person. It is important, therefore, that the coach attempts to interrogate and understand what it is about sport that provides such a powerful personal sense of purpose and well-being; that is, why sport is central to their pursuit of 'the good life'. Part of that interrogation requires the coach to contemplate the nature of sporting activity and its unique characteristics. Here, beyond the contingencies of particular sporting contexts in specific historical times, such an investigation reveals that a significant reason for sport's enduring magnetism is that it centres on game playing (Suits 1995). Despite the tendency to undervalue the play element in modern sports, it is important to understand that sport's principal attraction is that of experiencing a well-made game. Though many may play sport for the immediate psychological and material benefits of winning, sport's unique and enduring appeal lies in how it provides participants with opportunities to pursue a mutual quest of athletic excellence through challenge (Simon 1991). In this quest, coaches have a significant role in maximising the tactical and technical attributes of the participants to allow them to overcome the obstacles the game presents.

Following on from this point, then, it would appear important for coaches to fully understand the specific role that they play in facilitating quality sporting experiences for others. To do this coaches should develop and nurture a lasting appreciation in their players and athletes for core internal goods that can only be acquired through diligent and committed attention to the demands of the sport in question. These internal goods include the development of the fundamental skills, acquiring a sophisticated understanding of the tactical possibilities that the game presents, and also an understanding and respect for the proper social conventions of the game including the observation of good sportspersonship. In our opinion, a good coach will ensure such aspects of sport are prioritised ahead of external goods such as the acquisition of financial rewards, fame and prestige.

## APPLYING PHILOSOPHY TO COACHING

The following example attempts to demonstrate how an ability to reflect and articulate philosophical thinking may benefit coaches.

### SCENARIO: THE ETHICS OF PLAYER-ORIENTATED COACHING

You are a coach of an under-8, seven-a-side football team. There are significant differences in ability within your squad of ten players and it is clear that the overall level of team performance depends on who is on the field of play at any given time. Though you want to ensure that all players have equal playing time, you know that doing so will mean losing games you could win. You wonder what the right thing to do is.

Most coaches will find themselves initially coaching at a foundational level despite the fact that they may have been elite or sub-elite performers themselves. Usually this means working to develop young players during their formative experiences rather than fine-tuning high-level tactical and technical abilities. In such circumstances, a crucial starting point for philosophical reflection is to take into account the needs of various stakeholders (i.e. those who contribute to the coaching process generally). Here, while your interests as a coach and those of parents are important, we contend that the overriding concern is what is in the best interests of the players.

It is usually taken that, at a young age, the development of technical and tactical footballing abilities should be a relatively minor aspect of a child's overall needs. This gives rise to the often-used cliché that it is the development of persons that should be the primary focus of the coach rather than a specific set of footballing techniques and strategies. In practice, this means that the coach should focus on ensuring players have intrinsic enjoyment from football and begin to acquire an appreciation and understanding of the particular physical skills, competitive challenges and particular ethos of the game. Here, the coach tries to develop in children a commitment to, and love of, the game from which a desire for technical and tactical improvement will grow.

This approach suggests that the immediate demands of competitive success are relatively unimportant. However, this need not necessarily be the case. What is probably more important is that the coach is able to judge the extent to which the competitive environment provides each individual player with an appropriate opportunity to develop, first, as a person and, second, as a footballer. Under such conditions it is highly unlikely that any contest at this foundational level would warrant a coach not sharing playing time equally among his or her squad of players. Nevertheless, in accordance with such a principle, this does not mean that it is appropriate to ignore all differences between individual players. A coach will still need to take into account such things as physical, emotional and technical differences among his or her players and treat such individual differences accordingly. It is important to ensure that both stronger and weaker players gain as much from their playing experience as possible. Hence, they may be allocated proportionately more or less playing time depending on the quality of the opposition. The same adjustments may also be needed for less physically developed players when playing against physically stronger or weaker teams. The coach may also need to identify both positional and tactical responsibilities that best suit certain players. Though it is preferable that all players gain experience from playing in different positions, such challenges ought to be developed first through coaching sessions and sensitively implemented in game situations when the stresses of other challenges are diminished. Subsequently, experimentation with playing position and team tactics could best be carried out against weaker opposition.

Fortunately, many junior football leagues recognise such ideals and downplay com-petitiveness through regulatory structures (i.e. no need to report scores, no leagues or tables, no elimination competitions) and certain playing rules (no penalty kicks, unlimited substitutions). Furthermore, discerning coaches, recognising the different abilities and needs of the individual players within their squad, will organise coaching sessions in an appropriate manner to cater for these. Such coaches would possibly conduct aspects of practice in ability groups and, where exceptional talent is identified, seek out a further developmental environment for it (e.g. a regional academy). Within the context of the game, while playing time may be shared equally, this does not mean that time or playing position should be assigned randomly. Again, part of the coach's skill is to recognise which players playing in which positions provide effectual organisational structure to the team to enable as many players as possible to play effectively. Consequently, key players in core positions would get a little more playing time, while more limited players are played in positions and at stages in the game that are not overly demanding.

## CONCLUSION

The immediate preceding discussion is laden with philosophical significance, though no philosophical terminology was used. The first issue, the identification of key stakeholders and their particular developmental stage in the context of their overall lives, has distinct ontological significance. We contend, in line with much general thinking, that the most important guide for coaches here is to consider their players in terms of their development as persons. It then follows that if the development of players as persons is of primary importance, the values compatible with such a goal need to be identified. Here we suggest that the development of moral values (such as honesty, courage, perseverance, commitment, respect) is more important than that of non-moral ones, whilst the pursuit of certain non-moral values (such as health, skill, knowledge) is more important than that of others (such as winning). Appreciation and articulation of such values provide the basis for ethical coaching behaviour and guide decisions as to who plays where and when.

## REVIEW QUESTIONS

1. Discuss philosophically the premise that 'sport is good for your health'. In doing so, engage reflectively on what is meant by 'sport', 'good' and 'health'.
2. As outlined in the chapter, what are the philosopher's basic tools? How can they be used in the coaching context?
3. What are the morals or ethics of a good coach? Justify your answer.
4. What do you consider to be the meaning or the function of coaching? Why?

# CHAPTER SEVEN

# SPORTS DEVELOPMENT FOR COACHES

Nicola Bolton and Bev Smith

*It is important for coaches to understand how they fit into the bigger sporting picture be it in terms of increasing participation or developing performance, in addition to contributing to wider social objectives.*

Julian North –
Head of Research, Sports Coach UK

**Key sections:**

- Introduction
- Key concepts
- Policy context
- Insights for sports development and sports coaching
- Conclusion

## INTRODUCTION

Spend a couple of minutes thinking about your own sporting career, and consider the various sports you have both taken up and subsequently dropped. Ask yourself the following questions:

- How many sports have I tried?
- What were the reasons for trying out these sports and why did I drop them?
- Who did I rely on to be able to participate?

A typical response to the first two questions would be that you have tried numerous sporting activities and that your decisions for participating and perhaps giving up were governed largely by a mix of personal, social and structural or opportunity factors (Torkildsen 2005). The third question is of great significance to this chapter. Regardless of the opportunities or constraints affecting your choice of activity you will have relied on others, indeed you will have been dependent on others, to participate. There are some obvious examples to draw upon: school teachers providing extra-curricular opportunities, coaches taking sessions, facility managers providing venues, volunteers helping the club and, of course, parents and other adults prepared to provide transport and finance. When put together, sport becomes an intricate subject. Coaches, then, are certainly not alone in providing coaching.

Participation in sport is affected by where you live, your background and wider personal and social influences (Horne *et al*. 1999). Consequently, not everyone has the same opportunities to either participate or excel in sport. Collins with Kay (2003) provides a clear overview of the unequal participation patterns experienced by groups and within certain areas in the UK. Hence, there are many equality issues inherent within sport while, for many commentators, sport does not reflect the unequal social composition of society so much as perpetuate it (Hargreaves 1986). Sport's complex role in society, then, is being increasingly appreciated, a realisation that is reflected in ever greater political involvement. For example, within the UK there are two principal governmental aims for sport: to achieve international success (especially given the 2012 London Olympics) and to ensure that the UK population is physically active. Importantly, the expectation to make Britain physically active reaches across all age-groups and presents a major new challenge for sport providers. This is because, in the past, priorities for action have focused almost exclusively on young people.

The purpose of this chapter is to explore issues associated with developing sport in the community and how they impact upon coaching. To address these issues the chapter is divided into four sections. The first provides some definitions and discussion of the key, yet elusive, concepts of sports development and community development. This is followed by a review of the main policy shifts relating to sport that have impacted on coaching since the arrival in government of New Labour in 1997. Drawing on this contextual information, the third section provides insights into some of the issues associated with sports development and sports coaching, in particular how the former can inform the latter. A final section gives some concluding comments. The significance of the chapter lies in giving coaches an understanding of how coaching opportunities are defined, generated and provided. Such knowledge is important for coaches, as it can help them comprehend the often problematic and changing context in which they work and, subsequently, to manage it better.

## KEY CONCEPTS

### Sports development

Although sports development is often referred to as a new activity and an emerging profession, according to Houlihan and White (2002) its basic characteristics emerged in the 1950s and were broadly associated with those of the welfare state. Since that time sports development has evolved often in tandem with the political tides of the day. Houlihan and White (2002) provide a full and comprehensive account tracing this growth from the birth of sports development half a century ago to the present. This history, however, does not provide a single definition of sports development. Nevertheless, Bramham et al. (2001: 3) provide a useful starting point when they write, 'Those engaging in sports development must be in the business of devising better and more effective ways of promoting interest, participation or performance in sport'. Based on work undertaken by the UK Sports Councils (the bodies charged with the broad development of sport in the UK) in the early 1990s, sports development workers became associated with ensuring that appropriate pathways were in place, not only so that people could participate in sport but that they could also develop their competence to perform at higher levels and, in some cases, achieve excellence. The inclusion of the word development here was and continues to be important and reflects an ongoing emphasis on initiating change (Eady 1993; McDonald 1995).

Whilst many models of sports development have emerged, three are especially note-worthy. The traditional sports development continuum (Figure 7.1, cited in Houlihan and White 2002), initially developed by Derek Casey in 1988, helped conceptualise how participants could move from foundation to excellence. It also outlined how organisations with responsibility for developing sport could identify their roles and responsibilities in relation to each level of the hierarchical continuum, thereby facilitating a smooth process from foundation to excellence (Bramham et al. 2001). This basic model was adapted (Figure 7.2) in the early 1990s to reconsider the relationship between sport participation and performance. Here, greater recognition of the horizontal movement between participation and performance was made taking into account 'changes in lifestyle, family and employment circumstances' (Houlihan and White 2002: 42). The third model (Figure 7.3) developed by Cooke (1996) was termed the 'House of Sport' (Bramham et al. 2001: 4). It provides a more realistic way of depicting the sports development process by outlining separate pathways for recreation (participation) and performance, and the addition of a third floor and penthouse, which embrace elite levels of performance. There are two other features of the model worth noting. Firstly, it recognises that success is not predicated on a broad base of participation and, secondly, that many people are introduced to some sports for the first time in adult life. The point here is that sports development in practice is complex and multifaceted rather than a smooth continuum or hierarchy as purported by the earlier models.

## Community development

Probably the most contested term used in this chapter is community. The word has multiple meanings and is used in very different contexts. Often it is used to define places associated by a range of characteristics including geographical size, population and socio-economic standards. However, Jarvie (2006: 328) writes, 'communities exist beyond geography; they encompass a wide range of social ties and common interests which go beyond

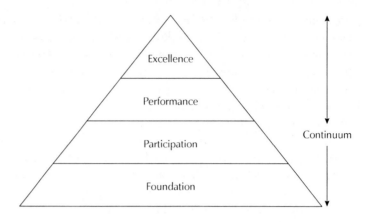

Figure 7.1
The traditional
sports development
continuum
(Hylton *et al* 2001)

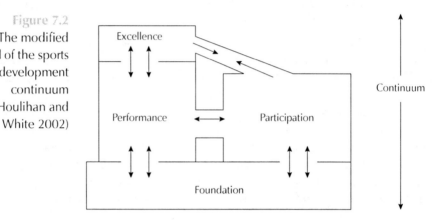

Figure 7.2
The modified
model of the sports
development
continuum
(Houlihan and
White 2002)

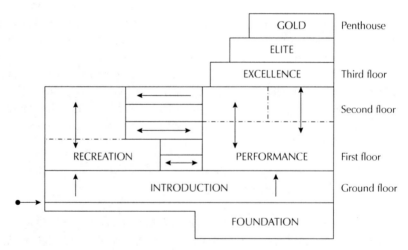

Figure 7.3
The house
of sport
(Hylton *et al*
2001)

proximity or common residence'. In similar vein, Hylton and Totten (2001) have concluded that the term community implies some notion of collectivity, commonality, a sense of belonging or something shared. Indeed, the notion of investing in each other has been loosely referred to as developing social capital (Collins with Kay 2003). Community development is a further expansion of this and suggests 'a more dynamic model of engagement whereby people themselves are empowered to take an active part in shaping their own community' (Hylton and Totten 2001: 69). Consequently, many writers draw on terms such as neighbourhood as a means of linking place and community together (Richardson and Mumford 2002). There is also the issue of community being associated with particular groups of people who have strong ties and a collective identity. For example, in sporting terms, Jarvie (2006: 327) writes of 'particular sporting communities be they local fans, places, national supporters or groups or people who wear a (common) badge of allegiance'.

Having addressed some key definitions, the focus of the next section is on policy and its implications. In the past decade, government policies have been particularly influential and have challenged organisations to create a more cohesive framework for the development of sport that is easily understood and avoids duplication. We contend that coaches are significant contributors to the sports development process and that a knowledge and understanding of this context is, therefore, important for them. Furthermore, coaches and the roles they perform are being increasingly differentiated and defined, and if government targets are to become a reality, a partnership approach between the two emerging professions of sport development and coaching is imperative. Central to this chapter, then, is the notion that coaches should look to sports development and the wider policy context regarding sport to inform their practice.

## POLICY CONTEXT

In the UK, the fate of sport during the post-war years (i.e. since 1945) has been linked to the political priorities set by various governments (Henry 2001). Not surprisingly, the importance of sport to government policy has varied during this time and, whilst a full account of these changes is beyond the scope of this chapter, it is reasonably straight-forward to track these historical developments (see, for example, Houlihan and White 2002; Henry 2001). It should be noted, however, that the relationship between national policy and local delivery in relation to sport has rarely been centre-stage. Hence, sport continues to be a discretionary service of the local state (Robinson 2004), with no mandatory requirement (unlike education and social services) for local authorities to fully address its provision and opportunities. However, although in reality most local authorities have chosen to provide sport as a service, because of this discretionary nature the outcome has been a variable pattern of provision.

Elected in 1997, the current Labour government produced a number of key policy documents relating to sport. These included:

- *A Sporting Future for All* (Department of Culture Media and Sport [DCMS] 2000);
- *The Government's Plan for Sport* (DCMS 2001); and
- *Game Plan* (DCMS/Strategy Unit 2002).

Devolution has also impacted on sports policy. Hence, both the Scottish Parliament and Welsh Assembly have produced their own strategies for sport. These include:

- *Sport 21* (Scottish Executive 1998); and
- *Climbing Higher* (Welsh Assembly Government 2005).

Taken together, these documents provide a long-term framework for sport to be developed. In the case of *Game Plan* and *Climbing Higher*, 20-year strategies inclusive of targets have been set. These policy documents all emphasise the twin objectives of making the UK more physically active (participation) and achieving international sporting success (excellence). Within this overall framework, the government is committed to 'Third Way' politics (Giddens 1997). This requires equality and social inclusion to be embraced as key principles within any public service reforms. This has led some commentators to write that sport for sport's sake is no longer relevant at the community level and that, alternatively, the value of sport is in its ability to serve other wider political interests (see, for example, Coalter 2001). Houlihan and White (2002: 4) also pick up on this issue by articulating:

> Perhaps most significant in policy terms has been the tension between *development through sport* (with the emphasis on social objectives and sport as a tool for human development) and *development of sport* (where sport is valued for its own sake).

So how does sports coaching fit into this wider policy context? Emerging from the government's original *Sporting Future for All* (DCMS 2001) report, a Coaching Task Force (CTF) was established in June 2001. It undertook a wide-ranging and detailed review of sports coaching and concluded that there was:

- not enough paid opportunities for coaches;
- too much reliance on volunteers within coaching;
- no proper career structure for coaches; and
- a lack of nationally recognised/transferable qualifications within, and in relation to, coaching.

As a result, Sports Coach UK, the body responsible for coach development in Britain, was charged with addressing these issues and significant funding was made available. Two initiatives, the UK Coaching Certificate (UKCC) and the UK Coaching Framework, were subsequently developed. Given the comments made earlier in relation to devolution, the fact that these initiatives have been agreed on a UK level is important. Each initiative will be considered briefly, but students are directed to the Sports Coach UK website to obtain more detailed information on both (http//www.sportscoachuk.gov).

## The UKCC

Those within Sports Coach UK charged with developing the UK Coaching Certificate (UKCC) are currently working with a number of national governing bodies to achieve a five-level UK framework of standards for coach education. This will help professionalise the role of the coach, enable movement between the home countries and provide opportunities to move between sports through the inclusion of core components. The current position of the UKCC is that 31 national governing bodies have agreed to be subject to this new coach education structure. The introduction of these 31 sports into the structure has been divided into three distinct phases. Phase one and phase two sports (totalling 21) received funding to implement the UKCC by the end of 2006. The other ten sports have received administrative and training support to enable them to lead the second wave of implementation.

An extensive monitoring and evaluation programme in relation to the success of the new structure has been undertaken by Marketing and Opinion Research International (MORI) on behalf of Sports Coach UK. Here, in 2004, a series of in-depth, semi-structured interviews were conducted with a number of relevant personnel, firstly to evaluate the delivery planning process, and later to assess the ongoing functioning of the UKCC. Research was also conducted to determine enablers as well as barriers that the governing bodies faced regarding the implementation of the UKCC. In summing up the delivery planning process, the perceived benefits included defining better the sports coach's role, standardising coach education and qualifications, raising the profile of coaching and producing knowledgeable and competent coaches. Similarly, the ongoing implementation study reported significant progress in several areas including the identification of tutors, verifiers and assessors, the employment of extra staff, and greater support from governing body senior management and external agencies (Sports Coach UK 2004). Perhaps most importantly, however, was the emergence of support shown for the new structure from existing coaches. On the other hand, several barriers were also identified, including the increased demand on lead officers, a delay in guidance materials and poor networking between sports.

## The UK Coaching Framework

The UK Coaching Framework is the long-term plan for coaching, and sets out its vision of establishing:

A cohesive, ethical, inclusive and valued coaching system where:

Skilled coaches support children, players and athletes at all stages of their development in their sport
And which is number one in the world by 2016
'bench-marked against international best practice'

(Sports Coach UK 2006: 3)

The UK Coaching Framework maps out the key goals to take place over the next 11 years to achieve this vision. They will be incorporated into three phases which will, in turn, run concurrently:

- Building the Foundation 2006–08 (3 years);
- Delivering the Goals 2006–12 (7 years); and
- Transforming the System 2006–16 (11 years).

The Framework also highlights the increasingly diverse roles expected of coaches. In seeking some clarity here in developing a coherent organisational system for sports coaching, the UK Coaching Model, which is subject to further detailed development, will be adopted. This recognises the need for long-term coach development (LTCD) and for it to sit alongside long-term athlete/player development (LTAPD), long-term sportsperson development (LTSD) and long-term disabled player development (LTDPD).

## INSIGHTS FOR SPORTS DEVELOPMENT AND SPORTS COACHING

Since the turn of the twenty-first century, sports-related employment opportunities have grown. Nowhere has this been seen more clearly than within the emerging profession of sports development (Anderson 2001; Hylton and Totten 2001). Equally, Lyle (2002) has claimed that coaching is gaining parity with other professions such as teaching. If one subscribes to the view that there is a pathway towards greater recognition of sports development and sports coaching as professions, then much can be learned from the work of Bayles (1988) who suggested three necessary conditions for a profession: extensive training, training that is intellectual in kind, and the delivery of an important service. Similarly, Chelladurai (1999) suggested four characteristics as defining a profession: an organised body of knowledge, professional authority, community sanction and a regulative code of ethics. Spend a little time thinking about sports development and coaching in light of the above conditions and characteristics, and answer the following questions. Do you view either in the same professional light as law, medicine or teaching? Alternatively, do you view either as a vocation or an occupation? Finally, what factors did you consider in coming to your conclusion?

Although some of you may consider both sports development and coaching to be professions, there are clearly areas of doubt. One of them surrounds the clear concep-

tualisation of what each involves; that is, do they meet Chelladurai's condition of being rooted in distinct bodies of knowledge? Indeed, the terms 'sports development' and 'coaching' are often used randomly and inappropriately; a tendency that undermines the credibility of both to be considered separate professions. This is particularly so when studying the relationship between sports development and sports coaching at the community level. Think of some adverts for jobs to develop sport in the community. Often they come with a mix of descriptors crossing the fields of coaching and sports development that serve to confuse potential candidates. Similarly, in practice there is frequently a blurring of roles between sports development and sports coaching. The following scenario provides an illustration of how the practice of sports development and sports coaching can become confusing and lack clarity of purpose.

## CASE STUDY 7.1

A graduate with a Master's qualification in a sports discipline is seeking employment. In addition to academic qualifications, she has a national governing body coaching qualification and experience of working with a sports team. She sees an advertisement for a sport-specific development officer to work in an identified geographical area. Some of the key objectives for the post-holder, against which the applications will be measured, include:

- increasing the size of the governing body membership (participants, coaches, officials and clubs);
- sustainable club development (increasing the capacity in clubs and identifying relevant training for club personnel); and
- increasing the size of the network (identifying and involving key partners to contribute to the sports development process).

Having been the successful candidate, she is given considerable freedom in creating a work programme. Being enthusiastic and relatively inexperienced, she develops an extremely busy schedule, networking between various schools and clubs and working many unsocial hours. On a visit to one of the area's clubs, it became apparent that one of the teams was likely to disband because they were unable to find a replacement coach. The club secretary made it quite clear that the best way a development officer (DO) could help them was to coach the team until they could find someone else. After much discussion, she, as the DO, agreed to find some extra hours in the work programme and coach the team for a period of three weeks, while the club looked for a replacement. In that period the team made progress and attracted additional players, whilst she thoroughly enjoyed working in the given coaching capacity. After three weeks the club had still not found a replacement so she, as a DO, agreed to stay on indefinitely (until another coach was found).

This illustration seeks to provide a real-life situation that many sports development officers experience. Now consider the following two questions. First, determine two advantages and two disadvantages of undertaking the role of the coach in this instance; and secondly, suggest one or two alternative solutions that the development officer could have explored to resolve the situation she found herself in. Although, as a DO, our graduate undoubtedly provided a good service to the club whilst thoroughly enjoying the coaching experience, we contend that filling the position indefinitely was in no-one's long-term interests. This is not to say, however, that sport development officers should never be involved in coaching. Indeed, in support of the work of Eady (1993) and Duffy (2006), we firmly believe that sports development workers and coaches have similarities, with both being considered agents of change. In this respect, both should seek to engage people in sport and physical activity, thus making a difference to people's lives. The significant distinction between them, however, lies in the fundamental roles they should play. For example, a sports development worker effects change in several places at one time with several groups of participants. This involves the employment or deployment of coaches and seeks a shift in the behaviour of individuals in the community. On the other hand, a coach effects change in one place at a time with a single group or individual participant through the delivery of coaching sessions.

The National Occupation Standards (NOS) developed by Skills Active (2005) are helpful, as they clearly differentiate sports development from sports coaching in determining the competencies required to work in both sectors. Additionally, whereas coaching starts at NOS Level 1 and progresses to Level 5, sports development commences at Level 3 and progresses to Level 5. The fact that sports development only starts at Level 3 is important as it indicates that management competencies are needed to work in this profession. Furthermore, not one of the sport development units at Level 3 focuses on the need to deliver sports sessions. Rather, the emphasis is on the need to recruit, select, motivate and retain colleagues and volunteers as coaches and other sport workers, alongside planning and managing projects and services. A focus for sports development practitioners, then, is the planning process in relation to assessing the need before building networks and co-ordinating successful implementation. Key to this are the recruitment, employment and deployment of coaches into a variety of surroundings.

Nesti (2001) identified the personal and psychological qualities possessed by many sports development workers as creativity, empathy, commitment, presence and authenticity. Given sports development's rather unique role to be proactive and interventionist, Nesti (2001: 210) suggested close links to counsellors, psychotherapists and educators. Similarly, there is an ongoing debate in coaching that suggests important shifts are occurring: from instruction to pedagogy and from a focus on the participant–performer divide to an emphasis on developing the individual (Jones 2006). Additionally, coaching is becoming increasingly recognised as 'an inherently non-routine, problematic and complex endeavour', particularly with regard to its complex leader–follower nature (Jones 2006: 3). Clearly, these two emerging professions have commonalities, and given the current agenda, if developed in a complementary and meaningful manner, could be instrumental in contributing to a new sporting landscape.

Recognising their complementary nature, it is important to examine how the concepts used in sports development can be used to support coaches in their practice. For example, for coaches to have a better conceptualisation of their evolving role, it would appear relevant for them to have a firm understanding of governmental agendas as related to increasing sport and physical activity opportunities in the UK over the next 20 years. Here, whilst there is some variation between the UK Home Countries, the overriding goal remains the same, i.e. to encourage greater participation, possibly by as much as 1 per cent per annum. This ambitious target will require sports development professionals and sports coaches to seek new participants – an agenda that focuses on getting existing participants to do more will be insufficient. For example, encouraging sport and physical activity to be undertaken at places of work, thus establishing employers as a priority partner for the future. Such initiatives will run parallel to the primary and secondary school participation programmes already being implemented. Sports development, thus, will have a key role in developing sustainable opportunities within local communities; in essence, providing opportunities for sports coaches to work or assisting coaches to develop such opportunities for themselves.

Sports coaches also need to determine their role within this wider agenda. Sports development will be seeking coaches to deliver sessions but, given that there will be new audiences, it is anticipated that the majority of sports coaching will not be primarily about improving performance to achieve game-related results. Hence, we believe there will be a need to look beyond a historic emphasis on coaching young people and performers and to consider the needs of the wider population. Coaches in the community will be required to deliver products that attract very different groups of people of all ages. The development menu of the future, then, needs to be varied, targeted and sustainable. Indeed, the UK Coaching Framework (Sports Coach UK 2006) establishes some clear expectations that coaches should address if interest in sport is to be engendered and sustained. These include welcoming children and adults into sport; making sport fun; building fundamental skills in participants; improving sport-specific skills; developing fair play; ethical practice; discipline and respect; enhancing physical fitness and positive lifestyle; guiding children, players and athletes through the steps to improved performance; placing a high value on the development of the whole person; and keeping children, players and athletes safe in sport. Such directives hold the potential to give coaches a clear future focus in relation to where they should concentrate their energies.

## CONCLUSION

Since the beginning of the twenty-first century, the sectors of sports development and coaching have received unprecedented levels of attention and investment from central and devolved government. Sport is now recognised as a tool that can assist in partially delivering the related governmental social agenda. Education and training for sports development professionals has been seen as a priority in official policy documents such as *Sporting Future for All* (DCMS 2000), while the recent launch of a new professional body, the Institute of Sport, Parks and Leisure (ISPAL) has signalled a step-change in improving the stature and profile of its members. Similarly, Game Plan (DCMS/ Strategy Unit 2002) sets out some key objectives and these have been supported by subsequent UK Home Country policy strategies. Coaching has emerged as one of the priorities and Sports Coach UK has been tasked with developing and implementing the UKCC and the UK Coaching Framework. No doubt sports development and sports coaching are emerging professions. Set within an overall policy context of increasing participation it is important that their roles remain complementary but distinct. Each comes with its own challenges but shares the need to remain people-centred and people-focused as change agents within the sports industry. Knowledge of the sport development context and how it shapes coaching policy is undoubtedly important for coaches, as it enables them to carefully consider their role as they respond to the wider developmental and social agenda.

## REVIEW QUESTIONS

1. Who enables you to participate in sport?
2. Write a job description for a Sports Development Officer. Rank the duties in order of importance. Justify your answer.
3. How has the governmental policy impacted on the development of coaching in the UK?
4. The chapter's authors argue that sport development officers and coaches should carry out largely separate, complementary roles. Do you agree? Why?

# PART 3

# CHAPTER EIGHT

# BIOMECHANICS FOR COACHES

David G. Kerwin and Gareth Irwin

*Knowledge about biomechanical principles is critical in understanding and explaining suitable technique to athletes.*

*Jon Grydeland – Head Coach,*
*Norwegian Beach Volleyball team*
*(3rd European Championships, 2006 [women];*
*3rd World Cup, 2006 [women])*

## Key sections:

- Introduction
- The conceptual model of technique and performance
- The coaching–biomechanics interface
- Types of analysis in sport biomechanics
- Modelling in biomechanics
- Concluding thoughts: the future

## INTRODUCTION

This chapter aims to outline the value of sports biomechanics for coaches. Biomechanics is the application of mechanical principles to biological systems. In this context, the focus is on how these principles apply to the human athlete taking part in sporting activities. Gymnastics, a highly technical sport, is ideal to illustrate many of the concepts being presented and so features strongly within the chapter. Other sports are referenced where appropriate, with several of the ideas being transferable.

Many established texts exist that provide a well-grounded, scientifically rigorous explanation of the basic concepts relating to sports biomechanics (e.g. Hay 1994; Hamill and Knutzen 2003; Robertson *et al.* 2004; Watkins in press). The content of this chapter

87

provides our perspective, and is supported by current research that has evaluated the link between the coaching process, training theory and the universal principles of biomechanics. In many ways, then, this chapter provides a platform to bridge the divide between science and coaching.

The first section introduces a conceptual model of technique and performance based on a recent article by Irwin et al. (2005), and includes a discussion of the ways in which coaches understand technique within the context of biomechanics. The second section introduces the notion of the coaching–biomechanics interface that details how biomechanics can help coaches in their work. This is followed by a third section that outlines different types of analyses currently practised in sport biomechanics. A note of caution, however, runs through the chapter concerning issues of (coach) interpretation and comprehension. This is particularly so in relation to the use of new video-based technologies where, at times, a false impression can be created with the images alone appearing to provide answers. Alternatively, we would like to emphasise the importance of understanding within biomechanics and its translation to coaching, which places biomechanical knowledge as a tool to be used critically by coaches. Finally, a brief view of future developments in biomechanics and coaching are presented to highlight the impact of new technologies on coaching practice.

## THE CONCEPTUAL MODEL OF TECHNIQUE AND PERFORMANCE

Knowing how to develop skills successfully in athletes is a crucial aspect of a coach's knowledge (Zinkovsky et al. 1976). To illustrate how elite coaches facilitate such improvements, we recently developed a conceptual model (Irwin et al. 2005) (see Figure 8.1).

This model is consistent with others (e.g. Côté et al. 1995) and represents a mental process illustrative of a coach's response to, and interpretations of, specific situations. The research that underpins it was carried out on elite gymnastics coaches and echoes previous findings within the more generic coaching literature (e.g. Gould et al. 1990). A key feature of the model is the development of a 'mindset' for a coach, which represents a conceptual understanding of the technical aspects of a skill. Over time, coaches develop this conceptual understanding that they associate with successful performance. The components underpinning the development of this mindset are, firstly, the refinement of techniques that are already known. For example, when in 2000 the gymnastic vaulting-horse was replaced by the vaulting-table, coaches relied on refining the training drills from the old horse to the new table. The second component that contributes to the mindset is current coaching knowledge. The importance of this has been well researched (Gould et al. 1990; Irwin et al. 2004) with the value of critical reflection and interactive mentorships being emphasised. The third aspect is to do with a coach's mental picture of the skill that is used to identify key phases, movement patterns and timings. Finally, a fourth component, biomechanical understanding of the final skill, relates to a descriptive understanding of how the performer organises his or her body segments to achieve a successful technique. The

biomechanics for coaches

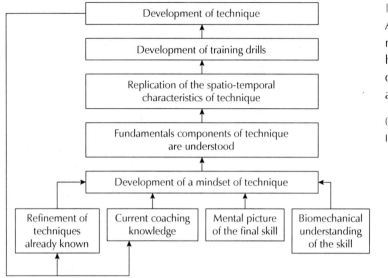

Figure 8.1

A conceptual model depicting how coaches develop skills in athletes

(adapted from Irwin et al. 2005)

development of the mental picture and the biomechanical understanding (i.e. the third and fourth components) are often aided by technology (e.g. a frame-by-frame analysis). From the resultant mindset, a coach can generate a clear grasp of the key phases of the skill in question.

When developing training regimes, coaches often attempt to replicate key aspects of technique in practice drills. This specificity allows adaptations to occur that assist in the effective and efficient development of particular skills. Importantly, Figure 8.1 also highlights the fact that the coach is managing the whole process and decides how and in what order aspects of the desired skill are going to be addressed. This ability to arrange the process of skill development is key, although, naturally, it relies heavily on technical knowledge being clearly understood in the first place. For example, an elite gymnastics coach would need to have precise knowledge of what he or she would expect from a gymnast in terms of the movement patterns and body positions to be performed (Irwin et al. 2005). If, on the other hand, the technical understanding is not accurate, it would be impossible for the coach to select training drills that would be effective. The potential benefit of the model depicted in Figure 8.1, then, echoing the case made in Chapter 2 ('Skill acquisition for coaches'), lies in uncovering the mechanisms that control skill development so that coaches can manage them better.

Similarly, the theoretically grounded science of sports biomechanics provides a mechanism that can help coaches better understand technique. It can do so through identifying the most effective skill development pathways, reducing the risk of injury and removing the trial-and-error of training. In essence, following the principles of overload and specificity (principles discussed in greater depth in Chapter 11 'Physiology for coaches'), sports biomechanics aims to make training more effective and efficient. Helping coaches to understand technique and, hence, providing the link between biomechanics and coaching has been a challenge for the last 30 years. Trying to identify how biomechanics can help coaches and how the knowledge requirements of coaches can be assessed has led us to what we have termed the coaching–biomechanics interface.

## THE COACHING–BIOMECHANICS INTERFACE

The coaching–biomechanics interface is a term that conceptualises how coaching can be informed from a biomechanical perspective. The process involved here is a continuous one, with each cycle starting and ending with the athlete. The process is based on a coach's tacit knowledge in relation to the practices that are routinely used to develop athletes' skills. This information, through systematic conversation with a biomechanist, is then turned into biomechanical variables that can either be measured or analysed theoretically. The key to these variables is that they are directly related to successful performance of the skill. Once understanding of the key aspects of skills and any associated progressions or drills has been understood, informed feedback can be delivered to the athletes via the coach. Integral to this process is the communication between the biomechanist and the coach and athlete. This cycle of extracting, processing and imparting new scientifically grounded knowledge or understanding represents the whole or the actuality of the coaching–biomechanics interface. Sometimes this new knowledge may simply reinforce existing practices or it can provide new insights that inform future skill development. The overall purpose of developing the coaching–biomechanics interface is to bridge the gap between biomechanical science and practice. The interface aims to make training more effective and efficient, particularly for athletes who are working near to their physiological limits. More specifically, the coaching–biomechanics interface can help coaches and the coaching process in five ways. Each of these will now be discussed in turn.

### 1. Enhancing coaches' technical understanding of skills

Input from biomechanics can enable coaches to gain a better appreciation of successful technique by providing an understanding of underlying principles of motion and how they apply to key phases of skills. In general, coaches' understanding of technique is based on a visual inspection of the skill in question. Here, in order to evaluate technique, a coach will look at the key aspects of performance that are considered to be directly related to success. For ease of interpretation, we shall call these variables performance indicators. These performance indicators fall into two main groups: continuous and discrete. The functional phases of the longswing in gymnastics have recently been shown to be a good example of a continuous performance indicator (Irwin and Kerwin 2006). The functional phases are characterised by a dynamic hip extension (opening) to flexion (closing) and shoulder flexion to extension, as illustrated in Figure 8.2. The left graphic (in Figure 8.2) shows the start and end of the gymnast's hip functional phase (linked by a double-headed arrow) while the right graphic depicts the corresponding phase for the gymnast's shoulders. The findings here demonstrated how both extension and flexion occurred as the gymnast passed underneath the bar and, consequently, that 70 per cent of the total musculo-skeletal work needed for the longswing was completed during this time. Coaches, then, should generally focus their attention on these phases of the swing, emphasising the extension and flexion of the hips and shoulders as the gymnast passes underneath the bar.

Discrete performance indicators are defined as single-outcome measures or measures at an instant in time during a skill, which are key to the successful performance of the skill in question. For example, Figure 8.3 illustrates a sprinter in the thrust phase of his start. The thrust phase of the sprint start is the result of a large impulse that is needed to accelerate the athlete from the blocks. Ideally, a straight line should be formed from the ankle to the shoulder, indicating that the drive is effectively transferred into a suitable forward and upward direction of motion. By identifying and/or confirming such key aspects of performance (as highlighted in Figures 8.2 and 8.3), biomechanical analyses can enhance coaches' understanding of skills and their application.

## 2.  Evaluation of coaching practices to enhance skills

This area of work is potentially sensitive because a biomechanist can sometimes be seen as challenging coaches in relation to what they know. This, however, should not be the case as both should be working together to enhance each other's knowledge. For example, during the build-up to the 2000 and 2004 Olympic Games, the UK sprinter Darren Campbell received biomechanical support for his sprint start technique. Based on the need to establish the most effective block setting, the coach, athlete and biomechanist devised a series of sessions that enabled them to determine which block setting (i.e. the distance between the blocks and the hands) was most effective for Darren. In addition to

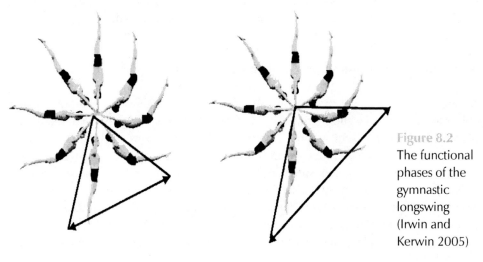

Figure 8.2
The functional phases of the gymnastic longswing (Irwin and Kerwin 2005)

Figure 8.3 Darren Campbell performing the sprint start showing extension into the 'thrust position': a key discrete performance indicator used by coaches as a measure of successful execution of the skill

this, a more detailed analysis of the thrust position (see Figure 8.3) and the forces and impulses produced by it was undertaken to enable the relationships between thrust mechanics and successful sprint start performance to be determined.

## 3. Evaluation of training practices to develop skills

As opposed to the specific advice on certain aspects of performance, the primary aim here is to inform the selection of training drills or preparatory activities for the development of skills. One approach for coaches is to mine information from academic research to identify the most effective training drills for the development of a particular skill. An example from our own work provides an illustration of this process. Here, as part of a series of linked research studies (Irwin and Kerwin 2005; in press a; in press b), one objective related to identifying more effective progressions (preparatory skills) for the development of the longswing in men's artistic gymnastics. We had previously identified that UK coaches have at their disposal 49 different progressions for this skill (Irwin et al. 2004). From a biomechanical analysis of these, two categories of progressions were identified; firstly, those that exhibited similarities in movement patterns (kinematics and co-ordination), and secondly, those that required similar musculo-skeletal work (kinetics) to the final skill. The progressions were then ranked in terms of difficulty within each category, enabling selection of appropriate ones to a gymnast's current stage of development.

### 4. Facilitating the evolution of technique within sport (i.e. through the development of new skills)

Biomechanics has directed the development of sport in numerous ways. The most obvious instances lie within equipment design (e.g. new javelins, soccer balls and golf clubs) and innovative techniques. An example in relation to developing new technique comes from the former Soviet Union (USSR), when it was decided that gymnastics was going to be an illustration of the country's alleged superior political and social system. Consequently, biomechanists and coaches worked together and theoretically derived a catalogue of skills that had never been attempted before (Malberg 1978). The most famous of these was the Tkachev (see Figure 8.4). The skill involves the gymnast rotating clockwise around the bar up to the point of release before travelling backwards over the bar whilst rotating anti-clockwise to re-catch the bar on the downswing. The skill can be performed in a straddled, piked or straight body shape; the shape adopted by the performer dictating the difficulty rating.

The skill was first performed in 1974 by the Russian gymnast Alexander Tkachev, after whom it was named. However, emphasising the link to biomechanics, it was first proposed not by a coach but by the Soviet biomechanist Smolevski in 1969. Similarly, recent work by Hiley and Yeadon (2005) has used computer simulation to address the question of whether a triple straight backward somersault dismount could be performed from the high bar. Their conclusion was that, although it is technically possible, the margins for error in both the preparatory circle and the exact instant of release are so minimal that it would be extremely risky for a gymnast to attempt the skill in competition.

### 5. Assisting in optimising performance (i.e. by theoretically justifying the modification of skills)

Computer models based on forward dynamics have been used increasingly to investigate and develop sports skills. A forward dynamics model uses information on forces applied within the body to predict the subsequent body movements. Through such means, sports biomechanics can begin to address questions such as, What is the optimal technique for a particular performer? An example of how this has worked comes from a study by Kerwin et al. (1990). At the 1988 Olympic Games (Seoul, South Korea) the Soviet gymnast Valerie Lukien (competitor #149 in Figure 8.5) performed his signature triple backward somersault

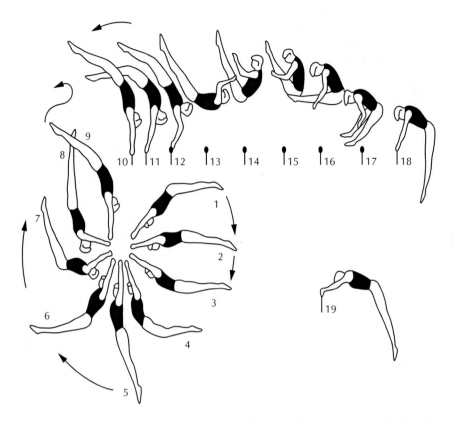

**Figure 8.4** The Tkachev move: the original Smolevski drawing (1969). Cited in Nissinen, M.A., Preiss, R. and Brüggeman, P. (1985) 'Simulation of human airborne movements on the horizontal bar', in D.A. Winter and R. Norman (eds) *Biomechanics IX-B.* Champaign, IL: Human Kinetics

dismount from the high bar. A simplified block-graphical reconstruction of this together with a recorded sequence from another competitor (#120) are shown in Figure 8.5.

To successfully execute a triple backward somersault, the gymnast needs to have generated substantial rotation (also known as angular momentum) as he releases from the bar (only male gymnasts carry out this manoeuvre). Importantly, once airborne, the magnitude of angular momentum will remain constant. The gymnast changes his body shape in order to control the somersault rate (also known as angular velocity). Whilst airborne, the rotation occurs around the gymnast's centre of mass. Because the gymnast needs to spin quickly to complete the triple somersault, he must grab his knees, thus pulling the body segments closer to the mass centre. This results in a reduction in the distribution of mass about the axis of rotation, with the reluctance to spin being decreased. This interplay between somersault rate (angular velocity) and resistance to rotate (moment of inertia) provides the performer with a control mechanism in flight.

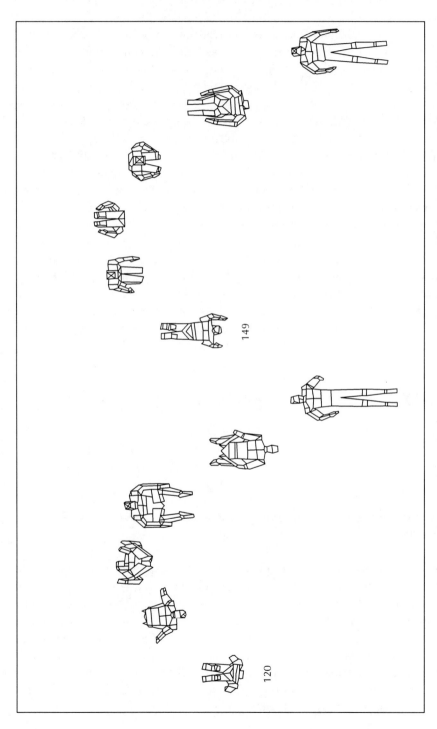

Figure 8.5 A graphical reconstruction of a triple backward somersault by Valeri Lukien (#149) and another gymnast (#120) at the 1988 Seoul Olympics

*Source* D.G. Kerwin, M.R. Yeadon, L. Sung-Cheol, 1985, 'Body configuration in multiple somersault high bar dismounts', *International Journal of Sport Biomechanics* 6 (2): 155, figure 2. 1990 by Human Kinetics Publishers, Inc. Reprinted with permission from Human Kinetics (Champaign, IL).

However, successful performance of this skill is dictated by the Fédération Internationale de Gymnastique (FIG) (the sport's international governing body), which states that the knees must not pass (i.e. be wider than) the width of the hips. Performer #120 in Figure 8.5 has the knees wider apart than the shoulders, whereas competitor #149 has adopted a (better) position with the knees being closer together. Officially, competitor #120 should lose marks; so what can be done to help him? One way would be for the coach to just advise him to tighten or close the tuck shape to avoid this penalty, leaving the gymnast to work things out further for himself. Alternatively, a much more detailed approach to solving the problem and help the gymnast achieve the desired aim would be through the use of computer simulation. By developing a set of equations of motion for the gymnast (who is of known physical dimensions) it is possible to model the skill in question. Firstly, it is necessary to check that the model works, i.e. that it reproduces an accurate representation of the skill performed. If this is satisfied, then it is possible to modify the movements made by the gymnast in subsequent runs of the computer model. The biomechanist can then see what happens to the theoretical gymnast as a result of closing the model's legs together in flight. The precise measures that come from this form of modelling can determine how much the angular momentum (i.e. the capacity to rotate) of the gymnast around the bar, prior to release, would have to be increased to enable a modified triple somersault dismount to be achieved. We believe that this approach to examining technique and modifying performance is certainly preferable to putting an athlete at risk of injury from a failed move resulting from inaccurate or inadequate advice. It is also preferable to wasting valuable training time on changes that, ultimately, may not improve performance.

## TYPES OF ANALYSIS IN SPORTS BIOMECHANICS

Building upon our notion of the coaching–biomechanics interface, we now turn to an examination of the types of analyses that can be undertaken within biomechanics to inform sports performance. These can be divided into three broad categories.

### 1. Qualitative analysis (e.g. matching observations to a mental image of a skill)

The increase in available computer and video technologies has provided opportunities for coaches to access a whole range of new techniques for analysis. As a result, areas of visual analysis that were once the province of the sports biomechanist have now become readily available to all interested parties. As also featured in Chapter 9 ('Notational analysis for coaches'), commercial software (e.g. Silicon Coach™ and Dartfish™) suitable for this type of analysis can run on a standard laptop computer and only require low-cost digital video cameras for input. They enable instant replay, slow-motion and frame-by-frame playback to be presented to the coach with ease. They also facilitate the production of sequential images of skills such as the rugby place-kick.

This form of video-based analysis is normally undertaken by coaches to inspect technical skills in detail or to compare performances from one session to another. It enables the coach to supplement and enhance his or her direct observational skills. As discussed in the section 'The conceptual model of technique and performance' on p. 88, coaches develop an understanding of what they consider to be the desired technique and by using new technologies such as these they have additional ways of comparing the current performance with an existing image of the ideal performance. The accuracy and effectiveness of any decisions made at this level of analysis, however, are dependent on the coach's mindset or subjective perception regarding that ideal performance. Hence, the coach may be able to see what is missing, but this does not necessarily result in understanding what needs to be changed to bring about the desired outcome.

## 2. Semi-quantitative analysis (e.g. analysis of angles and temporal aspects of movements)

This level of analysis is the first step to quantification, and provides an estimate of the key variables associated with performing any skill successfully. However, care has to be taken when using semi-quantitative analyses as only simple scaling (i.e. using a single object of known length to convert measures in the video image to real distances) can be achieved, while movements are largely assumed to occur in a plane, when, in reality, they are three-dimensional. The inaccuracies arising from such an assumption are particularly evident when angles are being estimated (Rodano and Tavana 1995). This leaves the validity of many measures recorded using semi-quantitative (and qualitative) analysis open to question. Qualitative and semi-quantitative analyses, then, whilst visually impressive and informative, do not provide coaches with the maximum benefit to be derived from such technology.

## 3. Quantitative analysis (e.g. full kinematic and kinetic analyses)

Kinematics is the general term used in biomechanics to describe temporal or sequential and spatial characteristics of movement. The variables in this category (i.e. kinematics) include position, velocity and acceleration of body parts (e.g. limbs) or the whole-body mass centre. Kinetics, on the other hand, is the generic description of forces that cause motion. Knowledge of the physical size of an athlete is added to the information on externally applied forces to complete the study of kinetics. Examples in sport would include an analysis of muscular forces producing joint flexion and extension necessary to determine the work done by specific muscle groups during dynamic activities like jumping or landing.

To conduct quantitative analyses requires a considerable step up in knowledge, technology and associated analysis procedures. For sport to benefit from the fruits of this category of analysis, close co-operation between coaches and biomechanists is necessary. The types of examination included here range from 2D video analyses to measure linear and angular positions (i.e. kinematics) to 3D inverse dynamics analyses (i.e. kinetics) to determine internal joint forces, muscle powers and musculo-skeletal work. A 2D video analysis might appear to be almost identical to one of the semi-quantitative studies listed above, but a true 2D video analysis needs very precise calibration of an image plane (Brewin and Kerwin 2003). Two-dimensional quantitative analyses, then, can be used when the apparatus constrains the movement or when both sides of the body move simultaneously in the same direction, as in vertical jumping. A longswing on high bar meets both these criteria and so illustrates a situation where 2D analysis is sufficient (Irwin and Kerwin 2001).

Biomechanists also use kinematics to describe and explain complex movement patterns involved in performances. This may be related to single joint analysis or to how joints and segments interact (Hamill *et al.* 2000; van Emmerik and van Wegen 2000). Conversely, kinetic analyses of internal joint forces are often used to produce insights into the musculo-skeletal demand of movements. Further, more advanced analysis can be derived from joint kinetics, including details of biomechanical energetic processes (Lees *et al.* 2004; Arampatzis and Brüggemann 2001). The information gleaned from these analyses can provide insights not available from observation or kinematics alone. A third form of quantitative biomechanics worth mentioning here is the description of neuromuscular activity through the use of electromyography. This is a specialist area of biomechanics that can provide information on the electrical activity in muscles, thus informing biological function (Clarys 2000; Komi *et al.* 2000).

## MODELLING IN BIOMECHANICS

The modelling most commonly referred to in biomechanics is the forward dynamic approach. The challenge in forward dynamics modelling is to build realistic and appropriate human body models with sufficient validity to enable techniques to be examined with confidence. A good example of this was the forward dynamics model developed by Wilson *et al.* (2006), which enables the fundamental mechanics of running jumps to be examined.

Ironically, from a mathematical point of view, modelling the airborne phase of a complex twisting somersault is actually easier than modelling a vertical jump take-off. The major reason for this is that to model a take-off or landing, the musculo-skeletal system has to be represented. The human can be simplified within a model but it still needs to be represented as a system of rigid and wobbling mass parts linked by springs with varying stiffness and compliance characteristics (Gittoes *et al.* 2006). The muscular contractions also have to be modelled to include complex dynamics to produce accurate skeletal muscle-force profiles.

Even something as apparently simple as pushing off from the floor in a jump is an immensely challenging computer modelling exercise. Despite these problems, computer simulation modelling offers great scope for future work in enhancing athletic performance.

Indeed, this approach has already been used in a variety of sports (e.g. soccer [Bray and Kerwin 2003], gymnastics [Arampatzis and Brüggemann 1999; Hiley and Yeadon 2005], athletics [Hubbard and Alaways 1987; Wilson *et al*. 2006], and tennis [Glynn *et al*. 2006]) to address theoretical questions such as, What will happen if we change a certain aspect of the movement?, or What are the implications on wrist mechanics of changing the stiffness of a tennis racket frame? Computer simulation modelling, then, represents a powerful tool and is, consequently, considered the only true method for identifying individualised optimal technique for a particular athlete performing a technically demanding skill.

## CONCLUDING THOUGHTS: THE FUTURE

From a coaching perspective, it is likely that the future holds great innovation in terms of immediate feedback technology. These include visual replays via new graphical plasma display screens and wireless-linked laptop computers. This form of immediate post-event feedback will be a principal future means of athlete enhancement. For example, instant biofeedback derived from a variety of sources will enable information on performance to be relayed to the athlete whilst training – greatly extending the simple measures in use today (e.g. heart rate). Additionally, the feedback timescale will stretch in the other direction to include overviews of seasonal and career-based tracking of performance. Athletes' training diaries will become totally electronic and contain not just calendars and dietary information but will also include training and competitive video records of performances. Trend analyses based on these electronic logs and other biomechanical and physiological measures of performance will assist in the future development of training programmes and planning of peaking regimes for optimising athletes' competitive performances.

From the purely biomechanics perspective, in addition to the ongoing developments and applications of simulation modelling, there are new technologies on the horizon in the fields of athlete-worn sensors that will impact sport. These new systems will expand the types of field-based measurements in qualitative and quantitative analyses, thus increasing the scope of activities that can be studied. The other result of these new technologies will be a many-fold increase in volume of fine-grained data. These, in turn, could better underpin athlete performance profiling and retrospective and prospective studies of injury, thus having the potential to greatly inform future coaching knowledge.

This chapter has provided an overview of the key role that biomechanics can play in a sports coaching context. It has also introduced a conceptual model of the coaching process and argued that biomechanics and coaching together can improve knowledge and understanding and, hence, enhance athlete performance. Different types of analysis used in sports biomechanics have been detailed with examples provided to help illustrate their relative strengths and weaknesses. Finally, a view of the future for both coaching and biomechanics has been presented, further highlighting their interdependency.

1. How do coaches generate a fundamental understanding of technique?
2. Summarise your understanding of the coaching–biomechanics interface. What is it? Why is it of importance to coaches?
3. Why is quantitative analysis often considered more effective than qualitative or semi-quantitative analysis within biomechanics?
4. Within the chapter, a bright future is predicted for biomechanics within coaching. Do you agree or disagree? Why?

# CHAPTER NINE

# NOTATIONAL ANALYSIS FOR COACHES

## Mike Hughes

*A successful coach is one who prepares his team to deal with all eventualities. Not only must your players be fully briefed on the game plan and understand their individual requirements but you must familiarise them with the particular strengths and weaknesses of the opposition.*

Graham Henry –
former Wales (1998–2002), British and Irish Lions (2001),
and current New Zealand All Black Rugby Union coach
(Henry 1999: 179)

**Key sections:**

- Introduction
- The purpose of notational analysis
- Starting the analysis: developing notational systems
- Examples of analysis in elite sport
- Video analysis and performance profiling as tools for coaches
- Conclusion

## INTRODUCTION

Coaching is about enhancing player or athlete performance. A principal means by which this is achieved is through feedback. However, researchers have consistently shown that human observation and memory, impressive though they are, are not reliable enough to provide the detailed information necessary to secure desired behavioural changes (e.g. Franks and Miller 1986). Consequently, in order to accurately capture complex aspects of the sporting context, more objective measuring tools are necessary. These can take the form of video analysis systems (in-event and post-event), and biomechanical or computerised notation systems. Such systems have generally been termed notational analysis, which can be defined as 'an objective way of recording performance so that key elements of that performance can be quantified in a valid and consistent manner' (Hughes 2005: 1).

Both hand notation (i.e. simple pen-and-paper recording) and computerised systems provide the same sort of data and are used for the same purposes; i.e. the recording of movement, tactics, technique and statistical compilation. Indeed, it has been argued that recent developments in both computer and video technologies have transformed the approach and role of notational analysts within the coaching process. This is as a consequence of the detail such systems can highlight, thus allowing coaches a high degree of specificity in their feedback. To ensure that accurate and reliable data are gathered for analysis by the coach, considerable training of notational operatives or data recorders is necessary, making the application of these systems a speciality (Hughes and Franks 2004). Consequently, it is unlikely that coaches themselves would undertake this task, but rather employ a notational analyst who can then pick out aspects of the game/contest as requested by the coach. The aim of this chapter is to give a basic outline of the rationale, application, design and theory behind notation systems, thus highlighting their value for coaching and coaches. In terms of content, following the introduction, the purpose of notational analysis is outlined before notation's position, and in particular the use of video, is clearly located within the wider coaching process. This includes a discussion of how to develop notational systems and their possible use by coaches. Finally, a conclusion summarises the main points made.

## THE PURPOSE OF NOTATIONAL ANALYSIS

The essence of the coaching process is to instigate positive changes in sports performance. Because coaching depends heavily upon analysis, to ensure that the feedback given as a consequence of such analysis is both precise and effective, informed and accurate measures are necessary. In most athletic events, analysis of the performance is guided by a series of qualitative assessments made by the coach. Figure 9.1 highlights and locates the role of analysis in this regard within the coaching process (adapted from Franks et al. 1983).

This represents the coaching process in observational, analytical and planning phases. For example, in an invasion-type game like hockey or football, the game is watched by the coach who will form a conception of positive and negative aspects of the players' performances. Often, information from previous games as well as the current one is then considered in planning for the following match. The next game is played and the process repeats itself. There are, however, problems associated with this process, most notably that it relies heavily upon the subjective assessment of game action. For example, during a game many occurrences stand out as distinctive features, such as exceptional technical achievements by individual players, which tend to distort the coach's recall and assessment of the total contest (Franks and Miller 1991). Similarly, human memory is limited so that it is almost impossible to remember all the events that take place during an entire match. For example,

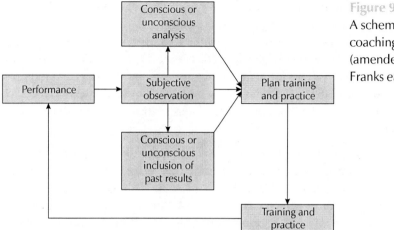

Figure 9.1

A schema of the coaching process (amended from Franks *et al.* 1983)

Franks and Miller (1986) showed that football (i.e. soccer) coaches are less than 45 per cent accurate in their post-game assessment of what occurred during a game. While there is considerable individual variability, this rapid forgetting is not surprising given the complicated process of committing data to memory and subsequently retrieving it (Franks *et al.* 1983; Hughes 1973). Furthermore, emotions and personal biases are significant factors affecting memory storage and retrieval. Carrying out accurate assessment and analysis of performances subjectively, then, is very difficult. So how can this problem be addressed?

One way much greater objectivity can be obtained is through the use of notational analysis. Notational analysis systems exist, and have existed in many forms throughout history; for example, hieroglyphic notation of Egyptian troop movements, medieval notation of music, and twentieth-century choreographic shorthand to record dance movement. More recently, sport has adapted some of these ideas and methodologies to explore the various details of individual and team performances. Such systems might notate the sequence of events leading to scoring in basketball open play, or those that follow short corners in field hockey. Alternatively, they might record the number (and length) of strides that players of various sports make walking, jogging, running, sprinting and so on during games; hence reporting on the time spent in each of these motions and the distances covered. Furthermore, they can record the shot sequences that lead to winning and losing rallies in racket sports, thus highlighting technical strengths and weaknesses of players when playing on different surfaces. All these ideas, and an infinite number more, can be explored using hand or computerised notation systems that can be modified according to specific requirements.

Hand notation systems are relatively accurate and cheap, but they do have disadvantages. The more complex ones involve considerable learning time, particularly if they are used in-event, whilst the data produced require many person-hours to process into output that is meaningful to coaches. For example, it can take as much as 40 hours just to process the data from a single squash match (Sanderson and Way 1979). The introduction of computerised notation systems has enabled these two problems, in particular that related to data processing, to be tackled positively. Using real-time analysis or with video recordings in post-event analysis, such systems enable immediate easy data access and presentation in graphical or other pictorial forms. Indeed, the increasing sophistication and reducing cost of video systems within the field of notation has greatly enhanced post-event feedback, a development that is examined in depth a little later (see Brown and Hughes [1995] for a fuller debate).

On the other hand, computers introduce extra problems. These include operator mistakes (e.g. accidentally pressing the wrong key), in addition to hardware and software errors that can similarly distort the collected data. Furthermore, perception errors, where the observer misunderstands an event or incorrectly fixes a position, are particularly problematic in real-time analysis when the data must be entered quickly. To minimise these problems, careful validation of computerised notation systems should be carried out. One way to do this is to compare the results from a computerised system with that of a hand system. In addition, reliability tests must also be performed on both hand and computerised systems to estimate the accuracy and consistency of the data collected by each observer. Ways to do this include repeat analyses of a video by a particular observer before comparing both sets of data for accuracy, or an intra-observer reliability test. If these data are then compared with those of the same performance by another observer, then these comparisons will give stronger evidence of reliability. This is called an inter-observer reliability test (Hughes and Franks 2004). In drawing this section to a close, it can be concluded that the three principal purposes of notation are to provide data and statistical analysis on:

1.  athlete movement (e.g. the ground covered in a game by an athlete and how it is covered);
2.  team and individual tactics; and
3.  individual technique.

The information derived can be used for several purposes, which include:

(i)   to provide immediate feedback;
(ii)  the development of a database;
(iii) to highlight areas requiring improvement;
(iv)  for additional evaluation; and
(v)   a mechanism for selectively searching through a video recording of a game.

(Franks *et al*. 1983)


### STARTING THE ANALYSIS: DEVELOPING NOTATIONAL SYSTEMS

The information that is available during a game is diverse and extensive. As the continuous action and dynamic environment make data collection difficult, any quantitative analysis of a sporting context must be structured effectively. As there are so many ways to collect information about any sport, when developing a notational instrument two very important points should be considered:

1.  There should be consultation about the purpose of the analyses with the best technical expert of the game (e.g. a coach). Issues that should be addressed in this context include, What is the question about the sport that needs answering? and, What are the important performance indicators?
2.  The potential use of the information should guide how the system will be designed, i.e. what is required from the analysis system should be completely determined before starting.

In conjunction with these, the first step is to create a flow-chart or logical structure of the game itself. This means defining the possible actions in the game, thus describing a sequential path that the game can take. For example, in a team sport such as field hockey, Franks and Goodman (1984) described the game very simply by a two-state model. Either team A has possession of the ball or the opposing team B does. This would be at the top of what Franks and Goodman termed the hierarchy. The next level of questions in the hierarchy would be:

1.  Where on the field did Team A or Team B gain and/or lose possession?
2.  Can these areas be easily identified (e.g. by dividing the field into six areas)?
3   Who on the team gained or lost possession?
4.  How was possession gained and lost (e.g. was it from a tackle, an interception, a foul)?

These questions can be included in a structure as indicated in Figure 9.2. While this level of analysis is obviously very simple, the questions posed can yield extremely useful

Figure 9.2

A hierarchically structured model for representing events that take place in an invasion team game such as field hockey, soccer, basketball or water polo

information. Furthermore, they can be easily produced and translated into pictorial representations. More detailed analyses might be concerned with specific techniques or include physiological and psychological parameters that are mapped along a time axis during the performance. No matter what the intended analysis is, it is advised to always start as simply as possible and gradually add other actions and their outcomes. Franks and Goodman (1984) go on to suggest three steps or tasks to be undertaken in the evaluation of performance. These are:

TASK 1:    Describe your sport from the general to the specific.
TASK 2:    Prioritise key factors of performance (see Figure 9.2).
TASK 3:    Devise a recording method that is efficient and easy to learn.

Detailed actions and outcomes (e.g. where and how possession was won and/or lost) can then be incorporated into a model for the events that take place.

Figure 9.3 demonstrates how such actions are subsequently built up into a picture of the game observed. Hence, as possession is gained by one of the players, a number of actions are available to him or her. The outcome of the action determines whether his or her side retains possession, scores a goal, gives away a free kick, etc. Inevitably this notational system (like any other) can be made more sophisticated. For example, the dribble, run, tackle or foul have not been included, nor have any actions when not in possession. The difficult decision to make in designing this type of model is knowing when the limitations of the model are acceptable within the terms of reference of the desired data.

The core elements of player, position and action are fundamental to most, if not all, analysis systems, although they do not need to be always included. For example, if the aim was to analyse the attacking patterns of a hockey team, we would not need to record the players' identities, only their position on the pitch, the actions undertaken and any outcomes. However, if we were examining the work rate of a particular player we would need to focus on the player in question, his or her position, action (stand, walk, jog, run etc.) and, possibly, the time. Building on this, the developed system in Figure 9.4 shows the simple logic needed to record and analyse the key elements of performance within the game of squash. The flow-chart (i.e. Figure 9.4) is complicated a little by the concept of lets and strokes. A let is when one player impedes the other in the process of his/her shot, which results in the rally being played again; no change in score, same server. A stroke is given against a player when he/she prevents the opponent from hitting the front wall with a direct shot or prevents a winner. Consequently, a stroke given against a player is equivalent to the player conceding an error.

Creating a model for the sequence of shot production and the respective positions from where shots are played is relatively straightforward. Hence, in most simple systems for racket sports, analysts will start with a winner/error analysis, recording the type of shots that were winners or errors and from where on the court they were played. However, to include the scoring system would require some additions to this flow-chart. The basis of

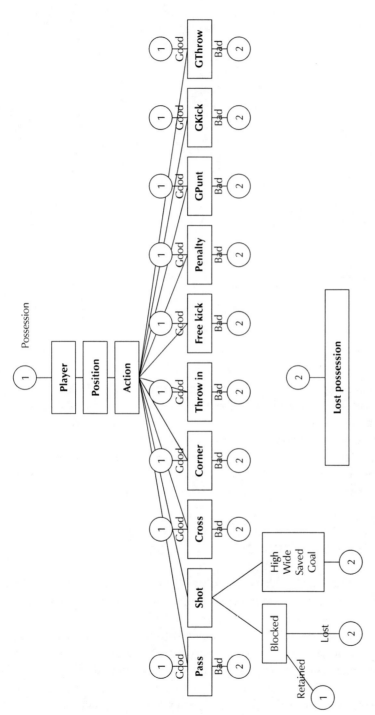

Figure 9.3 A simple schematic flow-chart of soccer

Figure 9.4
A simple
flow-chart
for squash

Figure 9.4 A simple flow-chart for squash

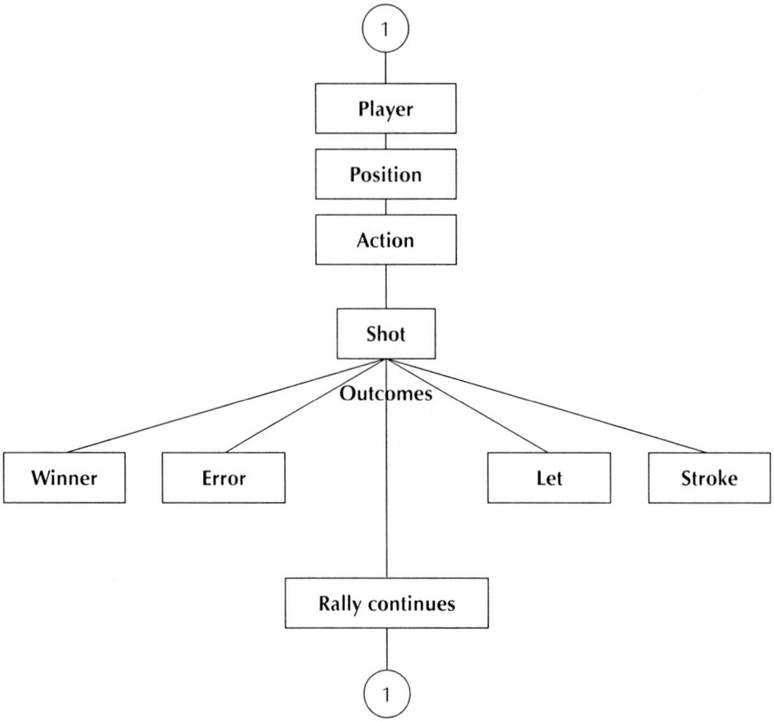

the so-called English scoring in squash is that the server receives a point if he or she wins the rally. If the non-server wins the rally he or she does not receive a point but wins the right to serve. One way of incorporating the logic of scoring, and who serves, into the model would be to keep the definition of the server and non-server throughout the rally. This would help clarify if the score increased at the end of the rally or not, depending on who won. The selection of these and other actions to be inserted into such models is determined by the degree of complexity required (Hughes and Franks 2004).

## EXAMPLES OF ANALYSIS IN ELITE SPORT

According to Hughes (2004), a performance analysis team should work closely with coaches. The gathered data should be shared so that both parties feel some ownership over them. In this way, coaches (and athletes) come to accept and understand the messages contained far more easily and readily. Through such involvement, coaches are able to keep the analysis systems live and relevant, coming up with new ideas of how to identify and evaluate the ongoing practices. Most of the support that is currently being offered to the coaches of England Squash (the National Governing Body of the sport in the UK) is based on the work of Murray and Hughes (2001). This research includes analyses ranging

Name of player: **Sarah Fitzgerald**

Of the three matches analysed, Sarah won two of them comfortably; an inherent problem in analysing top players.

- Sarah's overall winner/error (W/E) ratio was 83/38 (a very aggressive ratio). Against Michelle, it was 28/23 overall. On her own serve, the W/E ratio was 12/13, on her opponents' serve the W/E ratio was 16/10.
- In her tough match against Michelle, Sarah played more straight lengths (long, straight shots) (248:274) and proportionately less cross-court lengths (223:184).

**Positive profile**

- In the winners' distribution, Sarah is very strong across the centre of the court and strong on the short volley.
- The winners were distributed as follows: drives 10; drops 14; volleys short 11; cross drops 6; X-volley short 3.
- Sarah generated large numbers of errors from her opponents from the back of the court using straight and, particularly, cross-court drives.

**Negative profile**

- Sarah made more errors in the back of the court (there are always more shots in the back of the court).
- The errors were distributed as follows: drives 17 (9 b'hand all at the back, 8 f'hand all spread out); drops 5; volleys short 8 (7 on the b'hand); cross drops 3 (all f'hand at the back); boasts 8.
- The distribution of winners shows that most of these shots are from the backhand side for the easy matches, but against Michelle the distribution was more on the forehand at the back.
- This profile was also the same for the errors' distribution.

**Summary**

- Prepare well for the start of each rally – Sarah has a weak profile in short rallies.
- Sarah probably needs to play to a better length to stop opponent volleying; there is good width on the straight and cross-court lengths.
- Opponents tend to use a strong cross-court game to turn and pressure Sarah. Perhaps she can also use this tactic.
- Sarah is very good in the front half, particularly on the backhand, and uses the short shot appropriately.

**Figure 9.5** A summary of data used as feedback in a storyboard format to accompany edited video

from simple winner and error ratios to complex rally-ending patterns produced from computerised systems. More specifically, Murray and Hughes (2001) pooled information from five matches of a particular player into a single database. From this they were able to produce up to 300 different graphs illustrating the various combinations of shots played and the positions from which they were played. Acknowledging that this provided far too much information for coaches to use, the authors subsequently summarised it into bullet points that were used as a storyboard to accompany an edited video of the player under study. Figure 9.5 gives an example of the processed data in storyboard form as presented to the coaches.

The information gathered within the study by Murray and Hughes (2001) was subsequently normalised (i.e. standardised), converted into percentages and condensed onto a representation of the court. Here, the court was divided into 16 sections (in the same manner as the Simple Winner and Error Analysis Technology [SWEAT] system developed by Hughes and Robertson [1998]) with the areas of the court being analysed in respect of shot type. Not unnaturally, the coaches were, and continue to be, very receptive to this depth and relevancy of information, as it allows them to focus not only on the weaknesses of opponents but also on the performances of their own players.

In addition to building a general picture of players' performances, compact discs containing edited video material of unusual aspects of individual player profiles can also be provided for coaches. These can be created using sports analysis packages such as *Focus* (for further reading on the respective strengths and uses of the *Focus* and other software notation packages such as *Quintic*, *Dartfish* and *SiliconCoach*, see Murray and Hughes [2006]). As their use and value are being recognised, commercially available notational software systems are being used increasingly in many, particularly team, sports. For example, the *SportsCode* system can be used to track the performance of a footballer during a game. As opposed to *Focus*, which has a fixed categorisation, *SportsCode* allows any number and combination of variables to be used as codes. Each variable (e.g. action done [tackle, kick, intercept etc.]) is represented on the system by a button window. The shape, size and organisation of the buttons within the *SportsCode* window are not fixed and, hence, can be designed to suit the needs of the analyst, even to the colour of the buttons themselves. Furthermore, the text descriptors used in *SportsCode* to define actions can be activated in any number of ways, or not at all, so that novices as well as expert analysts can use the keys. Consequently, when an action is identified, the corresponding button is pressed. This builds up a comprehensive picture of the player and the game being observed.

## VIDEO ANALYSIS AND PERFORMANCE PROFILING AS TOOLS FOR COACHES

Systems such as *SportsCode* and *Focus* are capable of providing the fast and efficient feedback that Hughes and Franks (1997) identified as a pressing need within coaching. The successful application of these systems, however, depends upon the manner in which they are used (e.g. clearly determining what to analyse) as the quality of the output, although reliant on the information input, is without question. Additionally, the flexibility of the *SportsCode* system allows the coach to review performance and provide feedback both during and after the event. Figure 9.6 represents a flow-diagram modified from the work of Hughes and Franks (1997: 16), which illustrates such usage, thus locating notational analysis firmly within the coaching process.

Through such structured programmes of analysis, coaches are able to access vast amounts of detailed information not only on their own team and players but also on the opposition.

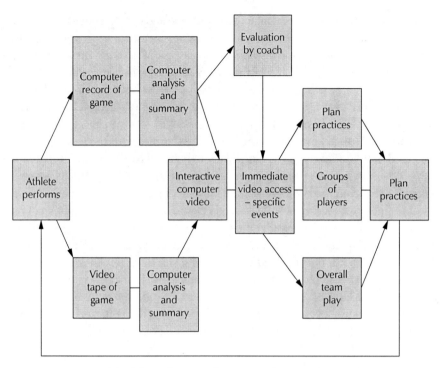

Figure 9.6 A modified flow-diagram illustrating the use of video feedback within the coaching process

Hence, the statistical data and video feedback gathered can be used to build up a database over a number of matches or even an entire season (Partridge and Franks 1993). This could potentially be made available to players and coaches across a network of computers. Indeed, the Welsh Rugby Union and a number of other national governing bodies and professional clubs are currently employing such systems to aid player development. This is because notational analysis, particularly through the use of video, gives coaches a chance to record, observe, reflect and check performances accurately through a medium that captivates both themselves and athletes (Lyons 1988).

The early work of Sanderson and Way (1979) and Hughes (1986) highlighted that a database of matches from sports such as football, rugby, hockey and netball could provide information regarding patterns of play that could be considered representative of the subjects used. The subsequent formation of profiles of different groups of players is proving to be a very powerful tool for coaches in their attempts to understand their respective sports better. As such, a number of studies over the years have attempted to profile both different player groups and aspects of sport. For example, Hughes et al. (2000) sought to answer the question of how many games should be observed before it could be concluded that a definite pattern had emerged. They replicated the earlier study of Hughes (1986) but used female squash players of three different standards as their subjects. They compared the profiles from databases containing eight, nine and ten matches to investigate when the profiles had become normative, that is stable. Statistical tests were used to ascertain the overall match totals, and distribution (i.e. location) of shots. They found that recreational players did not establish a normative playing pattern but county and elite players did. There was a difference, however, in the number of matches it took for the county and elite players' profiles to become normative. For county players it took eight to nine matches while for elite players it took six. However, more data were produced during the elite matches due to their longer duration, which could explain why the profiles of elite players stabilised more quickly. What is more likely is that as players improve in standard they are able to sustain set patterns of play due to their greater skill level. The opposite is true of recreational players, who generally are not skilful enough to play to fixed tactical patterns and so their profiles do not stabilise as quickly. The study showed that creating normative profiles is highly dependent on the nature of the data being collected and the ability of the performers. Such contextual factors, then, need to be considered carefully by coaches before they commission and/or interpret given data. Similarly, one would assume that the greater the number of matches in a database the more reliable the profile produced (Potter and Hughes 2001). However, recent work has suggested that as a database grows it becomes less sensitive to changes in playing patterns, and so becomes less accurate (Hughes et al. 2001). This, then, is currently a point of debate.

The number of recent research papers examining how a picture of athlete performance can be constructed demonstrates that this is an interesting and constantly evolving area of investigation. No doubt, methods of establishing how data stabilise leave a lot to be desired (Hughes et al. 2001), but at least they do give us some early signs of when performance-related patterns emerge. Additionally, the recent work of James et al. (2005) and O'Donoghue (2005) point the way to alternative ways of recognising and expressing patterned data, which could well bear fruit in future. Needless to say, the more accessible and understandable the data, providing its complexity is not lost, the better for the coach in the quest to improve athlete performance.

## CONCLUSION

Systematic notational instruments provide a method of collecting accurate, in-depth descriptive data on athlete performance. These data can be analysed and processed in a variety of ways thus providing a basis for detailed feedback regarding that performance. Furthermore, advances in both computer and video technology have recently made this observation process increasingly efficient. This chapter has attempted to illustrate how such systems and technology can help coaches. In this respect, through their careful and considered use, accurate and relevant data can be gleaned on any aspect of athletic competition. Such information is crucial in many ways, but particularly so in helping coaches to understand the performances of their own athletes and players, while developing realistic game plans to deal with future opposition.

1. What are the principal purposes of notational analysis? For what can the data gathered primarily be used?
2. Imagine you are charged with developing a new notational analysis system for an under-researched sport. Where do you start? Which factors should be taken into account in your thinking? Why?
3. Draw a flow-chart for any element of performance in a sport of your choice.
4. What is meant by 'performance profiling'?
5. When can a database of a racket player's actions become accepted as a profile? What are the factors that need to be considered when deciding this?

# CHAPTER TEN

# SPORTS MEDICINE FOR COACHES

## Andrew Miles and Richard Tong

*I am very concerned about injury preventive work. It enables me to challenge the specialists from a holistic perspective.*

Per Mathias Høgmo –
Director of Football, Norwegian Football Association;
Head Coach, Norwegian National Women's Football team (1997–2001);
Gold medal winners, Olympic Games, Sydney (2000).

**Key sections:**

- Introduction
- What is sports medicine and how can it help coaches?
- Defining and classifying sports injuries
- Injury prevention
- Injury management
- Rehabilitation from injury
- Summary

## INTRODUCTION

In recent years there has been a growing recognition of the role that sport and physical activity can play in enhancing the quality of life. Consequently, many different political, social and health agendas have targeted increased participation in related activities as a means of achieving government targets. These include the production of talented performers to underpin London's 2012 Olympiad; the reduction of coronary heart disease, obesity, diabetes and other illnesses; in addition to addressing issues associated with social exclusion, drug abuse and anti-social behaviour. Although such goals are generally seen as being worthy, developing widespread participation also holds the potential for under-prepared individuals to embark on sport and physical training without the necessary knowledge and support. Also, as established athletes aspire to achieve high performance levels, there is likely to be an increase in training loads and intensities. Both developments may result in a greater incidence of injury. Sports medicine, therefore, and in particular its relevance for coaches, is likely to become increasingly important in dealing with a subsequent anticipated upsurge in sport and physical activity related injuries.

Medicine has typically been associated with the diagnosis and treatment of illness or injuries. However, with an improved understanding of the mechanisms and causes of injury, there has recently been an increased focus on prevention. Such a changing stance is based on the belief that if society is to gain the desired benefits from increased involvement in physical activity and sport without overburdening existing resource infrastructures, everyone involved in their organisation and provision should be aware of the potential injury risks associated with them. Hence, they should be able to plan and prepare physical activity sessions that do not overstretch athletes and participants to the point of injury.

As the primary providers of organised sporting activities, coaches should be aware that participation in sport can easily lead to injury. Accordingly, we believe that the sports coach, whilst not being expected to treat all injuries, should have a good understanding of the factors that can lead to injury and how an injury should be managed in order to facilitate optimal recovery. The purpose of this chapter is to highlight the value that such an understanding of sports medicine and injury prevention, treatment and management has for coaches. The chapter starts by defining sports medicine before identifying and classifying common sports injuries. It then examines causal factors of such injuries and discusses strategies that coaches can utilise to reduce the risk of them happening. Issues relating to the treatment of an injury will then be addressed along with suggestions for the effective management of the recovery process.

## WHAT IS SPORTS MEDICINE AND HOW CAN IT HELP COACHES?

Many authors have sought to define sports medicine. Hollmann (1988: xi) offered an early definition that was adopted by the International Federation of Sports Medicine (FIMS) as including:

> . . . those theoretical and practical branches of medicine which investigate the effects of exercise, training and sport on healthy and ill people, as well as the effects of lack of exercise, to produce useful results for prevention, therapy [and] rehabilitation.

Additionally, Hollmann (1988) suggested that there are three facets to modern sports medicine; namely prevention, diagnosis and treatment/rehabilitation, with, as mentioned previously, prevention playing an increasingly significant role. In a society that is becoming more and more dependent on technology and automation whilst being consumed by a fast-food culture, there is a distinct drift towards a lack of physical activity. Hollmann

(1988) argued that the preventative aspects of sports medicine should use physical activity as an opportunity to restore normal physiological conditions, whilst using appropriate training to produce physiological adaptations that could prevent a range of diseases and age-related losses in physical capacity. In this way, an increasingly effective prevention strategy can reduce the need for treatment, although, inevitably, injuries will still occur and thus the need for diagnosis, treatment and rehabilitation will remain.

A more contemporary definition, offered by Brukner and Khan (2006: 3), suggests that sports medicine has developed into a broad area of study and service provision. They start by stating that sports medicine should be defined as the medicine of exercise, or, perhaps more accurately, as the total medical care of the exercising individual. This is further expanded to define the discipline as comprising:

> Injury prevention, diagnosis, treatment and rehabilitation; performance enhancement through training, nutrition and psychology; management of medical problems caused by exercise and the role of exercise in chronic disease states; the specific needs of exercising in children, females, older people and those with permanent disabilities; the medical care of sporting teams and events; medical care in situations of altered physiology, such as altitude or at depth; and ethical issues, such as the problem of drug abuse in sport. (p.3)

Aside from the rather confusing use of the words 'sport' and 'exercise', the most obvious observation arising from this extensive definition is the diversity of the discipline and the concept of total medical care provision. With this comes the recognition that any single practitioner is unlikely to be able to address all the issues associated with modern sports medicine. As such, almost all authors attempting to define modern sports medicine infer that the provision of good sports medicine services is characterised by a multidisciplinary approach; namely that the sports medicine needs of an exercising individual are best met through a team approach in which a number of specialists may be involved. Consequently, as in a typical medical model such as the UK National Health Service, where tiers of practitioner input exist, with a patient passing through a general diagnostic structure before being referred to more specialist support, in a sports medicine model an athlete's primary medical contact point would, more often than not, be the coach. The coach would then refer the athlete to an appropriate specialist – for example, a physiotherapist, physiologist or masseur. Consequently, it is imperative that coaches have a basic understanding of how to deal with injuries as they happen, and to whom they should subsequently refer an injured athlete.

According to Martens (2004), a coach's medical responsibilities are principally threefold:

- to ensure that an athlete's health is satisfactory prior to participation;
- to determine whether an illness or injury is sufficient for an athlete to stop participation; and
- to ensure that the athlete is ready to return to training and competition.

Although we agree with the points made here, as the earlier discussion outlines, we would like to expand them to emphasise the function of injury prevention. An awareness of sports medicine concepts, then, would appear to be important for coaches from a number of perspectives; from injury prevention, through diagnosing and referring injured or ill athletes to appropriate specialists, to monitoring and nurturing athletes' return to competition.

## DEFINING AND CLASSIFYING SPORTS INJURIES

In order to fulfil their responsibilities effectively in terms of preventing sports injuries, sports coaches need to have an understanding of the different types of sports injuries that can occur and, perhaps more importantly, be aware of the main causal factors associated with these injuries. If a coach knows what may cause an injury he or she will be better placed to develop training programmes and practice strategies that can prevent it from occurring. Defining sports injuries, however, can be problematic. An examination of the literature reveals that there is no single, widely accepted operational definition of a sports injury (Van Mechelen et al. 1992). Indeed, the literature offers a range of definitions suggesting that a sports injury can be anything from the occurrence of a new symptom during training or competition, to decreased athletic performance as a result of reduced functioning of a body part, to the cessation of participation that necessitates contact with medical personnel (Caine et al. 1996). Consequently, recording the occurrence of sports injuries and detailing their exact cause and nature is an issue with which sports injury epidemiologists are constantly grappling (Caine et al. 1996). This lack of agreement on terms and consistent reporting strategies has complicated the determination of injury rates (Pelletier et al. 1993). As a result, it is difficult to provide definitive data as to the most common sports injuries and the most prevalent sites for injury. However, the general consensus amongst the literature would appear to imply that, within the most commonly played sports, the knee and ankle are the predominant sites for sport-related injury (Caine et al. 1996).

Classifying the different types of sports injury can also be problematic, principally because there may be so many factors associated with one. The purpose of classifying a sports injury in relation to how, where, when and how often one occurs is to prevent future occurrences. For example, in the early stages of a recent Premiership soccer season, one top team reported a number of injuries to players' Achilles tendons. Analysis of the data led to the conclusion that a large volume of running on hard, dry surfaces while wearing inappropriate footwear was a major contributory factor. Such information cannot remedy existing injuries but it can certainly reduce the risk of future occurrences of similar ones. Additionally, keeping occurrence data over time can reflect the effectiveness of such and similar preventative measures and the impact of enhanced medical and training techniques.

Whilst the reason for classifying sports injuries is clear, the different forms of injury classification are not. Indeed, authors, researchers and practitioners alike adopt a wide variety of injury categorisations. For example, some studies simply report where on the human body the injury occurred. In practical terms this is a logical classification, but for such data to be meaningful there is also a need to consider the context, that is the sporting activity in which the injury occurred; i.e. quantifying the number of hand injuries in distance running is of less use than doing so in gymnastics. Other studies categorise injuries with reference to where, in an environmental sense, the injury occurred. These could record and compare indoor versus outdoor venues, hard (e.g. concrete) as opposed to soft surfaces (e.g. grass), as well as other factors such as climate, equipment and altitude. Classification in some studies is also made in terms of *when* an injury occurs, e.g. in training as opposed to competition, or during a warm-up as opposed to a fatigued state. These categorisations tend to be binomial in nature, in that they are either one thing or the other. Alternatively, there are some studies that report and classify injuries as being at some point along a continuum. The most obvious of these are classifications based on the longevity of the injury and its implications. Here, those injuries that do not prevent continued performance and from which an individual can recover relatively quickly are classed differently to those that have a longer-term effect and cause an individual to miss significant amounts of training or that may be permanently disabling. Van Mechelen *et al.* (1992) suggest that the severity of an injury is best measured against six criteria: (i) the nature of the injury, (ii) the duration and nature of the treatment required, (iii) the amount of sporting time lost, (iv) the amount of work time lost, (v) whether there is permanent damage, and (vi) the cost associated with the injury, both in terms of functional time lost and the resources expended in treating it.

These and similar forms of classification are useful in trying to identify the causal factors of injuries. However, we believe that the most meaningful categorisation is one that classifies injuries based on the type of injury that has occurred. This usually gives an indication of how the injury has been sustained. The literature widely utilises the terms 'acute' or 'sudden-impact' injuries to describe those injuries that have arisen as a result of some single traumatic incident. Similarly, the terms 'gradual onset', 'chronic' or 'overuse' injuries are used to describe those injuries that have occurred as a result of repetitive exposure to a stressor and have manifested themselves over a period of time.

Acute injuries are caused by one-off events that lead to a body part being damaged. They can be further classified as being caused extrinsically or intrinsically. Extrinsic acute injuries are those that result from contact with an external force. Typically, this may be through being struck by, or colliding with, another person, some equipment or implement, or the ground. Intrinsic acute injuries, on the other hand, are usually the result of some excessive internal force, e.g. a stretch, twist or pull that can lead to strains, sprains, ruptures or dislocation.

In contrast to those injuries that occur as a result of a sudden event, there are numerous injury types that may take time to develop symptoms. As with acute injuries, chronic or overuse injuries can be further sub-classified according to the nature of the predisposing factor. Extrinsic chronic injuries are those that typically result from continued exposure to a factor that lies outside the body. Obvious examples include excessive training

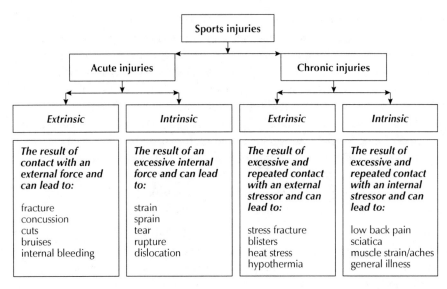

Figure 10.1 Summary of the categories of the most common sports injuries

loads, particularly on hard surfaces, inappropriate or poorly fitting footwear/clothing, inappropriate/wrong-sized equipment and hostile environmental conditions. Alternatively, intrinsic chronic injuries may result from some internal overstressing due to, for example, leg length discrepancies, muscular weakness or imbalance, limb malalignment, lack of flexibility, poor skill execution or genetic predispositions. Figure 10.1 gives a summarised categorisation of the most common sporting injuries.

Whatever the injury to athletes, coaches need to be aware of the nature of the injury and how their training methods could possibly have been responsible for its occurrence. Similarly, through successful classification and diagnosis, coaches are in a better position to respond to athlete injuries through considered rehabilitation and/or modification of the latter's training programmes. It is to this issue of injury prevention that we now turn.

## INJURY PREVENTION

The coach's role in injury prevention is to ensure that his or her actions prepare the performer and the coaching environment appropriately for training and competition. As has already been suggested, knowledge of what causes an injury can be of great help to the coach in preventing future injuries. It is essential, therefore, that a coach has a good understanding of the type and frequency of injury most commonly associated with their sport in order that they can reduce the risk of harm to athletes. The risk and severity of injury may vary with the level of performance and the type of population. For example, the incidence of injury in professional rugby is far higher than in amateur rugby due to the speed and intensity with which the game is played. At both levels, however, coaches need to be aware of typical injury sites so that they can develop fitness and skill levels that reduce the likelihood of such injuries happening. Similarly, coaches of young children need to be aware of the developmental factors affecting their charges' participation in sport. For example, intensive training of young children can delay the onset of puberty and skeletal maturation, thereby increasing the risk of damage to the heads of the bones (epiphysis). Additionally, in young women, heavy training increases the risk of the female triad syndrome of amenorrhea, osteoporosis and eating disorders. It is important that coaches understand these and other complex syndromes and recognise their symptoms, thus lessening the likelihood of occurrence. For those interested in more detail here, Dirix et al. (1988) provide a useful overview of sports injury perspectives in certain sporting populations such as children, women, the ageing athlete and athletes with disabilities.

Detailed knowledge and understanding of the physical (and mental) demands of their sport is important for coaches as it enables them to develop and design relevant training programmes. This is necessary, as inappropriate training can have two types of negative impact. Firstly, inadequate technique or fitness levels can lead to athletes being over-stretched by training or competition. Secondly, excessive training loads may lead to fatigue, a state that makes athletes increasingly susceptible to injury. Additionally, sustained heavy training loads with inadequate recovery periods can lead to the development of the pathological condition known as overtraining or unexplained underperformance syndrome (UUS). Indeed, Budgett (1998) reported that 10 per cent of endurance athletes per year experience overtraining symptoms that, in turn, further increase the risk of injury.

Since sport participation is much more to do with training than competition, it is more often the case that injuries occur whilst training. When preparing the training environment, then, the coach should identify any potential risks that may exist. For example, poor-quality training facilities can result in trivial injuries that can be easily avoided. Also coaches should familiarise themselves with emergency procedures and facilities both on and off site in case they are needed. Finally in this context, whilst it is not essential, it is highly desirable for a coach to have basic first aid and life-support training as it is often the coach who is the first person to attend to the injured athlete. Here, swift actions can often save a life or reduce the severity of athlete injury.

Selection of the most appropriate equipment and training terrain is also important for injury prevention. For example, the shoe in which an athlete trains should not only be dependent on the type of sport and surface but also on the individual's specific mechanical characteristics. The recent high-profile cases of injury to footballers' metatarsals (i.e. foot bones) highlight the influence that inappropriate footwear may have on increasing the possibility of injury. Other examples of inappropriate use of equipment include using the wrong grip size in tennis, which promotes tennis elbow, or incorrectly sized cycle frames, which increase the risk of back injury. Likewise, in contrast to the role of a running shoe (shock absorption and rear foot control), a tennis shoe is designed for lateral and cutting manoeuvres. Therefore, either running in a tennis shoe or playing tennis in a running shoe increases the risk of injury. Additionally, inappropriate techniques can further increase the risk of injury such as overpronation (i.e. the excessive inward roll of the foot before it leaves the ground) in running (Kibler 1991) or hyperextension (i.e. extending beyond the natural range of movement) whilst fast-bowling in cricket.

Although coaches are often responsible for the organisation of medical provision, the type of sport and level of competition influence their role in this regard. For example, at most major international competitions or mass-participation events, medical cover is normally provided by the organising body or sponsor. Here, it is the responsibility of the coach to find out about the existing medical cover and how to access it. However, at the lower levels of competition it is less likely that medical cover will be provided, leaving the coach responsible for organising medical support him or herself.

In terms of preparing an athlete for training or competition, there are a number of steps a coach can, and perhaps should, take to minimise the risk of injury. As well as ensuring that the training undertaken matches the capabilities of athletes so that they are not overstretched, coaches should also ensure that athletes are mentally and physically prepared for a training session through an effective warm-up routine. It is widely accepted that a general warm-up to elevate the heart rate and body temperature to optimal functioning levels followed by a specific warm-up to mimic the joint actions and muscle contractions to be performed during training can help reduce injuries (Gleim and McHugh 1997). Additionally, stretching is often reported to help prevent injury although the causal relationship here has yet to be proved definitively (Smith 1994).

Coaches should also be familiar with the screening requirements for their sport, thus identifying any individuals whom they consider to be at risk of injury. Such a strategy involves ensuring that athletes are fit enough to participate by, whenever possible, checking their medical histories. This includes becoming familiar with key indicators such as a personal history of cardiovascular disease, cholesterol levels and blood pressure. Additional factors that should be considered include previous head and musculoskeletal injuries, exercise-induced asthma, diabetes and heat-related illness (Scuderi and McCann 2005). For contact sports such as rugby, American football and boxing there are clear guidelines regarding pre-screening as well as the amount of time before athletes can return to competition following a head injury. In many other sports, however, the guidelines are less prescriptive and often are at the discretion of coaches.

## INJURY MANAGEMENT

The key to successful rehabilitation is the effective management of an injury from initial occurrence to complete recovery. To ensure long-term success, additional measures may be required to help prevent the injury re-occurring. This section will examine the key stages in injury management and identify the differing roles that coaches and others play in the process. There are several stages in the management of a sports injury. The first of these is immediate management. Here, either first aid is administered or an initial diagnosis and treatment are performed. This is followed by early management, where a more informed diagnosis is carried out with appropriate treatment administered soon after the injury. The third stage is that of detailed diagnosis. This is where an in-depth analysis is completed that may require arthroscopic surgery or x-rays. The penultimate phase is rehabilitation, where the athlete undertakes exercises to strengthen and rehabilitate the affected area. The final stage is the return to play, with the athlete being passed fit again. Each will now be outlined in more depth.

At the immediate management stage it is often the coach who takes the initiative. This may involve a decision related to the fitness of the athlete to continue participation, or that medical treatment is required. In some cases, coaches fail to realise the significance of the injury and allow the athlete to continue, often resulting in greater trauma to the injury site. For serious injuries to the head, neck or chest, additional specialist medical support should be called for immediately. To assist coaches in this context, Steele (1996) has produced a useful textbook entitled *Sideline Help: A Guide for Immediate Evaluation and Care of Sports Injuries*, which readers may wish to access to develop their knowledge further.

The early management phase tends to happen either on the field or in the changing room/medical room. It is normally completed either by a coach, physician or physiotherapist and can lead to referral to a specialist. This initial treatment falls into four categories; treatment of wounds, fractures, soft-tissue and head/neck injuries. The coach should be aware that for wound management the key aim is to reduce contamination and prevent blood loss. This is often addressed by dressing the wound. The initial treatment of fractures involves immobilising the joint, possibly using some form of splint. For soft-tissue injuries, the goal is to reduce or control swelling with the most effective way being that described by the acronym R.I.C.E.; Rest–Ice–Compression–Elevation. Generally, ice should be applied for 15 minutes every one to two hours in the 24 hours immediately after the injury occurring, whilst compression should be adequate enough to apply pressure but not to cause pain. Head and neck injuries often require immobilisation via the application of a neck brace or spinal board.

During the detailed diagnosis stage a specialist may become involved. This often depends on financial considerations rather than the severity of the injury. The diagnosis itself may require an x-ray or MRI scan, while for serious or complex injuries several opinions may be required. The resulting treatment could be surgery, the use of therapeutic drugs such as cortisone steroids and other anti-inflammatories, ultrasound stimulation, manipulation or massage.

Biomechanists, nutritionists, podiatrists or other specialists could also be called upon at this stage to contribute to an overall assessment and management of serious injuries. Such staff are useful in determining the underlying causes of injuries and can often provide advice or interventions that may help prevent any re-occurrence. For example, numerous knee, hip and Achilles tendon injuries in runners are the result of wearing the wrong type of running shoe. A podiatrist/biomechanist can analyse a runner's gait to determine any mechanical issues that need addressing and consequently can prescribe orthotics or specially designed running shoes for the athlete. The final phase of rehabilitation and return to play will be covered in more detail in the next section. This comprises a combination of treatments and interventions as outlined in the detailed diagnosis phase, combined with exercises to strengthen and regain flexibility in the injured region(s).

## REHABILITATION FROM INJURY

This section will examine the key issues associated with rehabilitation from injury and look at the processes involved in restoring full use to an injured body part. For successful rehabilitation to occur, a coach needs to appreciate that an injured athlete should be able to return to competition without any increased risk of the initial injury re-occurring. To achieve this, a rehabilitation programme needs to adhere to the general principles of training with specific focus on progression and individuality. The manipulation of key training principles for injured athletes involves paying particular attention to safe progression for each athlete in terms of frequency, intensity, overload and time. Unfortunately, there is no magic formula to achieve this. Consequently, these principles will vary with each case as all injuries are unique, whilst each individual has specific needs to ensure successful recovery. However, all rehabilitation programmes have a common aim; to allow the athlete back to full functional ability at the earliest possible opportunity with minimal chance of reoccurrence of the original injury. According to Brukner and Kahn (2006), factors that influence the rehabilitation process include:

- the type and severity of injury;
- the circumstances surrounding the injury;
- the external pressures (to return to play by the coach/media/team);
- the pain tolerance of the athlete;
- the psychological attributes of the athlete; and
- the coach–athlete support system.

In terms of this last point, the coach's role in supporting an injured athlete cannot be overestimated. Here, the coach's knowledge of the athlete's self-esteem and attitude to training adherence is essential, as all athletes respond differently to being injured. Those with high self-esteem and motivation levels often respond well to rehabilitation by focusing on their desire to play again. These individuals normally follow any rehabilitation programme religiously, although they may also try to progress too rapidly and overstretch at the initial stages of recovery. In contrast, athletes with low levels of self-esteem and poor adherence to training often fail to follow strict exercise regimes resulting in a longer rehabilitation phase. An injured athlete who understands what and why they are doing something, and has easy access to facilities and support, is more likely to adhere to a rehabilitation programme. Additionally, the setting of realistic and achievable targets by coaches will assist athlete compliance and adherence to the set course of action. The use of sports-specific activities can also help to maintain athlete interest and motivation, thus allowing the injured athlete to recover more rapidly.

A rehabilitation programme can be divided into four stages: initial; intermediate; advanced; and a return to competition. A coach needs to appreciate each of these stages so that he/she can support each athlete's return to full fitness. The initial stage involves getting the athlete to be pain-free and to have a full range of movement. This stage is often very frustrating for injured athletes, as the required rehabilitation exercises are often highly repetitive and non-sports-specific. Consequently, in team sports it is sometimes useful to allow injured athletes to involve themselves in other ways to ensure that they continue to feel part of the team. For example, they could help coach the less-able athletes/players or work with the development squads. Alternatively, some players rehabilitate better when isolated from distractions. Thus, they may benefit from attending specialist training/ rehabilitation centres away from the home club.

The main purpose of the intermediate stage is for the athlete to regain any deficiencies in strength/muscle imbalances associated with inactivity. Here, it is often useful for injured athletes to join specialised training groups. For example, professional soccer and rugby players often complete this stage in conjunction with strength-based sportsmen/women who often focus purely on strength rather than skill or technique development. Alternatively, at the advanced rehabilitation stage the injured athlete should be performing conditioning specific to the activity or sport in which they compete. The role of the coach is important here in ensuring that the rehabilitation exercises are sports-specific, thus placing the injured body parts under similar stresses to those encountered during competition. Finally, the coach has an important function in the return to competition stage of a rehabilitation programme in ensuring the injured player or athlete is ready to do so. This may involve setting up simulated match practice or getting the athlete in question to initially compete at a lower level than normal. For example, it is usual for games players to start the return to competition stage by playing in the reserves, with a gradual transition to playing a full match for the first team. Likewise, international athletes often compete at local club competitions prior to returning to the intensity of elite sport.

## SUMMARY

We believe that injuries, whilst being very prevalent in sports participation, are in many instances, preventable. A coach can assist in this prevention by developing a good understanding of the different types and causes of injury that may occur in his or her sport. Such an understanding can help coaches to develop the physical, psychological and technical capabilities of athletes, thus enabling the latter to better meet required demands. However, in some instances injuries to athletes will still occur. In such cases, coaches should be aware of the necessary steps to take to both reduce the severity of, and facilitate the recovery from, such injuries. Careful management of an injury will aid an athlete's recovery and subsequent return to training and competition. Once an athlete is on the road to recovery the coach should then give consideration to how and when the athlete will be re-introduced to normal training. Similarly, the possible causes of the original injury should be reflected upon to prevent the same injury occurring again. Developing such sports medicine-related knowledge, then, as associated with the prevention, treatment and management of injuries, allows the coach to better protect the health, well-being, fitness and, hence, the ultimate performance of athletes.

## REVIEW QUESTIONS

1. Define sports medicine. How can such knowledge be useful to coaches?
2. How can sports injuries be classified? What is the value of such classification?
3. Discuss how coaches can actively prevent and manage athlete injuries.
4. What are the factors that influence an athlete's rehabilitation from injury? What is the role of the coach in this process?

# CHAPTER ELEVEN

# PHYSIOLOGY FOR COACHES

Michael G. Hughes

*A working knowledge of physiology is essential for all good coaches. You have to know how different kinds of training affect the body so you can develop the optimal preparation programme for players.*

Julia Longville –
Welsh National Netball Coach (2002–6)

## Key sections:

- Introduction
- The physiological aspects of sports performance
- Assessing the physiological demands of sports
- Fitness assessment
- Training to improve physical performance: general considerations
- Training to improve physical performance: specific considerations
- Conclusion

## INTRODUCTION

Sports physiology is concerned with how the body reacts to physical training and competition. Many physiological characteristics impact on an athlete's performance, ranging from visible factors like gender and body size to the complex biochemical processes that cause muscle contraction at the molecular level. While a coach may not need to have an in-depth knowledge of all these processes and reactions, a grasp of the key aspects of physiology and how they relate to sports performance is essential for the optimal preparation of athletes. The aim of this chapter is to examine a number of these aspects, thus giving coaches an understanding of how to maximise the fitness levels of athletes. In terms of structure, the physiological processes that determine human performance over a range of durations are initially outlined. This is followed by a discussion of the value of assessing the physical demands of the sport in question and athletes' individual needs to maximise performance. Penultimately, training considerations and techniques aimed at improving both general and specific areas of fitness are highlighted, before a conclusion summarises the principal points made.

## THE PHYSIOLOGICAL ASPECTS OF SPORTS PERFORMANCE

The contraction of muscle is fundamental to all exercise performance. It is initiated by nerve signals that promote movement, provided that sufficient chemical energy is available to the muscle fibres. Indeed, exercise represents a challenge to a muscle's energy stores, with many physiological reactions conditioned to replenish such stores so that exercise can continue. These energy-releasing reactions range in complexity from very simple ones within the active muscle, to highly complex ones that require the co-ordinated responses of the respiratory, metabolic, cardiovascular, hormonal and muscular systems. An understanding of these systems and how they impact on different kinds of activity, both in competition and in training, is essential for coaches who wish to improve the fitness levels of athletes. Accordingly, the rest of this section outlines the physiological factors that have most impact on physical performance.

### Muscle contraction and the physiology of very short-duration exercise

The performance of very short-duration activity involves the least complex physiological processes. Here, a nerve signal initiates a series of reactions that cause contraction in a muscle, resulting in force production and movement. If exercise lasts less than a couple of seconds, then energy stores within the working muscles are sufficient to meet the demands of the activity. The very short duration of such activity negates the need for other more complex energy-producing processes to be activated. Consequently, muscle produces its highest possible force and power when exercise is very short. Table 11.1 lists a series of sports events of contrasting exercise duration. It should be appreciated that the activities with the shortest duration are also those that require the highest intensity of effort. The limiting factors for very short-duration exercise are mainly the muscle's maximal strength, size and power. Therefore, training to enhance strength, power and muscle size will be most effective in improving short-duration performance.

### The physiology of longer-duration performance

Once exercise lasts more than a couple of seconds, the need to continually supply the working muscle with energy begins to limit the levels of performance. Figure 11.1 shows the power output during sprint running, illustrating the point that once exercise lasts more than a couple of seconds, the performance of the muscle declines. In effect, muscles are

*Table 11.1* Sporting events and the physiological factors that limit their performance

| Exercise duration | Examples of sport/activity | Main physiological factors that determine performance |
|---|---|---|
| Up to 2 seconds | Shot putt, discus, weightlifting | Muscle size, strength and power |
| Up to ~ 15 seconds | 60m and 100m sprints (run), bobsleigh | Anaerobic energy production |
| ~ 15–60 seconds | Gymnastics, 200m and 400m run, 50m and 100m swim | |
| 1–10 minutes | 1500m run, Alpine skiing, figure-skating, rowing (2000m) | Anaerobic energy production Cardio-respiratory fitness |
| Longer than ~ 10 minutes | 5000m running and above, triathlon, cycle stage races | |

already experiencing fatigue even after three seconds of sprint exercise. This is because the muscles' most immediate supply of energy is beginning to be compromised, resulting in a decline in performance.

The processes that the body uses to supply the energy needs of exercise are usually classified into two broad categories: aerobic and anaerobic. Anaerobic processes refer to energy-producing reactions that happen without the need for oxygen at the muscle. Conversely, aerobic metabolism refers to energy-producing reactions that require oxygen. As identified previously, muscle produces its highest possible levels of performance when activity is performed over very short periods, but once exercise lasts more than two seconds or so, the muscle must derive its energy from either aerobic or anaerobic processes.

Anaerobic reactions convert energy within the working muscle, thus allowing movement to continue. These are relatively simple reactions, so they can happen very quickly. However, because these energy stores are limited, anaerobic exercise cannot last for very long, while also producing reactions within muscles that cause fatigue. The anaerobic processes are, therefore, only suitable for sustaining high-intensity exercise over a short period of time. Aerobic processes, on the other hand, require the integrated response of the lungs, heart and circulation (i.e. the cardio-respiratory system) to take oxygen to the working muscle. This delivery of oxygen from the lungs, however, is merely a precursor for the energy-producing reactions at the muscle site, which, in turn, sustain aerobic activity. As a result of these complex requirements, aerobic processes cannot supply energy as quickly as anaerobic ones. This is because aerobic metabolism is associated with the release of energy (as fats and carbohydrates) from all over the body, not just from the muscle site. Consequently, aerobic metabolism provides access to more energy stores with which to fuel prolonged exercise. Aerobic activity, therefore, can last for very long periods. However, the compromise of using aerobic as opposed to anaerobic metabolism is that only relatively low-intensity exercise is possible. The factors that

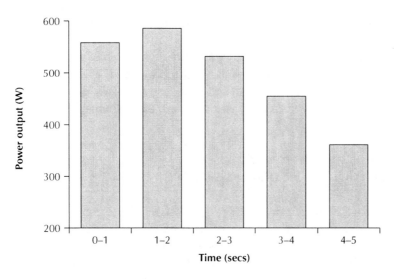

Figure 11.1 Power output during five seconds of sprint running (unpublished measurements from the author)

principally limit the performance of aerobic activity, then, are the capability of the cardio-respiratory system and the speed of the aerobic energy reactions at the muscle site.

### Repeated-sprint sports

The physiological demands described so far have focused on a situation where just one exercise bout of a specific duration is performed. However, many sports require athletes to perform several bouts of short-duration, high-intensity exercise interspersed with periods of relative recovery. These so-called repeated-sprint sports include football, hockey, rugby, basketball, volleyball and the racket sports. It has already been discussed how the performance of a single, short-duration, high-intensity bout of exercise is mostly determined by muscle strength, power and the anaerobic energy system. Consequently, these are also essential for success in repeated-sprint sports. However, the speed of recovery from such high-intensity bouts is related to aerobic fitness (Glaister 2005). Therefore, these sports not only require the strength, speed and anaerobic fitness for short-duration activity, but also high levels of aerobic fitness in order to promote recovery. As the repeated-sprint sports have mixed physiological demands, it is important that a wide range of training session activities is provided for athletes who participate in them.

In summarising this section, it is essential that a coach understands the so-called pay-off between exercise intensity and duration. With very short-duration exercise, the body can produce its highest levels of physiological performance. This is associated with the relative simplicity of the energy reactions that are required for such short bouts of activity. As the exercise duration increases, the delivery and maintenance of energy to working muscle tends to limit performance. Aerobic activity tends to be associated with the lowest exercise intensities but the longest exercise durations. If periods of high-intensity activity are interspersed with lower-intensity exercise, a combination of energy provision from the anaerobic and aerobic systems, in conjunction with strength, power and cardio-respiratory fitness, are required for optimal performance. An understanding of these issues is important in enabling coaches to devise training sessions that maximise the development of athletes' fitness.

## ASSESSING THE PHYSIOLOGICAL DEMANDS OF SPORTS

Where sports are made up of a single bout of all-out exercise, it is relatively straightforward to estimate their physiological demands using the principles outlined earlier. However, for most sports a wide array of characteristics is required in order to compete at a high level. A challenge for coaches is to establish the needs of competition so that athletes can be prepared accordingly. Valuable sources to consult here include textbooks, magazines and governing body publications. Additionally, more specific information can be derived from the use of notational analysis or the assessment of physiological responses to training and competition. The notational analysis of sports performance is covered in more detail elsewhere in this book (see Chapter 9), but the outcomes of such work lead directly to an understanding of the likely physiological consequences of participation. For example, in rugby union, contrasting demands between different playing positions have been demonstrated, information that can be used to devise specific training programmes for different playing positions (Deutsch et al. in press).

Physiological indices or measures can also be used to determine the demands of sports performance. The physiological factor most easily assessed by a coach is the heart rate of the athlete, which can be done through the use of a commercially available heart rate monitor. Although heart rate is useful, as it usually relates to the intensity of exercise, it is only an indication of the extent of cardio-respiratory stress. This is illustrated in Figure 11.2, where the heart rate graph of an athlete performing highly intense, explosive training is shown. Here, despite the intensity, a relatively low average heart rate (103 beats per minute) is recorded.

Alternatively, when exercise is comparatively prolonged (more than one minute of continuous activity), heart rate is a much more useful indication of exercise intensity. Indeed, a principal value of heart rate monitoring for athletes is its ability to demonstrate the exercise intensity of prolonged endurance training sessions (see Figure 11.3). By carefully monitoring an athlete's performance in training, an endurance coach is able to conduct sessions at an appropriate exercise intensity. More detail can usually be obtained by sport scientists, who can assess the concentration of blood lactic acid or the rate of oxygen consumption to determine the athlete's anaerobic or aerobic systems' contribution to the exercise undertaken.

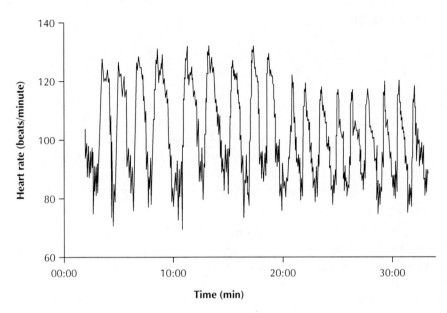

Figure 11.2  The heart rate response to a very high-intensity, short-duration training session (mean heart rate 103 beats per minute)

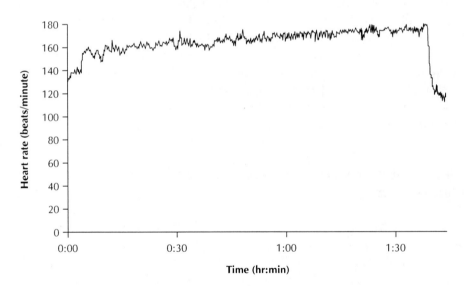

Figure 11.3  Heart rate response to a continuous, prolonged endurance training session

## FITNESS ASSESSMENT

The previous section discussed how physiological response measurements to competition and training can inform a coach about the requirements of a sport. This section refers to how knowledge of individual athletes can be matched to those requirements. Insight into the physiology of individual athletes can be achieved through assessing their fitness levels. Once a coach has an appreciation of the demands of a sport, it should be possible to identify the key elements of that activity and isolate them for the purposes of fitness assessment. For example, in a sport like football (i.e. soccer), a player needs high levels of power as well as speed, aerobic fitness and the ability to perform repeated-sprint activity. Accordingly, Table 11.2 shows fitness tests that could be suited for the assessment of fitness in football players (Tumilty 2000).

Fitness tests have a wide range of applications and should be used as part of a regular training plan. In all sports, fitness testing is used as a way of comparing an athlete's results to previous performances or to normative standards established in the sport. Fitness testing can thus be used to modify future training as appropriate. Once a battery of suitable fitness tests has been decided upon they should be performed regularly using constant procedures, in order that conclusions are valid and meaningful. In most cases it is normal to assess athletes' fitness around four times a year.

Once sufficient tests have been performed on enough athletes, it is possible to draw up a fitness profile of competitors in a specific sport. Table 11.3 contains a set of fitness test results from national squad athletes in the sport of badminton. Each result in the table represents a mean score derived from at least twenty players. Because these data are representative of a considerable number of high-level competitors, it is possible to compare them with results from other individuals in the same age-groups in order to judge a player's fitness level. Indeed, the relative strengths and weaknesses of tested individuals are easily identified once a profile of athletes in a sport has been established.

## TRAINING TO IMPROVE PHYSICAL PERFORMANCE: GENERAL CONSIDERATIONS

One of the essential roles of a coach is to facilitate the development of fitness levels so that athletes can compete effectively. In some sports, the physical development of an athlete may be the main function of a coach. This is especially so where the technical or tactical demands of a sport are relatively low and where success is judged by time or distance (e.g. athletics). In other cases, the non-physical demands of a sport may be so high that a coach may devote a smaller percentage of time to athletes' physical training. Irrespective of the sport, however, there are a number of key components of fitness training that a coach must be able to understand and apply. These include those of overload and variation.

Table 11.2  Suitable procedures for the assessment of fitness in football players

| Fitness component | Fitness test |
| --- | --- |
| Power | Vertical jump test |
| Speed | Timed 20m sprint |
| Repeated sprint ability | 10 × 40m sprints starting every 30 seconds |
| Aerobic fitness | Repeated 20m shuttle-run test |

Table 11.3  Mean fitness test results from age-group to senior, national squad female badminton players (unpublished data from the author, with permission from Badminton England)

| | 14 yrs | 16 yrs | 18 yrs | Senior players |
| --- | --- | --- | --- | --- |
| Vertical jump height (cm) | 47.8 | 45.7 | 48.8 | 50.0 |
| Standing long jump (cm) | 196 | 193 | 201 | 208 |
| Medicine ball throw (cm) | 526 | 597 | 650 | 612 |
| On-court agility test (sec) | 14.1 | 13.7 | 13.1 | 13.3 |
| Badminton aerobic test (level attained) | 11.4 | 11.9 | 12.9 | 14.3 |

The human body is highly adaptable and, with sufficient training, can be transformed in terms of performance. A key to achieving improvements is that a training programme must overload the physiological processes required for competition. A training programme that includes the overload principle will incorporate planned attempts to increase one or all of the key training variables (i.e. intensity, duration and frequency). For example, a training programme for an athlete who can only run for 30 minutes at a slow pace and wishes to simply complete a marathon race will predominantly involve an overload of the duration of training sessions. If the same runner wants to run the marathon in under three hours, he or she would have to be additionally trained for maintaining the significantly faster speed required. In this case the overload would need to be imposed in relation to the intensity of exercise as well as the duration. Similarly, the frequency of training could also be increased to provide an overload, e.g. from three sessions per week up to a target of five over a period of a few months.

Although small changes can happen over relatively short periods of time, the development of high fitness levels can take many years. If training only involved the performance of activity that was the same as the athlete's sport, the repeated stresses of this activity could lead to increased injury risk, while the athlete could become bored and unchallenged by their training schedule. It is essential, therefore, that an athlete experiences variation in training. Variation can be achieved by the use of alternative activities as well as by planning for periods of training that differ in intensity, frequency and duration.

## TRAINING TO IMPROVE PHYSICAL PERFORMANCE: SPECIFIC CONSIDERATIONS

In addition to the general considerations of overload and variation, a coach should also be aware of specific issues, or the principle of specificity, when physically preparing athletes for competition. The principle of specificity dictates that training should be relevant to the demands of the sport and the athlete in question. Once this has been ascertained, in order to maximise fitness, each element of physical performance should be considered and trained in isolation. Specificity also dictates that the physiological demands of an event must be replicated in training. For example, if a sport requires short bursts of high intensity, training should be planned to include such activity. Specificity is further enhanced when the movement characteristics of a sport are matched in training. For example, many sports (e.g. tennis, rugby, squash) involve repeated changes in direction; hence the strength and speed training for these sports should include activities that promote the required braking forces and leg muscle explosiveness that allow for quick directional changes. The rest of this section will examine strength and speed development in more detail before going on to discuss the value of tailoring training towards anaerobic and aerobic competitive demands.

Speed of movement (e.g. how quickly someone can run) is related to the type of muscle fibres that one has. Muscle can be categorised into two types: fast-contracting and slow-contracting fibres. The proportion of fast and slow fibres within a muscle is partly genetically determined. However, the existence of other influencing factors means that speed is still highly trainable. At the level of the whole body, speed can usually be enhanced by increases in muscle power and movement technique, as well as by a reduction in body mass. As discussed earlier, maximal speed can only ever be achieved over extremely short durations (see Figure 11.1). Hence, if the principle of specificity to speed training is to be applied, such training should incorporate very short periods of repeated maximal effort activity interspersed with long recoveries. Consequently, sprinters in athletics should have at least 5 minutes rest to allow for complete recovery after each exercise bout. Similarly, for most sports players, maximal speed training should involve sprints of approximately five seconds followed by around one minute of recovery before the next sprint is performed. The fact that speed is essential in many sports means that this type of training is an important component in developing the fitness of many athletes.

If an athlete is attempting to train for improvements in maximal speed, and he or she is experiencing a decline in performance, then modifications are perhaps needed to the rest (lengthened) or exercise duration (reduced) to suit that athlete. Similarly, if an athlete is experiencing high heart rates and heavy breathing during a speed session, it is likely that the session is causing too much activation of the cardio-respiratory system. The engagement of the cardio-respiratory system in this regard reflects use of aerobic as opposed to the desired anaerobic energy reactions. In either case, the athlete needs to be given more recovery or shorter sprint duration to allow the session to meet the aim of maximal-speed development. The example given earlier of an explosiveness training session (see Figure 11.2) shows a successful attempt to minimise the use of the cardio-respiratory system within it.

Maximal strength is rather like speed, in that very heavy demands are placed on the working muscles for very short periods of time. Also, like speed training, strength training requires very short bouts of activity followed by longer periods of rest that allows the muscle's energy stores to be replenished. Only when the muscle can produce relatively high forces in training will it adapt to become stronger in the long term. The development of strength is likely to be beneficial to athletes in all sports, due to the fact that muscle strength provides protection from injury and improvements in muscle control that can transfer to all activities. The main adaptations that can be achieved from training in this way are an increase in muscle size (known as hypertrophy) and maximal strength. Although they often go together, it is usually desirable to separate these two in terms of training goals. For example, in athletics, competitors in jumping events need to be extremely strong but may also want to minimise their body (and thus their muscle) mass. Their training, therefore, should focus on developing maximal strength while minimising the hypertrophy of the muscle. In contrast, forwards in rugby may want to develop both maximal strength and muscle mass. To concentrate on the development of maximal strength, an athlete should train with heavy weights followed by a long rest period to allow for recovery within the working muscles. On the other hand, muscle hypertrophy is best achieved by training with lighter weights and slightly shorter recovery periods (Kraemer et al. 1990).

Exercise that is classed as anaerobic is inherently related to strength and speed. The training of the anaerobic energy system, therefore, adopts similar principles to those used for developing strength and speed. Consequently, a training session to enhance anaerobic fitness will comprise repeated bouts of short exercise (e.g. five to around thirty seconds), with the interval between these being between around five to ten times the length of each bout (see Table 11.4).

When performing exercises to enhance anaerobic fitness, the use of the aerobic energy system should be low. By interspersing periods of work with long rest periods, there is less contribution from the aerobic system, which, in turn, allows anaerobic processes to be the main providers of energy. It is essential that anaerobic training is performed at a very high intensity; therefore the athlete must work as hard as possible during the exercise periods.

Table 11.4 Interval (running) training sessions to enhance anaerobic fitness

|  | Intended aim of session | Sprint duration | Rest between sprints | Number of repetitions |
|---|---|---|---|---|
| Short-sprint duration | i) Repetition of very high-quality sprinting | 5 seconds | 50 seconds | 10–15 |
|  | ii) Fatigue-resistance and speed-endurance | 5 seconds | 30 seconds | 15 |
| Long-sprint duration | i) Repetition of high-quality, sustained performance | 30 seconds | 150 seconds | 6 |
|  | ii) Fatigue-resistance in sustained performance | 30 seconds | 90 seconds | 10 |

The use of rest intervals between exercise bouts has been termed interval training. A selection of interval training sessions designed to improve anaerobic fitness is given in Table 11.4. If athletes find these sessions too easy or too hard, the coach should alter the rest periods to ensure the session provides the appropriate stimulus for training adaptations. The main aim of anaerobic training is to improve the ability of the athlete to perform sustained high-intensity activity for events such as 200m running, 50m swimming or even sports like rugby and football where short, high-intensity bursts are interspersed with longer periods of low-intensity activity. Anaerobic fitness is also essential as a component of longer-duration events such as Olympic rowing, middle- to long-distance running, and cycling, where a sprint finish may be required towards the end of a race.

Additionally, aerobic fitness is a requirement of most sports. For example, long-duration events, where activity is maintained at a relatively constant, low-intensity (such as triathlons, a 10,000m run or a 1500m swim) are almost exclusively aerobic. However, in repeated-sprint sports, aerobic requirements are also high. This is because aerobic fitness promotes recovery between high-intensity exercise bouts. Hence, most exercise will improve aerobic fitness, even strength and sprint training (Dawson et al. 1998; Kraemer et al. 1995). Consequently, although the traditional way of enhancing aerobic fitness has been to perform low-intensity exercise over prolonged periods of time, a whole range of activities can be used to develop it. A common factor in doing so, however, is the necessity to provide an overload of both exercise duration and intensity. Therefore, rather than just exercising at a low intensity for a longer time, optimal development of aerobic fitness also requires interval sessions where higher-intensity work is interspersed with rest periods. This allows for more use of fast-contracting muscle fibres (Dudley et al. 1982) and greater stress on the cardiovascular system (Billat et al. 2001). In turn, the fast-fibres and the cardio-respiratory systems adapt to the training and, with time, aerobic fitness improves. The differences between interval training sessions for aerobic and anaerobic fitness are that aerobic interval sessions are not usually performed at a maximal intensity, while the rest period between exercise bouts is usually a little shorter. Table 11.5 shows a selection of training sessions that would be suited to the development of aerobic fitness.

*Table 11.5* A selection of (running) training sessions to enhance aerobic fitness

|  | Intended aim of session | Details of session |
|---|---|---|
| Short-duration interval | To improve aerobic fitness at very high movement speed | 5 sets of (10 repetitions of [10 seconds hard run, 20 seconds walk recovery]) 2 minutes between sets |
| Medium-duration interval | To improve aerobic fitness at sustained high running speeds | 6 repetitions of (3 minutes hard run, interspersed with 2 minutes walking recovery) |
| Continuous exercise | To improve general aerobic fitness and endurance | 45 minutes of low-intensity, continuous exercise |

## CONCLUSION

The aim of this chapter has been to highlight how an understanding of sports physiology can help to inform coaching practice. Hence, a series of principles have been presented and discussed that should enable a coach to make decisions regarding the best strategies for enhancing the fitness of athletes in order to optimise their competitive performance. Although it is beyond the scope of this chapter to provide definitive answers in relation to precise fitness questions and demands of individual athletes and the sports they perform, through applying the principles discussed it is hoped that all coaches can approach the development of their athletes' fitness with a greater level of knowledge and confidence.

## REVIEW QUESTIONS

1. Using the general points highlighted in this chapter, devise exercise training sessions to enhance the following components of fitness relevant to your sport of choice:

   a) Movement speed
   b) Endurance fitness

2. Why is strength training important for the preparation of competitors in most sports? How would you draw up general training guidelines that would enhance the following aspects of strength?

   a) Maximal strength
   b) Muscle hypertrophy (muscle size)

3. How would you apply the principles of progression and variation to the training sessions that you have devised in answering questions 2 and 3 above?

# CHAPTER TWELVE

# TYING IT ALL TOGETHER

Robyn Jones, Kieran Kingston and Mike Hughes

## INTRODUCTION

In this book, we have introduced readers to the sport sciences that underpin coaching. No doubt it is somewhat at odds with previous introductory-type books, which have tended to portray coaching as a rather simplified, sequential activity. In this respect, it could be troublesome for many, with previously familiar concepts rendered strangely complex (Perkins 1999). We make no apology for this, as coaching is often problematic and hard to manage. To portray it otherwise would do the subject and those who study it an injustice. The book is also not meant as an ending but as a beginning; a first passport into the largely undefined field of coaching where numerous knowledges are constantly drawn upon by practitioners in attempts to improve the experience and performances of athletes. We have tried to make most of these knowledges explicit, in particular how they impact on coaching.

Although, in terms of presentation, we have divided the knowledges that underpin coaching along lines of sport science, this was done in the interests of clarity and not because we view the subject as a fragmented and multidisciplinary one (i.e. including distinct, separate disciplines that don't intersect). On the contrary, we see coaching as being predominantly interdisciplinary in character, with practitioners needing to draw on several knowledge sources simultaneously to address both anticipated and unforeseen issues. We also view coaching as a personal activity, with every coach having his or her own ideas about what works best for them. This, however, is not to say that we endorse a philosophy of 'anything goes', as the preceding chapters present plenty of lines of good researched practice. Such information, however, should be used to think with, rather than to apply in every situation without question or thought to the consequence. Here, we hope that readers actively engage with the knowledges presented and, in doing so, denting the myth that good coaches are born and not made. Indeed, although some practitioners have more aptitude than others for the job, with hard work and an inquiring mind we believe that most can become competent, even good, coaches.

Although we have highlighted specific notions within the book that we believe can help coaches to develop, the personal nature of coaching was brought home to us by just how difficult we found it to write this final chapter. Naturally, we agree on many things regarding coaching (otherwise we could never have written this book!), but when it came to deciding what to emphasise in the conclusion our individual differences and perspectives soon emerged. For example, while one of us wanted to highlight the importance of knowledges that can be more directly accessed and, hence, applied, another considered that the social-scientific knowledges deserved a higher billing. Meanwhile, our third member considered that, although still valuable, some knowledges are apt to be implicitly picked up by coaches and should be left for this to be done, while others can and should be accessed directly as explicit resources. The following problematic coaching scenario, and how each of us approached it, provides an illustration of the case in point.

### DIFFERING VIEWS OF COACHING KNOWLEDGE

You are the relatively new coach of James (a highly gifted 16-year-old junior tennis player) who aims to make a successful transition to open-age tennis in the near future. In appraising him, you notice he has a strong serve-and-volley game that has worked successfully in junior competitions. You also observe that James has neglected his backcourt game due to the ease with which he has succeeded so far with the aforementioned serve-and-volley tactic. To develop his game further, you focus on improving his ground strokes while encouraging him to carefully craft points during a rally. Although seemingly acknowledging the strategy, James has struggled in recent competitions. This has frustrated him. Last week, during practice with a 'baseliner', who continuously kept the ball deep in the court, James openly displayed frustration and impatience by venturing aggressively to the net repeatedly, even when inappropriate. He was plainly unhappy. Following the session he complained to you and anyone who would listen that he already had a successful game plan and didn't need to change things to succeed. After another first round loss earlier this week, James's father called, saying that James was threatening to quit the sport. Apparently, he was disillusioned and losing his motivation to compete. He was no longer enjoying playing tennis and was blaming you for his gloomy state of affairs. James's father reminded you that before you became his coach, James was a highly ranked junior, and very intense about his sport. He now appears to have lost this intensity. You are, not unnaturally, stung by the criticism, which you consider unfair. Still, the facts seem unavoidable. How should you react? Where do you go from here?

## Kieran's interpretation

I am sure that few will be surprised (having read the earlier chapters to which I contributed) at my proposed approach in addressing the scenario outlined. As someone involved in two of the more traditional sport sciences (i.e. sport psychology and skill acquisition), I undoubtedly have a bias towards those areas. Consequently, if I was the coach in question there seems to be obvious mileage in accessing knowledge regarding sport psychology (e.g. in relation to motivation) and skill acquisition (e.g. in terms of practice scheduling and an appropriate attentional focus). This is because I believe they can directly impact upon the antecedents or precursors to James's emotional state (and his father's interpretation of the situation). Furthermore, support could also be sought from performance analysts (e.g. biomechanists and/or notational analysts) to evaluate any potential technical or strategic deficiencies in James's game. This given, I can also see great benefit in having or developing a deeper understanding of the sociological/historical context in which James, as the performer, and the sport exist, as well as reflecting on how my personal philosophy, both as a coach and a human being, influences the decisions I make.

On the face of it, my focus (as a coach) may appear overly narrow. In response, I would argue that we live in the real world, with coaching decisions being made on the availability and applicability of existing resources. Therefore, while the objective of this text is to illustrate the multiple knowledges that could and should be applied to coaching, the reality may be that coaches make a judgement call (implicitly) on the relative tangible benefits and logistics of seeking 'expert' guidance (both in person and from written resources). In this situation, then, I would argue that a coach is more likely to choose to access what he or she considers to be more concrete information directly based on a perceived immediate need and potential impact. Naturally, I assume that such information would then be couched in a sensitive yet realistic coaching philosophy. That philosophy should be based on a sound moral and ethical code, an understanding of effective coaching styles and an empathy with the sociological and historical factors that impinge on the athlete and the context. Furthermore, the coach should be aware of the pertinent health-and-safety issues associated with the situation.

This view of accessing certain types of information might imply a hierarchy of status comprising two tiers of knowledge. This is certainly not my intention as, although layers are evident, no judgement is made as to their importance, with both needing each other if coaching is to be accurate, informative, dynamic, empathetic and socially appropriate. Rather, the structure given is founded on issues of access, with coaches being more familiar and, hence, comfortable with what they already know and can retrieve directly. This would include information related to physiology, performance analysis (notation and biomechanics), psychology and skill acquisition. The second tier, then, might consist of disciplines that contribute indirectly to coaching, or which are pervasive in good coaching practice. These might include: a personal philosophy of coaching (philosophy and ethics), an understanding of the historical and social context of the sport in question (history and sociology), the organisational structure of the sport (sport development) and sports medicine in terms of managing injury risk.

## Robyn's view

In many ways I agree with the above interpretation. I acknowledge that a number of knowledge sources need to be drawn on here to deal with this problematic scenario. These include those from the realms of psychology (related to intrinsic and extrinsic motivation), biomechanics and notational analysis (carefully examining James's technique), skill acquisition and pedagogy (in terms of learning and feedback) and sport development (in locating coaching practice within wider political initiatives), among others. However, from my perspective it would also mean drawing on sociological and historical knowledge to a much greater degree, particularly in terms of what James has invested in his tennis identity and how he feels now that this identity is under threat. Like Kieran's admission above, this betrays my sociological roots in relation to what I think is important within coaching. The difference, then, between Kieran and myself lies in my belief that knowledge from the so-called softer or social sciences can and should be made explicit to, and therefore accessed directly by, coaches. This is because it has the capacity to directly influence coach–athlete interaction and not exist as some assumed common sense or art of coaching. Indeed, being taught to think with social, historical and philosophical tools is crucial if a fruitful relationship between coach and athlete is to be established. This is necessary so that knowledge and conversations about how hard to run (physiology) and what to focus on mentally (psychology) and movement wise (biomechanics) can be appropriately couched, enabling the message given to be accepted as intended. Indeed, recent research has highlighted that coaches consider how they interact and relate to athletes, to engender their respect, as the most crucial aspect of their coaching practice. After all, if the relationship between the coach and the athlete is a dysfunctional one, then no matter what the information given by the coach, the chances are that athletes will simply disregard it. As I said, where I differ principally from Kieran is my view that the interaction responsible for relationship building is a skill and knowledge that can and should be taught explicitly, learned and worked on.

## Mike's analysis

As a coach in this situation, I have made two mistakes. The first is in trying to change James's technique and, therefore, tactics mid-season. Secondly, and more importantly, I had not discussed it sufficiently well with him and his parents. So how do I react and where do I go from here? The first step would be to consult the short-term goals already defined with James (next tournament, next national squad etc.), and discuss with him the importance of winning the next tournament. If he wants to win it, and all 16-year-olds usually want to win every tournament, then I prepare him the best way I can to do so. That will probably mean reverting to the tried-and-trusted serve-and-volley tactic. It is a strategy aimed at getting his confidence and motivation levels high again. Here, then, I agree with both Kieran and Robyn that psychology has a part to play. I would concentrate on getting him right mentally, which probably means consulting a little more with his parents and others to understand what 'makes him tick.' This would mean drawing on his personal history and sociology to get to know him a little more as a person (history and sociology). To ensure that James and his parents fully understand how important and necessary the proposed changes are, I would additionally consult with a number of experts to support my case. These could include performance analysts to show how the change in style and tactics can help him succeed at the highest levels (notational analysis), and a physiologist (physiology) to outline the altered demands on his body, among others. If James and his parents are agreeable, we can set a new long-term plan, with realistic short-term goals, that will help him make the transition in a competitive but enjoyable way. In summary, then, I don't think that rigidly imposed coach dictates or ideas work. Athletes and their support teams (i.e. most often parents) need to be won over to proposed changes, especially if such changes are far-reaching in nature. If the athletes are not convinced, then even the best-intentioned plans will soon come to grief (and here I agree with the main thrust of Robyn's point). However, to win athletes over, coaches need to rely on many, explicit knowledge sources to provide the hard evidence (from, for example, biomechanics, notational analysis, psychology and sports development) that he or she 'knows what they are talking about'. It is not enough though just to put forward the case, as it also needs to be presented through competent interaction (sociology), so that the athlete buys into it and into the ability of the coach to deliver it. So, in my view, the working coach is the ultimate applied sports scientist needing to know elements of most, if not all, the knowledge branches covered in this book. On reflection, my general analysis tends to side with Kieran, with more concrete knowledge being of greatest help to coaches, although still needing to be couched in a context-sensitive manner.

## FINDING AGREEMENT: CONCLUDING THOUGHTS

Presenting these differing interpretations highlights what an individual activity coaching is; that there is no right answer to every scenario that one faces as a coach. As we talked through these differences, we came to realise that the important thing was not to find absolute agreement on every issue, but to experience the process of thinking about how to react in different situations, while being bound by general expectations of what the job of coaching actually entails. The information and concepts given in the chapters are presented as resources we can use to deal with the unique problems that coaching consistently presents. Indeed, when we consider the variety of knowledge sources available to coaches, and their interaction in the activity of coaching, we can see that there is much more to coaching than that contained in fashionable, simplistic buzzwords or sound-bytes. This is in line with our belief that there is no coach-by-numbers formula to be had, but rather a requirement to think insightfully about how to solve problems that present themselves in each particular context. Consequently, even with the resources presented in this book (and others), there is still a need for you as students of coaching to address every issue faced with imagination, creativity and rigour (Stones 1998). Similarly, as each of us had a different approach to managing the coaching scenario outlined, you are encouraged to make your own decisions about how to negotiate coaching's choppy waters. After all, such decision-making is really what coaching is all about. We hope that the information contained in this book will enable these decisions to be made from a more informed perspective.

# REFERENCES

Adonis, A. and Pollard, S. (1997) *A class act: The myth of Britain's classless society*, London: Penguin.

Anderson, B. (2005) *Imagined communities* (3rd edn), London: Verso.

Anderson, D. (2001) 'Foreword', in K. Hylton, P. Bramham, D. Jackson and M. Nesti (eds), *Sports development: Policy, process and practice*, London: Routledge.

Ames, C. (1992a) 'Classrooms: Goals, structures, and student motivation', *Journal of Educational Psychology*, 84: 261–271.

Ames, C. (1992b) 'Achievement goals and the classroom motivational climate', in J. Meece and D. Schunck (eds), *Student perceptions in the classroom*, Hillsdale, NJ: Erlbaum.

Ames, C. (1992c) 'Achievement goals, motivational climate, and motivational processes', in G. C. Roberts (ed.), *Motivation in sport and exercise*, Champaign, IL: Human Kinetics.

Arampatzis, A., and Brüggemann, G.P. (1999) 'Mechanical energetic processes during the giant swing exercise before dismounts and flight elements on the high bar and the uneven parallel bars', *Journal of Biomechanics*, 32: 811–820.

Arampatzis, A. and Brüggemann, G.P. (2001) 'Mechanical energetic processes during the giant swing before the Tkatchev exercise', *Journal of Biomechanics*, 34: 505–512.

Armour, K.M. (2000) 'We're all middle class now: Sport and social class in contemporary Britain', in R.L. Jones and K.M. Armour (eds), *Sociology of sport: Theory and practice*, Harlow: Pearson Education.

Ashworth, S. (1983) *Effects of training in Mosston's spectrum of teaching styles on feedback of teachers*, unpublished doctoral dissertation, Temple University, Philadelphia, PA.

Baldwin, J. and Baldwin, J. (1998) *Behaviour principles in everyday life* (3rd edn), Upper Saddle River, NJ: Prentice Hall.

Bandura, A. (1986) *Social foundations of thought and action: A social cognitive theory*, Englewood Cliffs, NJ: Prentice-Hall.

Bandura, A. (1977a) *Social learning theory*, Englewood Cliffs, NJ: Prentice Hall.

Bandura, A. (1977b) 'Self-efficacy: Toward a unifying theory of behaviour change', *Psychological Review*, 84: 191–215.

Battig, W. F. (1966) 'Facilitation and interference', in E. A. Bilodeau (eds), *Acquisition of skill*, New York: Academic Press.

Battig, W. F. (1979) 'The flexibility of human movement', in L.S. Cermak and F.I.M. Craik (eds), *Levels of processing in human memory*, Hillsdale, NJ: Erlbaum.

Baumeister, R.F. (1984) 'Choking under pressure: Self-consciousness and paradoxical effects of incentives on skilful performance', *Journal of Personality and Social Psychology*, 46(3): 610–620.

Baumeister, R. F. and Leary, M. R. (1995) 'The need to belong: Desire for interpersonal attachments as a fundamental human motivation', *Psychological Bulletin*, 117: 497–529.

Bayles, M.D. (1988) 'The professional–client relationship', in J.C. Callaghan (ed.), *Ethical issues in professional life*, Oxford: OUP.

Bennett, S.J. (2000) 'Implicit learning: Should it be used in practice?' *International Journal of Sport Psychology*, 31: 542–546.

Berger, P. (1963) *Invitation to sociology*, New York: Anchor Books.

Bernstein, N. (1967) *The co-ordination and regulation of movement*, London: Pergamon Press.

Best, D. (1978) *Philosophy and human movement*, London: Allen and Unwin.

Billat, V.L., Slawinski, J., Bocquet, V., Chassaing, P., Demarle and A., Koralsztein, J.P. (2001) 'Very short (15s–15s) interval-training around the critical velocity allows middle-aged runners to maintain $VO_2$ max for 14 minutes', *International Journal of Sports Medicine*, 22: 201–208.

Billig, M. (1995) *Banal nationalism*, London: Sage.

Bjork, R. A. (1988) 'Retrieval practice and the maintenance of knowledge', in M.M. Gruneberg, P.E. Morris and R.N. Sykes (eds), *Practical aspects of memory*, London: Wiley.

Borkovec, T.D. (1976) 'Physiological and cognitive processes in regulation of anxiety', in G. Schwartz and D. Sharpiro (eds), *Consciousness and self regulation: Advances in research*, New York: Phelem Press.

Boutcher, S.H. (1990) 'The role of performance routines in sport', in G. Jones and L. Hardy (eds), *Stress and performance in sport*, Chichester: Wiley and Son Ltd.

Brackenridge, C. (2001) *Spoilsports: Understanding and preventing sexual exploitation in sport*, London: Routledge.

Brady, F. (2004) 'Contextual interference: A meta-analytic study', *Perceptual and Motor Skills*, 99(1): 116–126.

Bramham, P., Hylton, K., Jackson, D. and Nesti, M. (2001) 'Introduction', in K. Hylton, P. Bramham, D. Jackson and M. Nesti (eds), *Sports development: Policy, process and practice*, London: Routledge.

Bray, K. and Kerwin, D.G. (2003) 'Modelling the flight of a soccer ball in a direct free kick', *Journal of Sports Sciences*, 21: 75–85.

Brewin, M.A. and Kerwin, D.G. (2003) 'Accuracy of scaling and DLT reconstruction techniques for planar motion analyses', *Journal of Applied Biomechanics*, 19: 79–88.

Brown, D. and Hughes, M. (1995) 'The effectiveness of quantitative and qualitative feedback in improving performance in squash', in T. Reilly, M. Hughes and A. Lees (eds), *Science and racket sports*, London: E. and F.N. Spon.

Brucker, B. S. and Bulaeva, N. V. (1996) 'Biofeedback effect on electromyography responses in patients with spinal cord injury', *Archives of Physical Medicine and Rehabilitation*, 77(2): 133–137.

Brukner, P. and Khan, K. (2006) *Clinical sports medicine*, Sydney: McGraw-Hill.

Budgett, R. (1998) 'Fatigue and underperformance in athletes: The overtraining syndrome', *British Journal of Sport Medicine*, 32: 107–110.

Burley, M. and Fleming, S. (1997) 'Racism and regionalism in Welsh soccer', *European Physical Education Review*, 3(2): 183–194.

Burton, D., Naylor, S. and Holliday, B. (2001) 'Goal setting in sport: Investigating the goal effectiveness paradox', in R.A. Singer, H.A. Hausenblas and C.M. Janelle (eds), *Handbook of sport psychology* (2nd edn), New York: Wiley.

Cain, N. (2004) 'Question time for the coaches: The six men plotting their countries' fortunes on the best and worst of their jobs', *The Sunday Times*, Sport Section, p. 19.

Caine, C.G., Caine, D.J. and Lindner, K.J. (1996) 'The epidemiologic approach to sports injuries', in D.J. Caine, C.G. Caine and K.J. Lindner (eds), *The epidemiology of sports injuries*, Champaign, IL: Human Kinetics Publishers.

Capel, S. (2000) 'Physical education and sport', in S. Capel and S. Pitrowski (eds), *Issues in PE*, London: Routledge.

Carpenter, P. J. and Morgan, K. (1999) 'Motivational climate, personal goal perspectives and cognitive and affective responses in physical education classes', *European Journal of Physical Education*, 4: 31–41.

Carrington, B. (1999) 'Cricket, culture and identity: An ethnographic analysis of the significance of sport within black communities', in S. Roseneil and J. Seymour (eds), *Practising identities: Power and resistance*, London: Macmillan.

Carrington, B. and McDonald, I. (eds) (2001) *Race, sport and British society*, London: Routledge.

Carron, A.V., Hausenblas, H.A. and Eys, M.A. (2005) *Group dynamics in sport* (3rd edn), Morgantown, WV: Fitness Information Technology.

Cashmore, E. (1982) *Black sportsmen*, London: Routledge and Kegan Paul.

Cassidy, T., Jones, R.L. and Potrac, P. (2004) *Understanding sports coaching: The social, cultural and pedagogical foundations of coaching practice*. London: Routledge.

Chandler, T.J.L. (1991) 'Games at Oxbridge and the public schools 1830–1890: Diffusion of an innovation', *International Journal for the History of Sport*, 18(2): 171–204.

Chelladurai, P. (1999) *Human resource management in sport and recreation*, Leeds: Human Kinetics.

Chollet, D., Micallef, J. P. and Rabischong, P. (1988) 'Biomechanical signals for external biofeedback to improve swimming techniques', in B.E. Ungerechts, K. White and K. Reichle (eds), *Swimming science*, Champaign, IL: Human Kinetics.

Clarys, J.P. (2000) 'Electromyography in sports and occupational settings: An update of its limits and possibilities', *Ergonomics*, 43(10): 1750–1762.

Coalter, F. (2001) *Realising the potential for cultural services: The case for sport*, London: Local Government Association.

Collins, M. with Kay, T. (2003) *Sport and social exclusion*, London: Routledge.

Collins, T. (1998) *Rugby's great split: Class, culture and the origins of Rugby League Football*, London: Frank Cass.

Connerton, P. (1989) *How societies remember*, Cambridge: Cambridge University Press.

Cooke, G. (1996) 'A strategic approach to performance and excellence', *Supercoach: National Coaching Foundation*, 8: 10.

Côté, J., Salmela, J. and Russell, S. (1995) 'The knowledge of high-performance gymnastic coaches: Competition and training considerations', *The Sport Psychologist*, 9: 76–95.

Cronin, M. (1999) *Sport and nationalism in Ireland: Gaelic games, soccer and Irish identity since 1884*, Dublin: Four Courts Press.

Cury, F., Biddle, S. H., Sarrazin, P. and Famose, J. P. (1997) 'Achievement goals and perceived ability predict investment in learning in a sport task', *British Journal of Educational Psychology*, 67: 293–309.

Cushion, C., and Jones, R.L. (2006) 'Power, discourse and symbolic violence in professional youth soccer: The case of Albion F.C.', *Sociology of Sport Journal*, 23(2): 142–161.

Daniels, F.S. and Landers, D.M. (1981) 'Biofeedback and shooting performance: A test of disregulation and systems theory', *Journal of Sport Psychology*, 3: 271–282.

Dawson, B., Fitzsimons, M., Green, S., Goodman, C., Carey, M. and Cole, K. (1998) 'Changes in performance, muscle metabolites, enzymes and fibre types after short sprint training', *European Journal of Applied Physiology*, 78: 163–169.

DCMS (2000) *A sporting future for all*, London: Department of Culture, Media and Sport.

DCMS (2001) *A sporting future for all: The Government's plan for sport*, London: Department of Culture, Media and Sport.

DCMS and Strategy Unit (2002) *Game plan: A strategy for delivering the Government's sport and physical activity objectives*, London: Department of Culture, Media and Sport.

Deci, E., Koestener, R. and Ryan, R. (1999) 'A meta-analytic review of experiments examining the effects of extrinsic rewards on intrinsic motivation', *Psychological Bulletin*, 125: 627–668.

Deci, E. L., and Ryan, R. M. (1985) *Intrinsic motivation and self-determination in human behavior*, New York: Plenum Press.

Deci, E. L., and Ryan, R. M. (2000) 'The "what" and "why" of goal pursuits: Human needs and the self-determination of behavior', *Psychological Inquiry*, 11: 227–268.

Del Rey, P., Whitehurst, M., Wughalter, E. and Barnwell, J. (1983) 'Contextual interference and experience in acquisition and transfer', *Perceptual and Motor Skills*, 57(1): 241–242.

DES/WO (1991) *NCPE working group interim report*, London: Department of Education and Science.

DeSensi, J.T. and Rosenberg, D. (eds) (2003) *Ethics and morality in sport management* (2nd edn), Morgantown, WV: Fitness Information Technology.

Deutsch, M.U., Kearney, G.A. and Rehrer, N.J. (in press) 'Time-motion analysis of professional rugby union players during match play', *Journal of Sports Sciences*.

Dirix, A., Knuttgen, H.G. and Tittel, K. (eds) (1988) *The Olympic book of sports medicine*, Oxford: Blackwell Publishing.

Dishman, R. K. (1983) 'Identity crises in North American sport psychology: Academics in professional issues', *Journal of Sport Psychology*, 5: 123–134.

Drewe, S.B. (2000) 'Coaches, ethics and autonomy', *Sport, education and society*, 5(2): 147–162.

Duda, J. L. (2001) 'Achievement goal research in sport: Pushing the boundaries and clarifying some misunderstandings', in G. C. Roberts (ed.), *Advances in motivation in sport and exercise*, Champaign, IL: Human Kinetics.

Duda, J. L., Fox, K., Biddle, S. and Armstrong, N. (1992) 'Children's achievement goals and beliefs about success in sport', *British Journal of Educational Psychology*, 62: 309–319.

Dudley, G.A., Abraham, W.M. and Terjung, R.L. (1982) 'Influence of exercise intensity and duration on biochemical adaptations in skeletal muscle', *Journal of Applied Physiology, Respiratory and Environmental Exercise Physiology*, 53: 844–850.

Duffy, P. (2006) *Sports Coach UK annual report 2005–06*, Leeds: Sports Coach UK.

Dweck, C. S. and Leggett, E. L. (1988) 'A social-cognitive approach to motivation and personality', *Psychological Review*, 95: 256–273.

Eady, J. (1993) *Practical sports development*, London: Hodder and Stoughton.

Ebbeck, V. and Becker, S.L. (1994) 'Psychosocial predictors of goal orientations in Youth soccer', *Research Quarterly for Exercise and Sport*, 65: 355–362.

Epstein, J. (1989) 'Family structures and student motivation: A developmental perspective', in C. Ames and R. Ames (eds), *Research on motivation in education*, New York: Academic Press.

Fasting, K. (2001) 'Foreword', in C. Brackenridge (ed.), *Spoilsports: Understanding and preventing sexual exploitation in sport*, London: Routledge.

Feltz, D.L. (1988) 'Gender differences in causal elements of self-efficacy on a high avoidance motor task', *Journal of Sport and Exercise Psychology*, 10: 151–166.

Feltz, D.L. and Kontos, A.P. (2002) 'The nature of sport psychology', in T. Horn (ed.), *Advances in sport psychology* (2nd edn), Champaign, IL: Human Kinetics.

Filby, W.C.D., Maynard, I.W. and Graydon, J.K. (1999) 'The effect of multiple-goal strategies on performance outcomes in training and competition', *Journal of Applied Sport Psychology*, 11: 230–246.

Fitts, P.M. (1964) 'Perceptual-motor skill learning', in A.W. Melton (ed.), *Categories of human learning*, New York: Academic Press.

Fitts, P.M. and Posner, M.I. (1967) *Human performance*, Belmont, CA: Brooks/Cole.

Fleming, S. (1995) 'Home and away: Sport and South Asian male youth', Aldershot: Avebury.

Fletcher, D. and Hanton, S. (2001) 'The relationship between psychological skills usage and competitive anxiety responses', *Psychology of Sport and Exercise*, 2: 89–101.

Fletcher, D., and Hanton, S. (2003) 'Sources of organizational stress in elite sports performers', *The Sport Psychologist*, 17: 175–195.

Fletcher, D., Hanton, S. and Mellalieu, S.D. (2006) 'An organizational stress review: Conceptual and theoretical issues in competitive sport', in S. Hanton and S.D. Mellalieu (eds), *Literature reviews in sport psychology*, Hauppauge, NY: Nova Science.

Fox, K., Goudas, M., Biddle, S., Duda, J.L. and Armstrong, N. (1994) 'Children's task and ego profiles in sport', *British Journal of Educational Psychology*, 64: 253–261.

Franks, I.M. and Goodman, D. (1984) 'A hierarchical approach to performance analysis', *SPORTS*, June.

Franks, I.M., Goodman, D. and Miller, G. (1983) 'Analysis of performance: Qualitative or quantitative', *SPORTS*, March.

Franks, I.M. and Miller, G. (1986) 'Eyewitness testimony in sport', *Journal of Sport Behavior*, 9: 39–45.

Franks, I.M. and Miller, G. (1991) 'Training coaches to observe and remember', *Journal of Sports Sciences*, 9: 285–297.

Gallagher, J.D. and Thomas, J.R. (1980) 'Effects of varying post-KR intervals upon children's motor-performance', *Journal of Motor Behavior*, 12(1): 41–46.

Gardner, H. (1993) *Multiple intelligences*, New York: Basic Books.

Gentile, A.M. (1972) 'A working model of skill acquisition with application to teaching', *Quest (Monograph XVII)*: 3–23.

Gentile, A.M. (2000) 'Skill acquisition: Action, movement and neuromotor processes', in J.H. Carr and R.B. Shepherd (eds), *Movement science: Foundations for physical therapy* (2nd edn), Rockville, MD: Aspen.

Giddens, A. (1997) *The third way*, Cambridge: Polity Press.

Gilbert, W. and Trudel, P. (2001) 'Learning to coach through experience: Reflection in model youth sport coaches', *Journal of Teaching in Physical Education*, 21: 16–34.

Gittoes, M.R.J., Brewin, M.A. and Kerwin, D.G. (2006) 'Soft tissue contributions to impact forces using a four-segment wobbling mass model of forefoot-heel landings', *Human Movement Science*, 25(6): 775–787.

Giulianotti, R. (ed.) (2004) *Sport and modern social theorists*, Basingstoke: Palgrave Macmillan.

Glaister, M. (2005) 'Multiple sprint work: Physiological responses, mechanisms of fatigue and the influence of aerobic fitness', *Sports Medicine*, 35: 757–777.

Gleim, G.W. and McHugh, M. (1997) 'Flexibility and its effects on sports injury and performance', *Sports Medicine*, 24: 289–299.

Glynn, J., King, M. and Mitchell, S. (2006) 'Determining subject-specific parameter for a computer simulation model of a one handed tennis backhand', in H. Schwamsder, G. Strytzenberger, V. Fastenbauer, S. Lindinger and E. Muller (eds), *Proceedings of XXIV International Symposium on Biomechanics in Sports*, Salzburg.

Gould, D., Giannina, J., Krane, V. and Hodge, K. (1990) 'Educational needs of elite U.S. National team, Pan America and Olympic coaches', *Journal of Teaching in Physical Education*, 9: 332–344.

Gould, D., Udry, E., Tuffey, S. and Loehr, J. (1996) 'Burnout in competitive junior tennis players: I. A quantitative psychological assessment', *The Sport Psychologist*, 10: 322–340.

Griffin, J. and Harris, M.B. (1996) 'Coaches' attitudes, knowledge, experiences and recommendations regarding weight control', *The Sport Psychologist*, 10: 180–194.

Guadagnoli, M.A., Holcomb, W.R. and Weber, T.J. (1999) 'The relationship between contextual interference effects and performer expertise on the learning of a putting task', *Journal of Human Movement Studies*, 37(1): 19–36.

Hall, K.G., Domingues, D.A. and Cavazos, R. (1994) 'Contextual interference effects with skilled baseball players', *Perceptual and Motor Skills*, 78(3): 835–841.

Hamill, J., Haddad, J.M. and McDermott, W.J. (2000) 'Issues in quantifying variability from a dynamical systems perspective', *Journal of Applied Biomechanics*, 16: 407–418.

Hamill, J. and Knutzen, K.M. (2003) *Biomechanical basis of human movement*, London: Wilson and Wilson.

Hanton, S., and Jones, G. (1997) 'Antecedents of intensity and direction dimensions of competitive anxiety as a function of skill', *Psychological Reports*, 81: 1139–1147.

Hanton, S. and Jones, G. (1999a) 'The acquisition and development of cognitive skills and strategies: I. Making the butterflies fly in formation', *The Sport Psychologist*, 13: 1–21.

Hanton, S. and Jones, G. (1999b) 'The effects of a multimodal intervention program on performers: II. Training the butterflies to fly in formation', *The Sport Psychologist*, 13: 22–41.

Hanton, S., Thomas, O. and Maynard, I. (2004) 'Competitive anxiety responses in the week leading up to competition: The role of intensity, direction and frequency dimensions', *Psychology of Sport and Exercise*, 5: 169–181.

Hardy, L. (1990) 'A catastrophe model of anxiety and performance', in G. Jones and L. Hardy (eds), *Stress and performance in sport*, Chichester: John Wiley and Sons.

Hardy, L. (1997) 'The Coleman Roberts Griffith address: Three myths about applied consultancy work', *Journal of Applied Sport Psychology*, 9: 277–294.

Hardy, L., Jones, G. and Gould, D. (1996) *Understanding psychological reparation for sport: Theory and practice of elite performers*, Chichester: John Wiley and Sons.

Hardy, L., Mullen, R. and Jones, G. (1996) 'Knowledge and conscious control of motor actions under stress', *British Journal of Psychology*, 87: 621–636.

Hardy, L. and Parfitt, C.G. (1991) 'A catastrophe model of anxiety and performance', *British Journal of Psychology*, 82: 163–178.

Hargreaves, J. (1986) *Sport, power and culture*, Cambridge: Polity Press.

Hargreaves, J. (1994) *Sporting females: Critical issues in the history and sociology of women's sports*, London: Routledge.

Harter, S. (1978) 'Effectance motivation reconsidered: Toward a developmental model', *Human Development*, 1: 661–669.

Harvey, A. (2005) *Football: The first 100 years*, London: Routledge.

Hay, J.G. (1994) *The biomechanics of sports techniques*, Englewood Cliffs, NJ: Prentice Hall.

Hebert, E.P. and Landin, D. (1994) 'Effects of a learning-model and augmented feedback on tennis skill acquisition', *Research Quarterly for Exercise and Sport*, 65(3): 250–257.

Hebert, E.P., Landin, D. and Solmon, M.A. (1996) 'Practice schedule effects on the performance and learning of low- and high-skilled students: An applied study', *Research Quarterly for Exercise and Sport*, 67(1): 52–58.

Henry, G. (1999) *The X factor*, Auckland: Celebrity Books

Henry, I. (2001) (2nd edn) *The politics of leisure policy*, Basingstoke: Palgrave.

Hiley, M.J. and Yeadon, M.R. (2005) 'The margin for error when releasing the asymmetric bars for dismounts', *Journal of Applied Biomechanics*, 21: 223–235.

Hobsbawm, E. (1983a) 'Introduction: Invented traditions', in E. Hobsbawm and T. Ranger (eds), *The invention of tradition*, Cambridge: Cambridge University Press.

Hobsbawm, E. (1983b) 'Mass-producing traditions: Europe, 1870–1914', in Hobsbawm, E. and Ranger, T. (eds), *The invention of tradition*, Cambridge: Cambridge University Press.

Hobsbawm, E. (1992) *Nations and nationalism since 1790: Programme, myth, reality*, Cambridge: Cambridge University Press.

Hodge, K. and Petlichkoff, L. (2000) 'Goal profiles in sport motivation: A cluster analysis', *Journal of Sport and Exercise Psychology*, 22: 479–501.

Hollembeak, J. and Amorose, A. J. (2005) 'Perceived coaching behaviours and college athletes' intrinsic motivation: A test of self-determination theory', *Journal of Applied Sport Psychology*, 17: 20–36.

Hollmann, W. (1988) 'The definition and scope of sports medicine', in A. Dirix, H.G. Knuttgen and K. Tittel (eds), *The Olympic book of sports medicine*, Oxford: Blackwell Publishing.

Holt, R. (1992) *Sport and the British: A modern history*, Oxford: Clarendon Press.

Horne, J., Tomlinson, A. and Whannel, G. (1999) *Understanding sport: An introduction to the sociological and cultural analysis of sport*, London: E. and F.N. Spon.

Houlihan, B. and White, A. (2002) *The politics of sports development: Development of sport or development through sport*, London: Routledge.

Hubbard, M. and Alaways, L. W. (1987) 'Optimum release conditions for the new rules javelin', *International Journal of Sport Biomechanics*, 3: 207–221.

Hughes, M. (1973) *Tactics and teamwork*, Wakefield: E.P. Publishing.

Hughes, M. (1986) 'A review of patterns of play in squash at different competitive levels', in J. Watkins, T. Reilly and L. Burwitz (eds), *Sport science*, London: E. and F.N. Spon.

Hughes, M., Evans, S. and Wells, J. (2001) 'Establishing normative profiles in performance analysis', *International Journal of Performance Analysis in Sport*, 1: 4–27.

Hughes, M. and Franks, I.M. (1997) *Notational analysis of sport*, London: E. and F.N. Spon.

Hughes, M. and Franks, I.M. (2004) *Notational analysis of sport: A perspective on improving coaching* (2nd edn), London: E. and F.N. Spon.

Hughes, M. and Robertson, C. (1998) 'Using computerized notational analysis to create a template for elite squash and its subsequent use in designing hand notation systems for player development', in T. Reilly, M. Hughes, A. Lees and I. Maynard (eds), *Science and racket sports II*, London: E. and F.N. Spon.

Hughes, M., Wells, J. and Matthews, K. (2000) 'Performance profiles at recreational, county and elite levels of women's squash', *Journal of Human Movement Studies*, 39: 85–104.

Hughes, M.D. (2004) 'Performance analysis – a mathematical perspective', *EIJPAS, International Journal of Performance Analysis Sport (Electronic)*, 4(2), 97–139.

Hughes, M.D. (2005) 'Notational analysis', in R. Bartlett, C. Gratton and C.G. Rolf (eds), *Encyclopedia of international sports studies*, London: Routledge.

Hylton, K. and Totten, M. (2001) 'Community sports development', in K. Hylton, P. Bramham, D. Jackson and M. Nesti (eds), *Sports development: Policy, process and practice*, London: Routledge.

Intiso, D., Santilli, V., Grasso, M.G., Rossi, R. and Caruso, I. (1994) 'Rehabilitation of walking with electromyographic biofeedback in foot-drop after stroke', *Stroke*, 25(6): 1189–1192.

Irwin, G., Hanton, S. and Kerwin, D.G. (2004) 'Reflective practice and the origins of elite coaching knowledge', *Reflective Practice*, 5(3): 425–442.

Irwin, G., Hanton, S. and Kerwin, D.G. (2005) 'The conceptual process of progression development in artistic gymnastics', *Journal of Sports Sciences*, 23(10): 1089–1099.

Irwin, G. and Kerwin, D. (2001) 'Use of 2D-DLT for the analysis of longswings on high bar', in J. Blackwell (ed.), *Proceedings of oral presentations: XIX international symposium on biomechanics in sports*, San Francisco, CA.

Irwin, G., and Kerwin, D.G. (2005) 'Biomechanical similarities of progressions for the longswing on high bar', *Sports Biomechanics*, 4(2): 164–178.

Irwin, G. and Kerwin, D.G. (2006) 'Musculosketal work in the longswing on high bar', in E. F. Moritz and S. Haake (eds), *The engineering of sport 6, Volume 1: Developments for sports*, New York: Springer.

Irwin, G. and Kerwin, D.G. (in press a) 'Musculoskeletal work of high bar progressions', *Sports Biomechanics*.

Irwin, G. and Kerwin, D.G. (in press b) 'Inter-segmental co-ordination of high bar progressions', *Sports Biomechanics*.

Jackson, R.C., Ashford, K.J. and Norsworthy, G. (2006) 'Attentional focus, dispositional reinvestment and skilled motor performance under pressure', *Journal of Sport and Exercise Psychology*, 28: 49–68.

James, N., Mellalieu, S.D. and Jones, N.M.P. (2005) 'The development of position-specific performance indicators in professional rugby union', *Journal of Sports Sciences*, 23: 63–72.

Janelle, C.M., Kim, J.G. and Singer, R.N. (1995) 'Subject-controlled performance feedback and learning of a closed motor skill', *Perceptual and Motor Skills*, 81(2): 627–634.

Jarvie, G. (1990a) 'Towards an applied sociology of sport', *Scottish Journal of Physical Education*, 18: 11–12.

Jarvie, G. (1990b) 'The sociological imagination', in Kew, F. (ed.), *Social perspectives on sport*, Leeds: British Association of Sports Sciences and National Coaching Foundation.

Jarvie, G. (ed.) (1991) *Sport, racism and ethnicity*, London: Falmer Press.

Jarvie, G. (2006) *Sport, culture and society: An introduction*, London: Routledge.

Jarvie, G. and Maguire, J. (1994) *Sport and leisure in social thought*, London: Routledge.

Jones, G. (1991) 'Recent issues in competitive state anxiety research', *The Psychologist*, 4: 152–155.

Jones, G. (1995) 'More than just a game: Research developments and issues in competitive anxiety in sport', *British Journal of Psychology*, 86: 449–478.

Jones, G. and Swain, A.B.J. (1992) 'Intensity and direction dimensions of competitive state anxiety and relationships with competitiveness', *Perceptual and Motor Skills*, 74: 467–472.

Jones, R.L. (2000) 'Toward a sociology of coaching', in R.L. Jones and K.M. Armour (eds), *The sociology of sport: Theory and practice*, London: Addison Wesley Longman.

Jones, R.L. (2006) 'How can educational concepts inform sports coaching?', in R.L. Jones (ed.), *The sports coach as educator: Reconceptualising sports coaching*, London: Routledge.

Jones, R.L., Armour, K.M. and Potrac, P. (2002) 'Understanding the coaching process: A framework for social analysis', *Quest*, 54(1): 34–48.

Jones, R.L., Armour, K.M. and Potrac, P. (2003) 'Constructing expert knowledge: A case study of a top-level professional soccer coach', *Sport, Education and Society*, 8(2): 213–229.

Jones, R.L., Armour, K.M. and Potrac, P. (2004) *Sports coaching cultures: From practice to theory*, London: Routledge.

Jones, R.L., Glintmeyer, N. and McKenzie, A. (2005) 'Slim bodies, eating disorders and the coach–athlete relationship: A tale of identity creation and disruption', *International Review for the Sociology of Sport*, 40(3): 377–391.

Jones, R.L., Potrac, P., Cushion, C. and Ronglan, L.T. (2007) 'Making an impression, hiding a defect: How Erving Goffman can help sports coaches', manuscript submitted for publication.

Jones, R.L., and Standage, M. (2006) 'First among equals: Shared leadership in the coaching context', in R.L. Jones (ed.), *The sports coach as educator: Reconceptualising sports coaching*, London: Routledge.

Jones, R.L. and Wallace, M. (2005) 'Another bad day at the training ground: Coping with ambiguity in the coaching context', *Sport, Education and Society*, 10(1): 119–134.

Kavussanu, M. and Roberts, G.C. (1996) 'Motivation in physical activity contexts: The relationship of perceived motivational climate to intrinsic motivation and self-efficacy', *Journal of Sport and Exercise Psychology*, 18: 264–280.

Kay, W. (2003) 'Lesson planning with the NCPE 2000 – The revised unit of work', *Bulletin of PE*, 39(1): 31–42.

Kernodle, M.W. and Carlton, L.G. (1992) 'Information feedback and the learning of multiple-degree-of-freedom activities', *Journal of Motor Behavior*, 24(2): 187–196.

Kerwin, D.G., Yeadon, M.R. and Sung-Cheol, L. (1990) 'Body configuration in multiple somersault high bar dismounts', *International Journal of Sport Biomechanics*, 6: 147–156.

Kibler, W.B. (1991) 'Functional biomechanical deficits in runners', *American Journal of Sports Medicine*, 19: 66–71.

Kidman, L. (2001) *Developing decision makers: An empowerment approach to coaching*. Christchurch, NZ: Innovative Print Communications.

King, C. (2004) *Offside racism: Playing the white man*, London: Berg.

King, J. (2002) *Budweisers into Czechs and Germans: A local history of Bohemian politics, 1848–1948*, Princeton: Princeton University Press.

Kingston, K.M. and Hardy, L. (1997) 'Effects of different types of goals on processes that support performance', *The Sport Psychologist*, 11: 277–293.

Kingston, K. M., Harwood, C.G. and Spray, C. M. (2006) 'Contemporary approaches to motivation in sport', in S. Hanton and S.D. Mellalieu (eds), *Literature reviews in sport psychology*, Hauppauge, NY: Nova Science.

Knuttila, M. (1996) *Introducing sociology: A critical perspective*, Oxford: Oxford University Press.

Komi, P.V., Linnamo, P., Silventoinen, M. and Sillanpaa, M. (2000) 'Force and EMG power spectrum during eccentric and concentric actions', *Medicine and Science in Sports and Exercise*, 32(10): 1757–1762.

Kowal, J. and Fortier, M.S. (2000) 'Testing relationships from the hierarchical model of intrinsic and extrinsic motivation using flow as a motivational consequence', *Research Quarterly for Exercise and Sport*, 71: 171–181.

Kraemer, W.J., Marchitelli, L., Gordon S.E., Harman, E., Dziados, J.E., Mello, R., Frykman, P., McCurry, D. and Fleck, S.J. (1990) 'Hormonal and growth factor responses to heavy resistance exercise protocols', *Journal of Applied Physiology*, 69: 1442–50.

Kraemer, W.J., Patton, J.F., Gordon, S.E., Harman, E.A., Deschenes, M.R., Reynolds, K., Newton, R.U., Triplett, N.T. and Dziados, J.E. (1995) 'Compatibility of high-intensity strength and endurance training on hormonal and skeletal muscle adaptations', *Journal of Applied Physiology*, 78: 976–989.

Kretchmar, R.S. (1994) *Practical philosophy of sport*, Leeds: Human Kinetics.

Lee, M. (1988) 'Values and responsibilities in children's sport', *Physical Education Review*, 11: 19–27.

Lee, T.D. and Magill, R.A. (1983) 'The locus of contextual interference in motor-skill acquisition', *Journal of Experimental Psychology: Learning Memory and Cognition*, 9(4): 730–746.

Lee, T.D. and Magill, R.A. (1985) 'Can forgetting facilitate skill acquisition?', in D. Goodman, R.B. Wilberg and I.M. Franks (eds), *Differing perspectives in motor learning, memory, and control*, Amsterdam: Elsevier.

Lees, A., Vanrenterghem, J. and Dirk, D.C. (2004) 'Understanding how an arm swing enhances performance in the vertical jump', *Journal of Biomechanics*, 37(12): 1929–1940.

Lemert, C. (1997) *Social things: An introduction to the sociological life*, New York: Rowan and Littlefield.

Liao, C. and Masters, R.S.W. (2002) 'Self-focused attention and performance failure under psychological stress', *Journal of Sport and Exercise Psychology*, 24: 289–305.

Lirgg, C.D., and Feltz, D.L. (1991) 'Teacher versus peer models revisited: Effects on motor performance', *Research Quarterly for Exercise and Sport*, 62: 217–224.

Long, J., Carrington, B. and Spracklen, K. (1997) 'Asians cannot wear turbans in the scrum: Explorations of racist discourse within professional rugby league', *Leisure Studies*, 16 (4): 249–259.

Lyle, J. (2002) *Sports coaching concepts*, London: Routledge.

Lyons, K. (1988) *Using video in sport*, Huddersfield: Springfield Books.

McDonald, I. (1995) 'Sport for all – RIP?', in S. Fleming, M. Talbot and A. Tomlinson (eds), *Physical education policy and politics in sport and leisure* (LSA publication no. 55), Eastbourne: Leisure Studies Association.

MacIntyre, A.C. (1984) *After virtue*, London: Duckworth.

Macionis, J. (2007) *Sociology* (11th edn), Upper Saddle River, NJ: Pearson Edu International.

McNamee, M.J. (1995) 'Sporting practices, institutions and virtues: a critiqu restatement', *Journal of Philosophy of Sport*, 22: 61–82.

McNamee, M.J. (1997) 'Values in sport', in D. Levinson and K. Christenson (eds), *Encyclopedia of world sport*, Oxford: ABC-Clio Inc.

McNamee, M.J. and Parry, S.J. (1990) 'Notes on the concept of "health"', in J. Long (ed.), *Leisure, health and well-being*, Brighton: LSA Publications.

McNevin, N.H., Shea, C.H. and Wulf, G. (2003) 'Increasing the distance of external focus of attention enhances learning', *Psychological Research*, 67: 22–29.

Magill, R.A. (2004) *Motor learning and performance: Concepts and applications* (7th edn), Boston, MA: McGraw-Hill.

Magill, R.A. and Hall, K.G. (1990) 'A review of the contextual interference effect in motor skill acquisition', *Human Movement Science*, 9: 241–289.

Magill, R.A. and Schoenfelder-Zohdi, B. (1996) 'A visual model and knowledge of performance as sources of information for learning a rhythmic gymnastics skill', *International Journal of Sport Psychology*, 27(1): 7–22.

Malberg, E. (1978) 'Science innovation and gymnastics in the USSR', *International Gymnast*, 20: 63.

Marsh, I., Keating, M., Eyre, A., Campbell, R. and McKenzie, J. (1996) *Making sense of society: An introduction to sociology*, London: Longman.

Martens, R. (2004) *Successful coaching*, Champaign, IL: Human Kinetics.

Martens, R., Burton, D., Vealey, R.S., Bump, L.A. and Smith, D.E. (1990) 'Development and validation of the Competitive State Anxiety Inventory-2 (CSAI-2)', in R. Martens, R.S. Vealey and D. Burton (eds), *Competitive anxiety in sport*, Champaign, IL: Human Kinetics.

Masters, R.S.W. (1992) 'Knowledge, knerves and know-how: The role of explicit versus implicit knowledge in the breakdown of a complex motor skill under pressure', *British Journal of Psychology*, 83: 343–358.

Masters, R.S.W. (2000) 'Theoretical aspects of implicit learning in sport', *International Journal of Sport Psychology*, 31: 530–541.

Mawer, M. (1995) *The effective teaching of physical education*, Harlow: Longman.

Maynard, I.W. and Cotton, P.C.J. (1993) 'An investigation of two stress management techniques in a field setting', *The Sport Psychologist*, 6: 357–387.

Mazur, J. (1990) *Learning and behaviour* (2nd edn), Englewood Cliffs, NJ: Prentice-Hall.

Mellalieu, S.D., Hanton, S. and Fletcher, D. (2006) 'A competitive anxiety review: Recent directions in sport psychology research', in S. Hanton and S.D. Mellalieu (eds), *Literature reviews in sport psychology*, Hauppauge, NY: Nova Science.

Merkel, U. and Tokarski, W. (1996) (eds) *Racism and xenophobia in European football*, Aachen: Meyer and Meyer Verlag.

Metzler, M. (2000) *Instructional models for physical education*, Boston, MA: Allyn and Bacon.

Mills, C. Wright (1959) *The sociological imagination*, New York: Oxford University Press.

Mitchell, M. and Kernodle, M. (2004) 'Using multiple intelligences to teach tennis', *Journal of Physical Education, Recreation and Dance*, 75(8): 27–32.

Moore, W.E. and Stevenson, J.R. (1994) 'Training for trust in sport skills', *The Sport Psychologist*, 8: 1–12.

Morgan, K. and Carpenter, P.J. (2002) 'Effects of manipulating the motivational climate in physical education lessons', *European Journal of Physical Education*, 8: 209–232.

Morgan, K. and Kingston, K. (in press) 'Development of a self-observation mastery intervention programme for teacher education', *Physical Education and Sport Pedagogy*.

Morgan, K., Sproule, J., Weigand, D. and Carpenter, P. (2005a) 'Development of a computer-based measure of teacher behaviours related to motivational climate in Physical Education', *Physical Education and Sport Pedagogy Journal*, 10: 113–135.

Morgan, K., Sproule, J. and Kingston, K. (2005b) 'Teaching styles, motivational climate and pupils' cognitive and affective responses in Physical Education', *European Physical Education Review*, 11(3): 257–286.

Morgan, L. and Fleming, S. (2003) 'The development of coaching in Welsh Rugby Union Football', *Football Studies*, 6(2): 39–51.

Morris, L., Davis, D. and Hutchings, C. (1981) 'Cognitive and emotional components of anxiety: Literature review and revised worry-emotionality scale', *Journal of Educational Psychology*, 75: 541–555.

Morris, M. (1998) *Too soon too late: History in popular culture*, Bloomington, IN: Indiana University Press.

Mosston, M. (1966) *Teaching physical education*, Columbus, OH: Merrill Publishing Co.

Mosston, M. and Ashworth, S. (2002) *Teaching physical education* (5th edn), Columbus, OH: Merrill Publishing Co.

Mullen, R. and Hardy, L. (2000) 'State anxiety and motor performance: Testing the conscious processing hypothesis', *Journal of Sport Science*, 18: 785–799.

Murray, S. and Hughes, M. (2001) 'Tactical performance profiling in elite level senior squash', in M. Hughes and I.M. Franks (eds), *pass.com*, Cardiff: CPA, UWIC.

Murray, S. and Hughes, M. T. (2006) *The working performance analyst*. Paper presented at the First International Workshop of Performance Analysis, International Society of Performance Analysis of Sport (ISPAS), Cardiff, January.

Nesti, M. (2001) 'Working in sports development', in K. Hylton, P. Bramham, D. Jackson and M. Nesti (eds), *Sports development: Policy, process and practice*, London: Routledge.

Newell, K. M. and Walter, C. B. (1981) 'Kinematic and kinetic parameters as information feedback in motor skill acquisition', *Journal of Human Movement Studies*, 7(4): 235–254.

Nicholls, J.G. (1989) *The competitive ethos and democratic education*, Cambridge, MA: Harvard University Press.

Nissinen, M.A., Preiss, R., and Brüggemann, P. (1985) 'Simulation of human airborne movements on the horizontal bar', in D.A. Winter and R. Norman (eds), *Biomechanics IX-B*, Champaign, IL: Human Kinetics.

Nolte, C. (2002) *The Sokol in the Czech lands to 1914: Training for the nation*, Basingstoke: Palgrave Macmillan.

Ntoumanis, N. and Biddle, S.J.H. (1998) 'The relationship between competitive anxiety, achievement goals and motivational climate', *Research Quarterly for Exercise and Sport*, 69: 176–187.

O'Donoghue, P. (2005) 'Normative profiles of sports performance', *International Journal of Performance Analysis in Sport*, 4(1): 67–76.

Ommundsen, Y., Roberts, G.C. and Kavussanu, M. (1998) 'Perceived motivational climate and cognitive and affective correlates among Norwegian athletes', *Journal of Sport Sciences*, 16: 153–164.

Ost, L.G. (1988) 'Applied relaxation: Description of an effective coping technique', *Scandinavian Journal of Behaviour Therapy*, 17: 83–96.

Papaioannou, A. (1997) 'Perceptions of the motivational climate, beliefs about the causes of success, and sportsmanship behaviours of elite Greek basketball players', in R. Lidor and M. Bar-Eli (eds), *Innovations in sport psychology: Linking theory and practice. Proceedings of the IX World Congress in Sport Psychology: Part II*, Netanya, Israel: Ministry of Education, Culture and Sport.

Partridge, D. and Franks, I.M. (1993) 'Computer-aided analysis of sport performance: An example from soccer', *The Physical Educator*, 50: 208–215.

Patel, D.R., Greydanus, D.E., Pratt, H.D. and Phillips, E.L. (2003) 'Eating disorders in adolescent athletes', *Journal of Adolescent Research*, 18: 280–296.

Pelletier, R.L., Montelpare, W.J. and Stark, R.M. (1993) 'Intercollegiate ice hockey injuries: A case for uniform definitions and reports', *American Journal of Sports Medicine*, 21: 78–81.

Perez, C. R., Meira, C. M. and Tani, G. (2005) 'Does the contextual interference effect last over extended transfer trials?', *Perceptual and Motor Skills*, 100(1): 58–60.

Perkins, D. (1999) 'The many faces of constructivism', *Educational Leadership*, 57(3): 6–11.

Perkins-Ceccato, N., Passmore, S.R. and Lee, T.D. (2003) 'Effects of focus attention depend on golfer's skill', *Journal of Sports Sciences*, 21: 593–600.

Pichert, J., Anderson, R., Armrustro, S., Surber, J. and Shirley, L. (1976) *A report: An evaluation of the spectrum of teaching styles*, Champaign, IL: University of Illinois, Laboratory for Studies in Education.

Pigott, R.E., and Shapiro, D.C. (1984) 'Motor schema: The structure of the variability session', *Research Quarterly for Exercise and Sport*, 55(1): 41–45.

Polley, M. (1998) *Moving the goalposts: A history of sport and society since 1945*, London: Routledge.

Poolton, J.M., Maxwell, J.P., Masters, R.S.W. and Raab, M. (2006) 'Benefits of an external focus of attention: Common coding or conscious processing?', *Journal of Sports Sciences*, 24: 89–99.

Potrac, P. and Jones, R.L. (1999) 'The invisible ingredient in coaching knowledge: A case for recognising and researching the social component', *Sociology of Sport Online*, 2(1) [On line]. http://physed.otago.ac.nz/sosol/home.htm

Potrac, P., Jones, R.L. and Armour, K.M. (2002). '"It's all about getting respect": The coaching behaviours of an expert English soccer coach', *Sport, Education and Society*, 7(2): 183–202.

Potter, G. and Hughes, M. (2001) 'Modelling in competitive sports', in M. Hughes and F. Tavares (eds), *Notational analysis of sport IV*, Cardiff: UWIC.

Powers, C.H. (2004) *Making sense of social theory: A practical introduction*, Lanham, MD: Rowan and Littlefield.

Premack, D. (1965) 'Reinforcement theory', in D. Levine (ed.), *Nebraska symposium on motivation*, Lincoln: University of Nebraska Press.

Pribram, K.H. and McGuinness, D. (1975) 'Arousal, activation and effort in the control of attention', *Psychological Review*, 82: 116–149.

Prinz, W. (1997) 'Perceptions and action planning', *European Journal of Cognitive Psychology*, 9: 129–154.

Purdy, L.G. (2006) 'Coaching in the "current": Capturing the climate in elite rowing training camps', Unpublished PhD dissertation, University of Otago, NZ.

Richardson, L. and Mumford, K. (2002) 'Community, neighbourhood and social infrastructure', in J. Hills, J. Le Grand and D. Piachaud (eds), *Understanding social exclusion*, Oxford: Oxford University Press.

Roberts, G.C. (2001) 'Understanding the dynamics of motivation in physical activity: The influence of achievement goals on motivational processes', in G.C. Roberts (ed.), *Advances in motivation in sport and exercise*, Champaign, IL: Human Kinetics.

Roberts, G.C., Treasure, D.C. and Kavussanu, M. (1996) 'Orthogonality of achievement goals and its relationship to beliefs about success and satisfaction in sport', *Sport Psychologist*, 10: 398–408.

Roberts, K. (2004) *The leisure industries*, Basingstoke: Palgrave Macmillan.

Robertson, G., Caldwell, G., Hamill, J., Kamen, G. and Whittlesey, S. (2004) *Research methods in biomechanics*, Champaign, IL: Human Kinetics.

Robinson, L. (2004) *Managing public sport and leisure services*, London: Routledge.

Rodano, R. and Tavana, R. (1995) 'Three-dimensional analysis of instep kicks in professional soccer players', in T. Reilly, J. Clarys and A. Stibbe (eds), *Science in Football II*, London: E. & F.N. Spon.

Rogers, C.A. (1974) 'Feedback precision and post-feedback interval duration', *Journal of Experimental Psychology*, 102(4): 604–608.

Rothstein, A.L. and Arnold, R.K. (1976) 'Bridging the gap: Application of research on videotape feedback and bowling', *Motor Skills: Theory into Practice*, 1: 36–61.

Ryan, R.M., and Deci, E.L. (2000) 'Self-determination theory and the facilitation of intrinsic motivation, social development, and well-being', *American Psychologist*, 55: 68–78.

Salmoni, A.W., Schmidt, R.A. and Walter, C.B. (1984) 'Knowledge of results and motor learning: A review and critical reappraisal', *Psychological Bulletin*, 95(3): 355–386.

Sanderson, F.H. and Way, K.I.M. (1979) 'The development of objective methods of game analysis in squash rackets', *British Journal of Sports Medicine*, 11(4): 188.

Schmidt, R.A. (1975) 'Schema theory of discrete motor skill learning', *Psychological Review*, 82(4): 225–260.

Schmidt, R.A. (1991) 'Frequent augmented feedback can degrade learning: Evidence and interpretations', in J. Renquin and G.E. Stelmach (eds), *Tutorials in motor neuroscience*, Dordrecht, The Netherlands: Kluwer Academic Publishers.

Schmidt, R.A. and Wrisberg, C.A. (2000) *Motor learning and performance* (2nd edn), Champaign, IL: Human Kinetics.

Schunk, D. (1999) 'Social self interaction and achievement behaviour', *Educational Psychologist*, 26: 207–231.

Scottish Executive (1998) *Sport 21 2003–2007: The national strategy for sport: Shaping Scotland's future*, Edinburgh: Scottish Executive.

Scuderi, G.R. and McCann, P.D. (2005) *Sports medicine: A comprehensive approach*, Philadelphia, PA: Elsevier Mosby Books

Sharpe, T. and Koperwas, J. (1999) *BEST: Behavioral evaluation strategy and taxonomy software*, Thousand Oaks, CA: Sage Publications, Inc.

Shea, C.H. and Kohl, R.M. (1990) 'Specificity and variability of practice', *Research Quarterly for Exercise and Sport*, 61(2): 169–177.

Shea, C.H. and Kohl, R.M. (1991) 'Composition of practice: Influence on the retention of motor-skills', *Research Quarterly for Exercise and Sport*, 62(2): 187–195.

Shea, J.B. and Zimny, S.T. (1983) 'Context effects in memory and learning in movement information', in R.A. Magill (ed.), *Memory and control of action*, Amsterdam: North-Holland.

Shoenfelt, E.L., Snyder, L.A., Maue, A.E., McDowell, C.P. and Woolard, C.D. (2002) 'Comparison of constant and variable practice conditions on free-throw shooting', *Perceptual and Motor Skills*, 94(3): 1113–1123.

Shumway-Cook, A., Anson, D. and Haller, S. (1988) 'Postural sway biofeedback: Its effect on reestablishing stance stability in hemiplegic patients', *Archives of Physical Medicine and Rehabilitation*, 69(6): 395–400.

Siedentop, D. (1991) *Developing teaching skills in physical education* (3rd edn), Mountain View, CA: Mayfield.

Simon, R.L. (1991) *Fair play*, London: Westview Press.

Singer, R.N. (1985) 'Sport performance: A five-step approach', *Journal of Physical Education and Recreation*, 57: 82–84.

Singer, R.N. (1988) 'Strategies and metastrategies in learning and performing self-paced athletic skills', *The Sport Psychologist*, 2: 49–68.

Skills Active (2005) *National occupational standards: NVQ/SQV Level 3 in sports development*, London: Skills Active.

Slavin, R. (2003) *Educational psychology: Theory and practice* (7th edn), Boston, MA: Allyn and Bacon.

Smith, A.D. (1991) *National identity*, London: Penguin.

Smith, C.A. (1994) 'The warm-up procedure to stretch or not to stretch: A brief review', *Journal of Orthopaedic Sports Physiotherapy*, 19: 12–17.

Smolevskij, V. (1969) *Masterstvo gimnastov*, cited in Nissinen *et al.* (1985).

Solmon, M.A. (1996) 'Impact of motivational climate on students' behaviors and perceptions in a physical education setting', *Journal of Educational Psychology*, 88: 731–738.

Spray, C.M. (2002) 'Motivational climate and perceived strategies to sustain pupils' discipline in physical education', *European Physical Education Review*, 18: 5–20.

Spray, C.M., Wang, C.K.J., Biddle, S.J.H. and Chatzisarantis, N.L.D. (2006) 'Understanding motivation in sport: An experimental test of achievement goal and self determination theories', *European Journal of Sport Sciences*, 6: 43–51.

Sports Coach UK (2004) *UK coaching certificate monitoring study: learning from the early stages of implementation: Phase 2 report*, Leeds: Sports Coach UK.

Sports Coach UK (2006) *UK action plan for coaching: Consultation draft*, Leeds: Sports Coach UK.

Standage, M., Duda, J.L., and Ntoumanis, N. (2003) 'Predicting motivational regulations in physical education: The interplay between dispositional goal orientations, motivational climate and perceived competence', *Journal of Sports Sciences*, 21: 631–647.

Steele, M.K. (1996) *Sideline help: A guide for immediate evaluation and care of sports injuries*. Champaign, IL: Human Kinetics.

Stones, R. (1998) 'Tolerance, plurality and creative synthesis in sociological thought', in R. Stones (ed.), *Key sociological thinkers*, Basingstoke: Macmillan.

Suinn, R.M. (1987) 'Behavioural approaches to stress management in sports', in, J.R. May and M.J. Asken (eds), *Psychology of motor behaviour and sport*, Champaign, IL: Human Kinetics.

Suits, B. (1995) 'The elements of sport', in W.P. Morgan and K.V. Meier (eds), *Philosophic inquiry in sport*, Leeds: Human Kinetics.

Swain, A.B.J. and Jones, G. (1993) 'Intensity and frequency dimensions of competitive state anxiety', *Journal of Sport Sciences*, 11: 533–542.

Swinnen, S.P., Schmidt, R.A., Nicholson, D.E. and Shapiro, D.C. (1990) 'Information feedback for skill acquisition: Instantaneous knowledge of results degrades learning', *Journal of Experimental Psychology: Learning, Memory and Cognition*, 16(4): 706–716.

Taylor, M. (2005) *The leaguers: The making of professional football in England, 1900–1939*, Liverpool: Liverpool University Press.

Thomas, O., Maynard, I. and Hanton, S. (2004) 'Temporal aspects of competitive anxiety and self-confidence as a function of anxiety perceptions', *The Sport Psychologist*, 18: 172–187.

Tinning, R., Kirk, D. and Evans, J. (1993) *Learning to teach physical education*, London: Prentice-Hall.

Torkildsen, G. (2005) *Leisure and recreation management*, (5th edn) London: Routledge.

Treasure, D. (1993) 'A social-cognitive approach to understanding children's achievement behavior, cognitions, and affect in competitive sport', unpublished doctoral dissertation, University of Illinois, Urbana-Champaign.

Tumilty, D. (2000) 'Protocols for the physiological assessment of male and female soccer players', in C.J. Gore (ed.), *Physiological tests for elite athletes: Australian Sports Commission*, Champaign, IL: Human Kinetics.

Vallerand, R.J. (1997) 'Toward a hierarchical model of intrinsic and extrinsic motivation', in M.P. Zanna (ed.), *Advances in experimental sport psychology*, San Diego, CA: Academic Press.

Vallerand, R.J., and Losier, G.F. (1999) 'An integrative analysis of intrinsic and extrinsic motivation in sport', *Journal of Applied Sport Psychology*, 11: 142–169.

van Emmerik, R.E.A. and van Wegen, E.E.H. (2000) 'On variability and stability in human movement', *Journal of Applied Biomechanics*, 16: 394–406.

Van Mechelen, W., Hlobil, H. and Kemper, H.C. (1992) 'Incidence, severity, aetiology and prevention of sports injuries: A review of concepts', *Sports Medicine*, 14: 82–99.

Vealey, R. S. (1986) 'Conceptualization of sport-confidence and competitive orientation: Preliminary investigation and instrument development', *Journal of Sport Psychology*, 8: 221–246.

Vealey, R. S. (2001) 'Understanding and enhancing self-confidence in athletes', in R.N. Singer, H.A. Hausenblas, and C.M. Janelle (eds), *Handbook of sport psychology*, New York: John Wiley and Sons Inc.

Vealey, R.S., Hayashi, S.W., Garner-Holman, M. and Giacobbi, P. (1998) 'Sources of sport-confidence: Conceptualization and instrument development', *Journal of Sport and Exercise Psychology*, 21: 54–80.

Vlachopoulos, S.P. and Biddle, S.J.H. (1997) 'Modelling the relation of goal orientations to achievement-related affect in physical education: Does perceived ability matter?' *Journal of Sport and Exercise Psychology*, 19: 169–187.

Vygotsky, L. (1978) *Mind and Society*, Cambridge, MA: MIT Press.

Walker, J.E. and Shea, T.M. (1999) *Behavior management: A practical approach for educators* (7th edn), Upper Saddle River, NJ: Merrill.

Walling, M.D., Duda, J.L. and Chi, L. (1993) 'The perceived motivational climate in sport questionnaire: Construct and predictive validity', *Journal of Sport and Exercise Psychology*, 15: 172–183.

Watkins, C. and Mortimer, P. (1999) 'Pedagogy: what do we know', in P. Mortimer (ed.), *Understanding pedagogy and its impact on learning*, London: Paul Chapman.

Watkins, J. (in press) *An introduction to the biomechanics of sport and exercise*, Edinburgh: Elsevier.

Weinberg, R. and Gould, D. (2003) *Foundations of sport and exercise psychology* (3rd edn), Champaign, IL: Human Kinetics.

Welsh Assembly Government (2005) *Climbing higher: The Welsh Assembly Government, strategy for sport and physical activity*, Cardiff: Welsh Assembly Government.

Whannel, G. (1992) *Fields in vision: Television sport and cultural transformation*, London: Routledge.

White, A. and Bailey, J. (1990) 'Reducing disruptive behaviour of elementary physical education students with sit and watch', *Journal of Applied Behaviour Analysis*, 3: 353–359.

Williams, J. (2003) *A game for rough girls? A history of women's football in Britain*, London: Routledge.

Williams, J.M., and Straub, W.F. (2001) 'Sport psychology: Past, present, future', in J.M. Williams (ed.), *Applied sport psychology: Personal growth to peak performance* (5th edn), Mountain View, CA: Mayfield.

Wilson, C., King, M.A. and Yeadon, M.R. (2006) 'Determination of subject-specific model parameters for visco-elastic elements', *Journal of Biomechanics*, 39: 1883–1890.

Winstein, C. J. and Schmidt, R.A. (1990) 'Reduced frequency of knowledge of results enhances motor skill learning', *Journal of Experimental Psychology: Learning Memory and Cognition*, 16(4): 677–691.

Woodman, T. and Hardy, L. (2001a) 'Stress and anxiety', in R. Singer, H.A. Hausenblas and C.M. Janelle (eds), *Handbook of research on sport psychology* (2nd edn), New York: Wiley.

Woodman, T. and Hardy, L. (2001b) 'A case study of organizational stress in elite sport', *Journal of Applied Sport Psychology*, 13: 207–238.

Wulf, G., McNevin, N.H., Fuchs, T., Ritter, F. and Toole, T. (2000) 'Attentional focus in complex skill learning', *Research Quarterly for Exercise and Sport*, 71: 229–239.

Wulf, G. and Prinz, W. (2001) 'Directing attention to movement effects enhances learning: a review', *Psychonomic Bulletin and Review*, 8: 648–660.

Wulf, G. and Schmidt, R.A. (1994) 'Contextual interference effects in motor learning: Evaluating a KR-usefulness hypothesis', in J.R. Nitsch and R. Seiler (eds), *Movement and sport: Psychological foundations and effects*, Sankt Augustin, Germany: Academia Verlag.

Zimmerman, B.J. and Kitsantas, A. (1996) 'Self-regulated learning of a motoric skill: The role of goal setting and self-monitoring', *Journal of Applied Sport Psychology*, 8: 60–75.

Zinkovsky, A.V., Vain, A.A. and Torm, R.J. (1976) 'Biomechanical analysis of the formation of gymnastic skill', in P.V. Komi (ed.), *Biomechanics VB, International Series on Biomechanics*, Champaign, IL: Human Kinetics.

Zinsser, N., Bunker, L. and Williams, J.M. (2001) 'Cognitive techniques for building confidence and enhancing performance', in J.M. Williams (ed.), *Applied sport psychology: Personal growth to peak performance*, Mountain View, CA: Mayfield.

# INDEX

Page numbers in *italics* refer to figures and **tables**.